# FIND CLARITY, EASE, AND TRUST IN YOUR MOTHERHOOD JOURNEY

# MOTHERING *from* WITHIN

Always trust your instincts —
they are your superpower !

♡ Kaili

Toronto, Ontario, Canada

Copyright @ 2022 Kaili Ets

*Mothering From Within: Find Clarity, Ease, and Trust in Your Motherhood Journey*

YGTMedia Co. Publishing Press Trade Paperback Edition

ISBN trade paperback: 978-1-989716-90-8

eBook: 978-1-989716-91-5

Published in Canada, for Global Distribution

by YGTMedia Co. Publishing

www.ygtmedia.co/publishing

To order additional copies of this book:

publishing@ygtmedia.co

Editors: Rachel Small and Christine Stock

Book Designer: Doris Chung

eBook Edition: Ellie Sipilä

Author photo by Sara Tanner

FIND CLARITY, EASE, AND TRUST IN
YOUR MOTHERHOOD JOURNEY

# MOTHERING
# *from* WITHIN

## KAILI ETS

# TABLE *of* CONTENTS

Dear Reader,

This book is for you, beautiful mama, or mama-to-be.

You are doing your very best.

You may be exhausted from all those sleepless nights.

Or find yourself comparing and worrying about your baby's development.

But your desire to give your baby the best start in life is strong.

Truth is, babies are hard. Parenting is hard.

There will be ups and downs in each new stage.

But you are on a journey . . .

From feeling overwhelmed to empowered.

From confused to confident.

From who you are now to who you will become.

What you seek isn't magic answers but support and credible information.

Meet this book: *Mothering from Within.*

A place for you to connect with and learn to trust your mama instincts.

Think of this book as a guide, a mentor, a therapist, and a small part of your village of support.

In this book I strive to provide holistic, attachment-focused, developmentally driven, and evidence-based information—never judgment.

Come as you are.

Leave empowered, inspired, and ready to lead your family with confidence.

XO,

*Kaili*

# AUTHOR'S NOTE

Congratulations on becoming a mama! Whether you have a fresh newborn or an active toddler, know that I've been where you are, and I'm here for you.

And congratulations on taking the first step toward getting better sleep, gaining confidence in your baby's feeding and development, building a closer bond with your baby, and returning to trusting your instincts.

The first two years of motherhood will forever change you. You'll discover superpowers you never knew you had. While you'll do the very best for your baby, I want you to remember that you don't have to do that at the expense of yourself. Promise me that you will also prioritize yourself, nurture yourself, take care of yourself—just the way you take care of everyone else in your life—and do your best to remember who you were before baby.

Before we get started, I want to tell you a little bit more about me.

I'm Kaili. I'm a mama of two, a self-proclaimed natural-wellness guru, and the founder of Kaili Ets Family Wellness. I always knew I wanted to be a mama, and now, I also know how hard motherhood can be. When I got pregnant with my firstborn, Kristjan, I was overjoyed. And with many years of pediatric occupational therapy experience under my belt, I thought it would be a breeze. "No problem, I got this whole mom thing!"

Well, I did . . . sort of.

Yes, I knew how to play with my baby, and I knew how to encourage him to meet his milestones on time. I talked and sang to help him in his language development, and I bounced and rocked him to calm him. But what I didn't know about or anticipate was the pure exhaustion and brain fog of sleep deprivation, the fear of him choking when we started solids, the worry and guilt that would come from comparing him to other babies, the loneliness of having no one but your little person to talk to day in and day out. There were definitely (many) days when it just seemed easier to not get dressed and not leave the house.

My son wasn't what you would call a good sleeper—at least I didn't think so at the time. In fact, he was the classic twenty- to thirty-minute napper who'd wake up the second the stroller stopped or his head hit the bassinet mattress. He could sleep for three hours on or next to me but rarely alone in his own sleep space. He never slept for more than two or three hours in a row until he was eight and a half months. And I was exhausted. I started dreading the nights and therefore going to bed later, essentially self-sabo-taging. I started to dread responding to my son when he woke at night, and even felt as if I hated him at times. It was awful!

Then I got help. Help that felt supportive and in line with my values. That didn't make me leave my baby to cry and "figure it out" alone. And with more sleep, the mama-brain fog lifted a bit and I felt as though I could think and be again—and I recognized that mamas needed more knowledge and support. So I set out on a new journey, to help reduce the overwhelm of motherhood, one mama and baby at a time.

Mama, I see you, I hear you, I have worked with you, and I have walked in similar shoes.

While having a baby was exciting, joyful, and a dream come true, my start to motherhood was also stressful, full of worrying, questioning, comparing, googling, reading, analyzing, and, ultimately, wanting to do the best for my baby. I was confused, even though I had tons of training and experience in infant and child development. I was totally stressed out from reading all the blogs and books and downloading the various schedules, feeling as if these were all things I was "supposed to do." They all said something different and I was so overwhelmed—until I stopped. I stopped caring about what the schedules and outdated books said. I stopped caring about the fact that my baby wasn't quite the same as other babies in terms of sleep, and rolling, and demeanor.

I stopped stressing and started being.

I started watching my baby with the intention of enjoying the moments, however small. I tuned in to my knowledge of what IS normal for baby sleep and development. And I watched the stress melt away. The self-trust came back—the knowing that I understood what was best for my baby (and ultimately for me). As long as I followed this knowing, he would be fine. We would both be fine!

Now I'm on a mission to help you feel the same way. To help you go from overwhelmed and confused to confident and thriving! To help you tune in and trust your mama instincts—they're there, I promise!

**Important Note:** While I use the term "mama" throughout the book, please know that the word is intended to be inclusive of all those who identify with mothering or caregiving.

# SIX BUILDING BLOCKS

At the core of my work with mamas and their babies are six concepts that I refer to as the building blocks. You can think of them as the six Cs of motherhood. These building blocks are ultimately what help you move from that state of overwhelm and confusion to feeling confident and as though you've got this whole motherhood thing.

I invite you to keep these in the back of your mind as you read this book.

## 1.   COURAGE

Courage is about finding your voice and saying no. It's about being open to learning and growing. It's about stepping into the unknown, making mistakes, and moving forward. To be courageous is to listen to and be present with your child or even with family members who might not agree with your way of doing things. Courage is choosing love and being kind and respectful to your baby, to your family, and, most of all, to yourself. Courage is accepting your imperfections and leaning in to them while showing yourself compassion and understanding. It takes courage to do motherhood YOUR way, especially if it's different from the norm or what others in your life are recommending or advising.

 *Courage is the power to be you against all odds.*

—Dr. Shefali Tsabary

## 2.    COMFORT

Providing comfort through loving intention, gentle touch, and responding to our children's needs isn't creating "bad habits" or "spoiling them," as our society can lead us to believe. In fact, it's doing the opposite. Providing comfort is often the very thing that your instinct is leading you to do, that you do automatically, without thinking. It's what helps our babies and children know that they're loved and that they can always count on us to support them. It's what helps them grow into confident, independent, and resilient individuals.

## 3.    CONNECTION

Life boils down to connection, which is love. Connection is the thing that our children seek the most, and that doesn't stop once they reach adulthood. Connection is often the antidote to the very things we want to protect our children from—anger, fear, loneliness, and, yes, even all those "behaviors" and peer pressure. It's important to prioritize connection in every aspect of our lives but especially when it comes to the youngest, most vulnerable people in them. True connection requires us to tune in to the other person—their feelings, their desires, their needs. By focusing on connecting with your child, you'll start to become tuned in to their smiles (when they're working on a big poop, for example!), their cries, and their signals for when they're tired and overwhelmed. Focusing on connection will also help you maintain a secure attachment with your baby, which is essentially what we all want.

## 4.   CLARITY

Gaining clarity is about bringing more awareness to whatever is causing you confusion or overwhelm. This could involve researching what is "biologically normal" or typical for babies in their development and sleep, or perhaps learning about why breast-feeding can feel so hard, or maybe even realizing that there's always a reason for a baby's reflux. Perhaps it involves learning about new concepts, such as sensory processing, that finally help to explain your baby's unique temperament. Each new phase of babyhood brings with it a whole host of new questions and worries. Of course it does! It's something new, to both you and baby, and it takes time to figure it all out. Whatever it is, gaining clarity is much less stressful when you're learning from trusted sources rather than information found during a random Google search at 3:00 a.m. when your baby is up for the tenth time (yup, I've been there—trust me, you do not want to go down that rabbit hole).

5.  ## CONSISTENCY

Consistency is key! I homed in on this way back in my occupational therapy days, when I was treating children and giving parents home programs. The only way you'll see any progress is through consistency. This concept is such an important one for growth and development milestones but also for getting more sleep, making changes, and building new habits. When we're consistent with something, it becomes familiar and predictable, and our primitive brain then views it as "safe." Consistency allows our babies and children to know what to expect. The brain views new things as "unsafe" or "scary," thereby triggering our fight-or-flight alarm system to keep us safe and help us survive. So again, consistency is key, okay? (Note that this doesn't mean consistently leaving your baby to cry in an effort to teach them to self-soothe or sleep. Being in a consistent state of distress can lead to chronic stress and a whole host of other problems later in life.)

6.  ## CONFIDENCE

We all want more confidence. Confidence is what allows us to hold our heads high and live our lives without second-guessing ourselves. Confidence is essentially trusting yourself, and this is so important in motherhood! For some, confidence comes quite easily, but for many of us it takes time to build. I've found that building confidence requires the right mindset (deciding to trust yourself and your baby), repetition and practice (consistency), and being willing to be perfectly imperfect (yup, you'll make mistakes because we all do; it's part of the human experience). I also know that if you focus on the first five building blocks—courage, comfort, connection, clarity, and consistency—you'll be building and strengthening your confidence and ability to trust in yourself (and your mama instincts) throughout your motherhood journey and beyond.

I've been on a journey to believing and trusting in myself, my knowledge, my skills, and even my motherhood journey for a while now. I have come to understand (and accept) that confidence comes with time, and the first step is courage. Courage to follow your heart. Courage to do things YOUR way. Courage to trust yourself and your baby. Courage to trust that you've got this, Mama! Because you do. My hope is that by focusing on these six building blocks, or six Cs of motherhood, you'll start to realize that in fact you do know what's best for your baby and your family. And that by following your heart, your mama instincts, you'll be able to take imperfect action day after day and finally feel like the supermom you are who CAN do this parenting thing.

## TRUST YOUR INTUITION

It's likely that at least one person in your life has told you to follow your instincts or that a mother's intuition is never wrong. This is so true! But if you're anything like me, you might be so focused on keeping your baby alive while trying to figure out breast-feeding and the whole sleeping thing that the last thing on your mind is following that feeling in your gut (or heart).

We're all intuitive. We just need to slow down enough to tune in and listen to our intuition, and we need the courage to trust it. This book will guide you in this.

Did you know that moms' (and dads') brains are physically altered during pregnancy and childbirth? Yup, this is why your newborn baby's cries elicit a much stronger reaction in you than your friend's baby's do. Your baby's cry is meant to trigger your survival instinct—to make you go to your baby and care for or protect them. Evolution has designed us this way! A hormone called oxytocin (or "the love hormone") is responsible for this. This is also the hormone responsible for bonding, attachment, and feeling loved. New parents have high levels of this hormone in their system. Oxytocin production is activated by the right orbitofrontal cortex (ROFC) and the auditory cortex of the brain, which is why we parents have a heightened responsiveness to our baby's cries.

I can attest to this. With both my children, I had heightened sensitivity to their cries, sometimes to the point where I'd think I'd heard them and wake up only to have my husband tell me they were sleeping. Funny thing though—often my babies would cry only moments later. It's as if my body (or my mother's intuition) knew and was rousing me in preparation to go to them.

Though this heightened sensitivity might feel strange or perhaps even annoying at times (e.g., those phantom cries), it's an important tool to facilitate bonding between you and your baby. By experiencing your baby's cries so strongly, you feel empathy for your baby, you're focused on helping them, and you pay careful attention to their needs. But it's not just about being sensitive to their cries. You also have a strong biological desire to take care of your baby. This desire, this sensitivity, this instinct makes you more observant, helping you understand their cues, wants, and needs. Of course this all takes a lot of trial and error in those first few days and weeks, but eventually you start to develop a deep understanding of the little person in front of you. With my first baby, it took me a long time to figure out his cues and I often found myself doing the "are you hungry, wet, tired, bored?" dance. Whereas with my daughter, because of the practice with my first, things were easier and came more naturally.

Your intuition is always there, even during times of stress, confusion, or exhaustion. You may not always be aware of it, or you might even disregard it, but it's there. And everyone is unique in the way they experience intuition.

Sometimes it's a feeling or inner knowing. Other times it comes through our senses in visions, auditory messages, or smells.

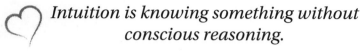

> *Intuition is knowing something without conscious reasoning.*
>
> –Kaili Ets

Learning to trust our intuition takes time. It takes slowing down and tuning in to our baby and also ourselves and how we're feeling. And it takes courage to trust and follow that intuition. Focusing on your breath is one of the easiest ways to slow your mind, relax your body, and be in the present moment, all of which will help your intuition come through. Another wonderful technique is to focus on your heart and connect with the state of love. But really, any activity that gets you into a relaxed state will help you tune in to your intuition, and the more we tune in, the stronger it gets. Any of the self-care activities in Chapter Twenty-Four: You Matter Too, Mama, will help you access this intuition.

I invite you to embrace this resource inside you—your mama intuition. Nobody will know your baby (or your family) as well as you, so if you feel as if your baby needs something or that something is wrong, don't suppress that feeling, even if someone (yes, that includes your doctor) says otherwise. If your mama heart aches, follow it! Trust yourself and your baby. Your intuition will never steer you wrong.

Being a new parent means constantly balancing protecting and letting go. There will likely be people who judge you for your various decisions, whether it's to bed-share or have your baby in a crib, to nurse or formula-feed, to nurse in public, to baby-wear, and more. The decisions are endless, and unfortunately, so are the judgments. Throughout this book I return to the concept of trusting your mama instincts and doing what feels right for you and your baby. Think about your values, your family, your baby. Always run any advice through the filter of those values and how something feels in your heart. If anyone (including me) tells you to do something that isn't in alignment with your values, don't do it!

*Does it align with my values?*
*Does it feel right in my heart?*
*Does it feel light?*
—*Kaili Ets*

It's also so important to find not only your community of like-minded mamas (whether in person or online), but also a roster of professionals you trust and whose advice resonates with you. Because, Mama, we were never, ever meant to do this alone. My hope is that reading this book will be like having a good friend, therapist, and mentor by your side—one you can go to for help any time of the day or night.

## WHAT THIS BOOK IS AND WHAT IT ISN'T

This book, like motherhood, isn't one-size-fits-all. Every human is unique, which means that every baby is unique. What works for one baby may not work for another. I recommend reading, tuning in to what strategies resonate with you, and then trying them. Promise yourself that you'll give the strategy a good try, being consistent with the approach for at least three to five days, assuming it still feels good instinctively, before deciding that it doesn't work.

In the past, I read many parenting books that had pretty titles and started off sweet and science-y, talking about sleep cycles, circadian rhythms, and homeostatic sleep pressure, and then bam—on to the sleep-training techniques. I felt duped. These books caused me stress when I was reading them for help with my son's sleep, and I now find them frustrating and disheart-ening. The authors use gentle-sounding words to essentially disguise their true approach: behavioral and separation based.

And I haven't seen many books that go into detail about your baby's development and what you should be looking for in terms of milestones at each age while also addressing red flags that might alert you to something more going on with your baby. Baby books are often quite general and include only a few paragraphs on physical development and milestones, or they outline the age ranges for various skills but not how you can actually encourage your baby to meet those skills in a way that's developmentally appropriate. And though there are books on breast-feeding, tongue-ties, baby-led weaning, and even picky eating, I haven't found a book that speaks to all of them.

This book came out of my realization that I have so much knowledge to share based on training and experiences in my professional and personal life, and that I can shed light on many of the "mama pain points," as I like to call them. I haven't seen another book out there that covers all these topics in some depth.

My intention with this book is to be by your side as you navigate the wild ride of the first few years of motherhood. It's full of evidence-informed, developmentally appropriate, attachment-focused information on develop-mental milestones, sleep, reflux, feeding/solids, mama mental health, and more. I guide you but also empower you to lean in and trust your mama instincts. To tune in to the baby you have in front of you and what reson-ates with you and your family—what feels right in your heart. To tune in so that you can start to tune out all the unsolicited advice from well-meaning family, friends, social media influencers, and, yes, sometimes even doctors.

My aim is to

- Help you feel more connected to your baby and have a happier baby as a result of harnessing your intuition
- Encourage you to respond to, support, and soothe your baby in a way that feels good to you
- Give you all the knowledge, tools, and strategies you need to establish healthy sleep for your family
- Guide you to tune in and lean in to your mama instincts rather than urging or forcing you to go against them

The information in this book isn't just based on my opinions and experience, although these do come into play. It's also informed by scientific evidence regarding topics such as sleep, sensory processing, reflux, and feeding, as well as from knowledge gained from my years of experience as a pediatric occupational therapist, my advanced certifications in pediatric sleep, reflux, and craniosacral therapy, and my many dozens of continued professional development courses on a variety of topics over the years. Rest assured that the information presented here is evidence informed while also relatable and easy to digest.

There's also never any intended judgment on my part. There may be times where I advise you not to do something and you think, "Oh my gosh, I've done that." Please remember what Maya Angelou said: "Do the best you can until you know better. Then when you know better, do better." I'm not perfect either—it's okay! We're all the very best parents we can be. As long as we keep learning with an open mind and make it a goal to always improve, our children will grow up to be fully functioning adults.

Here are a few reminders before you dive in, to set the stage for what's to come.

1.   **You are the best parent for your baby.**

Sometimes parenting is hard and you might feel as if you're failing miserably. Maybe you're exhausted, worried about every little noise, and haven't experienced any of this before. Rest assured, Mama, you ARE amazing! You're doing the very best you can and that's enough. So repeat after me:

*I am enough! I have done enough! I am doing enough! I am Superwoman! I am AMAZING!*

2.   **Babies wake up at night. Sometimes a lot. It means they're doing their job of being a baby.**

While waking up at night with your baby is biologically normal and necessary, I totally understand the sleep deprivation that comes from many, many months of hourly wake-ups (remember, my first didn't sleep for more than two or three hours until eight and a half months). Many layers may need to be worked through to optimize sleep, so put your detective hat on and get curious about your baby. My aim with this book is to provide you with information to help you figure out if what's going on with your baby is normal and to offer some things to look for and strategies to put in place to optimize sleep while trusting your instincts about what feels good and right in your heart.

3.   **Babies are a lot of work, but you're also allowed to have fun.**

So go out for coffee (or wine) dates with your friends, have a dance party in the living room amid the unfolded laundry, or catch up on a juicy Netflix show while eating popcorn as your baby has a contact nap on your chest. And try to not take each day so seriously. Laugh until you cry, be silly, find that inner child, and do your best to get back to some of the things that brought you joy before you had a baby. And if you're stressing about naptimes, worried that your baby isn't getting restorative sleep, or feeling guilty because you're formula-feeding . . . stop! Remember this:

If something is working for you and your baby, keep doing it. If it's no longer working, you're stressed out about it, or you hate it, then change it (FYI, you can make changes that feel good in your heart while still responding to your baby and also getting better sleep— day and night!).

4.     **Sometimes making a change means accepting that, in the short term, things may seem as if they're getting worse.**
This is totally normal. Change is hard for all of us (babies included), and it takes time to form habits that stick. And remember, change sends our stress system into high gear. It can be scary for our babies. They may start waking more often after you make a change (i.e., bed-sharing to crib, or weaning some night-feeds). Consistency will be key with this—and of course, following your heart!

This book will help you set realistic expectations around development, sleep, and babyhood in general. If you're anything like I was, you've probably printed out or saved all the different freebie sleep schedules from Internet land, read a few books on how to get your baby to sleep better and more, watched IG reels to see how to teach your baby to crawl, sit, and walk, and are trying to figure out how to fit these all into your day without feeling overwhelmed. Stop reading those articles, throw out the schedules, and focus on the information in this book. This isn't about following a rigid plan that's supposed to work for all babies. This is about figuring out what is biologically normal or typical and works for YOUR baby (not your neighbor's baby) and what feels good for you.

You already have all the answers inside of you. You might just need some help listening to and trusting them. That's what this book is for!

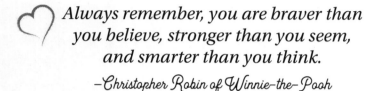

*Always remember, you are braver than you believe, stronger than you seem, and smarter than you think.*

–Christopher Robin of Winnie-the-Pooh

# THE INFANT BRAIN, ATTACHMENT, AND DEVELOPMENT

When I finally got to hold my son, Kristjan, in my arms (or rather on my chest), just minutes after he was born, I was crying tears of joy and distinctly remember feeling this overwhelming desire to protect him. I knew in that moment that I would do my very best to provide him with the best start to life and care for him in the best way I knew how.

At the time, I had eight and a half years of experience as a pediatric occupational therapist and knew quite a bit about infant and child development. I knew about the importance of skin-to-skin and baby-wearing. And I was also very conscious about the products I was using, wanting to eliminate as many toxins from our lives as possible. All to give him the best start.

In the weeks following Kristjan's birth, I experienced so many emotions—ups and downs—and the mama bear claws came out on numerous occasions as I fulfilled my duty to protect this precious little baby who couldn't yet protect or speak up for himself. During this time I was also very overwhelmed from lack of sleep, from breast-feeding pain and trying to get the perfect latch, and from having a baby that was happiest on or next to me. He seemed to hate tummy time and cried whenever we tried, and he rarely ever slept in his own sleep space (but put him on my chest and he could stay there for hours). I was torn because I loved the cuddles, but I also just wanted my own space and body back.

It wasn't until I started reading more about babies and the fourth trimester that I learned that babies are born even more vulnerable than I'd initially thought. His need for body contact made sense. Then, when I took my first pediatric sleep certification, I learned more about attachment, why it's so important, and how it develops in babies and young children—and my mind was blown. This information changed the way I thought about all my past occupational therapy clients! During my second sleep certification course, I really dug into the infant brain and how it differs from ours as adults. Again, holy cow! How had I never learned this in any of my schooling before? It was so fascinating and really helped me understand why loving and responsive parenting is key, both day and night.

In this first section of the book, I'll share some of the key takeaways I've gleaned over the past seven years of researching and learning about babies' brains and development. I hope it gives you a good foundation for starting to understand your baby and why your mama instincts are leading you to respond to, hold, kiss, and hug your baby all day (and night) long.

# Chapter One

# PARENTING THE INFANT BRAIN

If human babies gestated inside the womb for eighteen months and came out with the ability to stand and walk, like most other mammals, development would be a whole other ball game.

Because of this "prematurity," human babies are born with only a fraction of their brain developed (about 25 to 29 percent).[1,2] And so, human babies are born vulnerable and dependent on us, their caregivers, for survival and safety. The additional brain growth required to stay alive and thriving happens outside the womb. Most occurs in the first three years of life, but a huge amount happens during the fourth trimester.[1] What a big job our babies have!

It can be so hard in those first few months and years to feel as if you're the only person who can meet the needs of your baby, especially if you have a highly fussy or sensitive baby who seems to function best when *you* are the one caring for them. It's hard to be needed 24/7 when you're physically tired, emotionally and energetically depleted, sore or in pain while you heal from either a vaginal or a belly birth, and feel as if you've become a different person—when you're trying to come to terms with who you are now, in this new role as a mom, responsible for this entirely new person. It's hard to go from being fun, free, independent, social, and productive to being consumed by thoughts of which breast you fed from last, how many dirty diapers you're seeing in a day, how to best coax your baby to sleep, and when you last showered.

It's hard, no question about it. But guess what? You're not the only one who's gone through a change. Put yourself in your baby's shoes and see the transition from their point of view.

Your baby comes into this outside world after nine to ten months of being enveloped in the warmth of your womb, where they float freely, sounds are muffled, and the lights are dim. They're rocked to sleep with the rhythmical and comforting movements your body makes while you go about your day. Then, they get the signal that it's time to end that journey and start a new one. They twist, turn, and push to find the exit, with your body helping them gain momentum through the squeezing of contractions. They experience pressure and input through their head and feet as they make their way down the path toward the light. First their head, then their shoulders and body, and finally their feet. And then they land . . .

In the middle of the chaos of life outside the womb.

All of a sudden that warm, soothing, huglike environment is gone and they're bombarded with sensations—cold air on their skin, air instead of liquid in their lungs, bright lights above them, sounds that are no longer muffled but loud and happening all at once. They feel their bodies touched and pulled by strong, rough, or maybe soft hands. Their senses are on high alert, and their survival instincts kick in. "Where is my safe person?" they wonder. "That person whose smell, heartbeat, and voice are familiar?" Everything is new, and now is when the hard work really begins.

They must work with gravity now, and it's difficult to move. They no longer have a steady stream of nutrition coming in, so they have to find the food source and learn to suck and swallow. Sometimes that comes easily and sometimes it takes a lot of effort. It's tiring. They're exhausted from the journey, everything is unfamiliar, and they're not quite sure what to make of it all. All they want is to be back in their happy place, next to you. Perhaps they want to sleep but can't because they're being poked and prodded, perhaps suctioned or pricked, wrapped in stiff fabric, or even separated from the one thing, the one person they know. What a transition that is!

This is why in those first few months, often called the fourth trimester, or even the first six to nine months, your baby's favorite place is next to you. Your smell, the heat of your body, your heartbeat, your breath rate, and even all the gurgling sounds your body makes are what help your baby feel as if everything is right in the world. Being close to you helps them regulate their body temperature and their heart and breath rates, and it helps them feel a sense of safety and security.

This is normal, and I urge you to embrace it.

Your baby being happiest next to you is normal—and exactly what they (and you) need. No, you aren't creating any bad habits or causing them to be dependent on you forever. What you're doing is nurturing your baby's brain, supporting their development and well-being, and laying the foundation for a strong, secure attachment with you.

I know that it can be hard to hold your baby all the time. You worry that they'll become too dependent on you, and sometimes you just want time to yourself. This is normal! Perhaps you can wear your baby while you read to your toddler or make yourself a meal; maybe your baby can do some tummy time on the floor while you fold laundry next to them; or maybe you can hand off your baby to another loving caregiver while you have a nap or a shower or just some time for you! As the saying goes, "The days are long but the years are short." There will be a day in the not-so-far future that your child won't want to be constantly attached to you. And then will come the day when they head off to school. And eventually, they'll move out. So enjoy the snuggles, Mama, but don't forget to take care of you.

## COMFORT, COMFORT, COMFORT

As parents, we want to do our best for our children, and we're the perfect people to help with this big transition from the womb. Unfortunately, we're often met with conflicting advice and information—from the people we trust, our middle-of-the-night Google searches, or that random person we follow on social media—and we get confused. With confusion comes worry, stress, and eventually overwhelm.

I'm here to remind you to pay close attention to comfort. Comforting your baby is a powerful, simple way to form, build, and strengthen the attachment relationship with your little one. And no, you cannot spoil a baby by holding them too much, or by picking them up every time they cry. Believe me, I've heard all of this, even from a nurse in the hospital when my firstborn was only hours old! You cannot go wrong with comfort, and as we'll look at later in this section, connection is the antidote to pretty much everything.

## YOUR BABY'S BRAIN

Your baby's brain is different from yours, at least initially. Remember, your baby is born with only 25 to 29 percent of their brain formed. Understanding these differences might just help you trust yourself and your instincts a bit more and allow you to sift through and even tune out all the confusing, often conflicting, information that comes your way (no matter how hard you try, some will still get through your filters, but you can wave it off and move on).

The brain develops in three stages. Our survival brain, which is housed in the brain stem, is developed and functioning at birth. The brain stem controls breathing, heartbeat, digestion, sleeping, crying, startling, blinking, sucking, and smelling, and it's also what allows us to orient ourselves toward smell, sound, faces and expressions, and eye contact. Next to develop is the emotional brain, which is where our limbic system is housed. This part of the brain is immature at birth and develops during the first three years of life and beyond, through relationships. The emotional brain regulates our mood, how we respond to stress, and shapes our lifelong mental health. Finally, we have the thinking brain, also known as the prefrontal cortex, which is housed in the frontal lobe. This is where true self-regulation happens. This part of the brain is immature at birth. It develops more slowly than the other parts of the brain and isn't fully mature until our twenties.

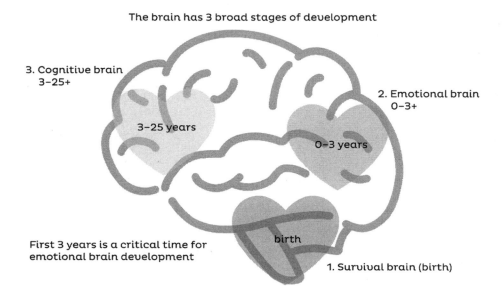

The brain has 3 broad stages of development

3. Cognitive brain
   3–25+

2. Emotional brain
   0–3+

3–25 years

0–3 years

First 3 years is a critical time for
emotional brain development

birth

1. Survival brain (birth)

# SELF-REGULATION

Let's talk about self-regulation for a minute. This is a term that gets thrown around in the "baby market" and particularly in the sleep-training culture. Self-regulation is the ability to monitor and modulate your behavior, emotions, or thoughts. It's actually a developmental skill, just like crawling, standing, and walking. There are even regulation milestones. It develops gradually, as our thinking brain develops and "turns on." This isn't something we can somehow "train" our children to do or even understand in the first years of life.

Self-regulation requires the awareness to evaluate our external environment and the current state of our body, then compare this information to what is already known and plan a response. And since the area of the brain (frontal lobe) responsible for self-regulation doesn't start to develop until around age three, it's up to us as parents to act as our infants' brains. We must be sensitive to the cues from their survival brain, nurture their emotional brain, and take over the jobs of their thinking brain by providing responsive, reliable, and positive care, day and night.[3]

# STRESS

To put the concept of self-regulation into perspective, we need to consider stress. Stress is key for survival, but too much of it can be detrimental.

There are two types of stress. Eustress is "good stress," and it motivates us and keeps us productive. Distress, or "bad stress," on the other hand, involves things like excessive worrying and anxiety. All stress increases our cortisol levels. Some cortisol is needed during the day to keep us awake and alert, but high levels of cortisol and adrenaline (both of which are activated when our survival instincts kick in) can mess with our hormonal balance, wreak havoc on our immune system, and negatively affect sleep. We aren't meant to have high cortisol levels for a long time. They return to normal once the cause of the stress has been removed.

When we talk about stress we also have to talk about the nervous system, specifically the autonomic nervous system. There are three branches to this system: the parasympathetic nervous system, the sympathetic nervous system, and the social engagement system (from Stephen Porges' polyvagal theory). Together, these branches affect how we function in our daily lives, and it's important to keep them in balance.

The parasympathetic nervous system is often referred to as our "rest, digest, and heal system." The sympathetic nervous system, also known as our "fight, flight, or freeze system," gets activated in response to a perceived threat. The social engagement system is specific to humans. We use it to assess the safety of a situation (before fight, flight, freeze comes into play), and it's associated with connection, calmness, and engagement in daily activities. We read facial expressions, listen to voices, and generally read the behavior of other humans to determine whether we're safe or not. This system is strengthened by relationships and helps us navigate our sympathetic and parasympathetic systems.

Our ability to regulate is how we manage our arousal level among these three systems.

The sympathetic nervous system includes the amygdala, hypothalamus, pituitary gland, adrenal glands, hippocampus, and prefrontal cortex. Together, these make up the limbic hypothalamic pituitary adrenal (LHPA) axis, the most well-studied part of the emotional brain in relation to early life experience.

## HOW OUR STRESS SYSTEM WORKS

| Adults | Babies |
|---|---|
| 1. External threat from the environment or an internal threat from the mind activates an alarm in the amygdala | 1. External threat from the environment or an internal threat from the mind activates an alarm in the amygdala |
| 2. Brain sends signals to release cortisol | 2. Brain sends signals to release cortisol |
| 3. Brain and body are mobilized to respond to threat | 3. Brain and body are mobilized to respond to threat |
| 4. Prefrontal cortex can think and rationalize the threat and send stop signals to the amygdala | 4. The end. Baby's brain is underdeveloped and cannot shut off the stress. |

*Adapted from Kirschenbaum, Greer, PhD. Bebo Mia's Infant & Family Sleep Specialist Certification program. Attended 2021.*

Did you catch the difference between the baby and adult stress responses? At first glance they seem the same, but the most important part is step 4, which is tied to the prefrontal cortex (the thinking brain). Remember, that part of the brain doesn't really start to develop until about age three. This is a huge difference between the baby brain and the adult brain. Again, this is why it's so important that we "parent" the infant brain. We are their stress regulators!

# BABIES AND STRESS

Okay, so you might be wondering, what causes stress for a baby? I hear you. Their life does seem pretty great: getting fed on demand and being constantly held and snuggled and loved by everyone they meet—who wouldn't want that? But babies do experience stress, often more intensely than we do, and it starts the moment labor starts. After the stress of the birth and then the change in the sensory environment comes the stress of their daily lives. Are you (and baby) always on the go? Are there loud noises and crowds in your environment? Is your active baby being strapped in a stroller or car seat? Are you constantly meeting new people while your baby is with you? Over-tiredness, overstimulation, feeling scared, sensory processing differences, and more can all cause stress in our bodies.

Understanding who your baby is and what causes their stress is critical. Our stress reactivity is set in the first year of life. What we do and how we help our baby manage and regulate stress determines whether our baby will be easily set off by stressors. For example, constant exposure to stress can lead to a heightened stress reactivity later in life.

It's also important to remember that sometimes babies cry no matter what you do. This is simply how they communicate their needs to us. They cry to let us know they're hungry, wet, tired, cold, overstimulated, need some closeness and connection, etc. We'll talk about crying in more depth later—getting comfortable with and allowing tears while supporting the emotion behind them is so important for our children's development.

Babies will of course be exposed to different stressors on a daily basis, and this will cause some stress in their body, but if we can shorten the duration of stress, then it's more along the lines of eustress and won't have the same negative consequences as distress. This is why it's vital to be responsive and support your baby in regulating their bodies and arousal levels and to teach them that they can trust you to respond, to help, to care—day *and* night. It's through this responsiveness and the loving intention to support them that we take over the role of our baby's immature LHPA axis and thinking brain and stop the stress.

What happens if we don't respond (i.e., during some version of cry-it-out sleep training) and leave the baby alone to "figure it out" or "self-soothe"? Baby gets flooded with stress, is unable to shut it off on their own (because their brain isn't capable of that), and eventually shuts down and falls asleep.

I'm passionate about this topic and believe that all parents need to understand this (even at the basic level I've described here) so that they can make informed decisions around sleep training. The reality is, most parents don't know this and are somewhat blindly following the outdated sleep books, the advice (mostly well meaning) from their mothers, midwives, or even pediatricians, or the gazillionth sleep blog or free e-book because they're exhausted, desperate, and think their baby *should* be sleeping through the night.

Your baby's nervous system is slower than yours, which means it's slower to "correct" itself when it goes out of balance.[4] You just learned that their brains aren't fully formed or able to self-regulate, and they're still learning (through experience) about all the sensory input coming in from their environment, about how everything feels in their bodies, about what they like and don't like, how to suck, swallow, and even breathe. They need time to process it all, to have their brain figure out what to do with the information. So go slow with your baby while you play—slow down your movements, your speech. Avoid the "hustle and bustle" of rushing from task to task. And when you're doing an activity with them, be it diaper changing or playing in tummy time, remember that their body and brain are processing it. Allow them time to integrate it.

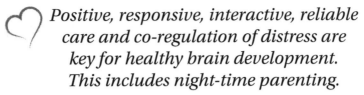

*Positive, responsive, interactive, reliable
care and co-regulation of distress are
key for healthy brain development.
This includes night-time parenting.*

*—Dr. Greer Kirschenbaum, ISE Sleep Certification*

Consistent, responsive care develops attachment, and nurturing interaction lays the foundation for key aspects of self-regulation (i.e., attention, impulse control, cortical development, and ability to modulate stress).

## SELF-SOOTHING AND SELF-SETTLING

Self-soothing is the ability to calm and comfort yourself and diminish negative emotions and distress. It's a form of emotional regulation (or self-regulation). The concept is popular in today's Western culture, particularly when it comes to a baby's sleep but also in terms of just being with and interacting with our babies. The claim is that you must teach your baby to self-soothe if you want them to fall asleep and stay asleep during the night, and that you shouldn't pick them up every time they cry. The reality is, you can't teach your baby to self-soothe. They develop the ability over time.

When babies wake up normally, with no sleep training, they signal a caregiver because they have a need (thirst, hunger, discomfort, loneliness, temperature regulation, fear, comfort). Waking with a need means they're experiencing a rise in stress. They signal a caregiver to meet the need, lower their stress, and help them to fall back to sleep.

As we've discussed, due to their brain structures, babies (and young children) are incapable of calming down from a place of stress. If babies were capable of self-soothing, it would mean that they'd wake up with a need, somehow lower their stress, either meet or ignore the need, and fall back asleep on their own. Infants can't do this during the day or night. Heck, if you've ever met a toddler in the throes of a meltdown because they got the pink cup and not the blue cup, you'll know that they don't have the capacity to regulate their emotions. We need a functioning prefrontal cortex to self-soothe or self-regulate. Even as adults we can't self-regulate all the time.

> *When a child is capable of controlling their own emotions, only then are they truly able to self-soothe or settle themselves when they're anything but calm.*
>
> —Sarah Ockwell-Smith, The Gentle Sleep Book

*Self-soothing* is often confused with and used interchangeably with *self-settling*, but they're quite different. Self-settling describes a child's ability to regulate their bodies without support, usually from a calm, awake state to sleep (for example, falling asleep at the beginning of the night or back to sleep after a transition between sleep cycles). It's a physiological process—an ability to organize and regulate their bodies by adjusting their body temperature, changing their breathing, and bringing themselves midline. This can only happen when a baby's needs have been met (both physically and emotionally), they are already in a calm state, and they feel safe and secure. The key here is that a baby is regulating their physiological state from a state of calm, without stress or tears, whereas self-soothing is the process of calming oneself from a state of distress (which requires much more cognitive and thinking-brain power).

Self-settling also isn't something you can necessarily train someone to do, though you can start supporting your baby to do so by creating a peaceful environment that's conducive to sleep. Through a calming bedtime routine (perhaps involving a special lovey or comfort toy) and the security of knowing you'll always come if they need you, your baby will start to practice self-settling. This might look like sucking on their hands, babbling or singing to themselves, blowing bubbles, rubbing their cheek against the crib mattress, or even vigorously sucking on their soother. My kids loved to chew on the ears of their loveys (we love the Angel Dear ones).

While we can't teach or train babies to self-soothe, at least not until they have the cognitive ability for this, we can help them learn this important life skill *through experience*—specifically through the experience of co-regulation, so that they learn what positive soothing experiences feel like. We can help them move into calm states with the power of our own regulation and ability to calm ourselves. By experiencing this, our babies can draw on these skills later on in life, independently, when they're developmentally ready.

## PRIORITIZE CO-REGULATION

Co-regulation is like a dance between caregiver and baby. We act as the regulator for our children. When they cry, we pick them up and comfort them. When they're hurt, we rub or kiss their bumps and bruises. When they're dysregulated and in the throes of a toddler tantrum, we hold space for them or wrap them in a big, warm, loving hug. Although it may seem as if we're doing the work for them and thus they aren't learning anything (this is an old paradigm that exists from the way we or our parents were parented), we now know that co-regulation (which is how we parent the infant brain) offers a lot of input to the developing brain and nervous system that helps it learn how to regulate.[5-8]

Though you likely already co-regulate with your baby naturally, through your mama instincts, one of the ways we can consciously tune in to this dance of co-regulation with our babies is to learn what dysregulation looks like. And one of the best ways to measure dysregulation is in the face. Facial cues will usually happen before crying. Many of these cues are similar to tired cues as well. This is where you need to put your detective hat on to figure out what your unique baby or toddler needs—are they tired, hungry, stressed, bored, overstimulated? Maybe they're uncomfortable due to the position they're in or something going on in their gut (maybe they're working on a big poop). Or maybe they're highly sensitive and have some underlying sensory processing differences causing this feeling of dysregulation.

## WHAT DOES DYSREGULATION LOOK LIKE?

### BABIES

- Frozen, empty eyes; squinting eyes
- Wide-open eyes (deer in headlights) /mouth
- Turning away
- Flushed skin; dilated pupils
- Biting, chewing, pressing, making fists with hands
- Finger/hand sucking (can also be a hunger cue, so tune in to your baby: when they last had a feed and what is going on in their environment
- Straightening legs/bracing body against crib or caregiver
- Curling more into a fetal position

### TODDLERS

- Running away
- Crying, screaming, squirming, fidgeting
- Giggling (a nervous vs. happy giggle)
- Tantrum/meltdown

The key is to recognize dysregulation then understand the underlying need and address it, initially through co-regulation, which can help your child return to a calm state again. Back to the concept of parenting the infant brain and being their stress regulator—if we're focused on tuning in to our babies and their unique cues and needs, we can consciously take action to prevent dysregulation. We can build rest periods into the day or leave an overstimulating environment.

## SYNCHRONY

Part of the power of co-regulation comes from something called synchrony (also referred to as emotion contagion). As parents, we have a positive synchronous relationship with our children. When they're upset, we tend to follow suit, and when we get upset, they tend to follow us there as well. This doesn't just happen behaviorally but also at a physiological and energetic level. If we cannot regulate ourselves, we cannot co-regulate. To truly regulate ourselves, we must be aware of our thoughts, feelings, and arousal levels throughout the day. We need to pay attention to and get curious about our triggers, and we need to experiment with various regulating tools that can help us maintain balance and calm so that we can have more clarity and control while we parent our children.

I encourage you to find something that you enjoy and that helps you feel regulated and calm. Perhaps it's breath work, going for a walk, doing yoga or some other form of exercise, journaling, crafting, meditating, or simply being present in the moment. These all sound a bit like things you can also do for self-care, am I right? Self-care is so important for us as parents. We need to fill our own cups so that we have a greater ability to regulate ourselves and in turn can better care for and co-regulate those we love.

*Take responsibility for the energy you bring into this space.*

*—Dr. Jill Bolte Taylor*

---

# SELF-REGULATION STRATEGIES

Some self-regulation techniques that don't cost any money and that you can take advantage of even while nursing your baby include:

**Movement Before Breathing**

Movement reduces stress. Do a few jumping jacks, run in place, or do some burpees. Dancing also works great. Then choose a breathing technique.

**Belly Breathing**

Close your eyes and put one hand on your belly and the other on your heart. Take slow deep breaths, expanding belly like a balloon. Repeat for ten breaths or several minutes.

**Breath Work**

Close eyes and put one hand on belly, the other on heart. Breathe in slowly for four seconds, hold for four seconds, exhale slowly for six seconds. Repeat ten times.

**Name Your Emotions**

Do breath work. Observe your thoughts, your emotions, what your body feels like. Say the feeling out loud: "I am overwhelmed." Relax your body, face, jaw, shoulders, etc. You can name your baby's emotions in the same way.

**Body Scan**

Slowly relax every part of your body from the head down to feet, one part at a time.

**Meditation**

Meditation is known to help improve mood, deepen sleep, and develop a sense of inner peace and calm. It creates lasting brain changes while facilitating self-regulation. Use an app like Calm, Headspace, or Gentle Birth.

**Mindful Observation**

Choose a natural object in your immediate environment and focus on watching it for a minute or two: flower, plant, clouds, moon, etc. Practice relaxing and using your attention to observe the object. Look at every detail.

*Chapter Two*

# SENSORY PROCESSING

Sensory what? This is what most people think, while looking at me with wide-eyed confusion, when I start talking about sensory processing.

Sensory processing differences are something I assess with every client I work with—blame it on my OT brain and the lens through which I view development and overall functioning. They even inform my work with infant reflux and sleep. Sensory processing is an integral part of our being, and it can have a lot to do with our daily stress. And guess what: sensory processing starts in the womb, so it can affect our babies and children as well—perhaps even more, because their brains aren't yet as skilled at filtering out all the input.

We live in a sensory-rich world. We learn about and take in our environment through our senses, specifically through sensory receptors. Sensory processing is our brain's ability to register this input, interpret the information, and form an appropriate response: either motor, language, cognitive, or emotional.[9]

Most of us are familiar with the five senses, but many people are surprised to learn we actually have eight!

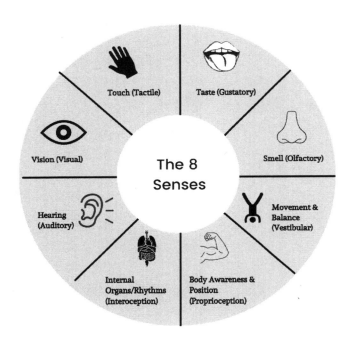

## THE FIVE EXTERNAL SENSES

We receive sensory input from the external world through five senses: tactile (touch), visual (vision), auditory (hearing), olfactory (smell), and gustatory (taste).

Our tactile system, which receives input from the skin (our largest organ with countless receptors), gives us information about temperature, pain, pressure, and touch. Touch gives us a sense of our bodies and tells us whether we're being threatened or comforted. Touch is crucial to a baby's physical, cognitive, and emotional development. It starts in utero but is even more important outside the womb.

Our visual system receives input through our eyes and allows us to see objects, light, and color. As this sense matures, we can view things near and far and in varying colors, as well as perceive depth and dimensions.

Our auditory system is activated when receptors in the ear pick up and register sounds carried through airwaves. We learn to identify (process) where sounds come from and then attach meaning to them, allowing us to distinguish background noises from speech, for example, and which sounds are important to focus on at any one time.

Smells are perceived via receptors in our nose. Our olfactory system is the only one that allows input to go right through to the limbic system, or emotional center, in the brain, which is why smells can evoke such strong emotions or memories. The smell of freshly baked cookies might bring warm, tingly, happy feelings as you remember your grandmother baking in the kitchen. Or maybe the smell of lavender helps you feel relaxed because it reminds you of being at the spa. On the flip side, maybe the smell of tar makes you cringe or brings on nausea as you remember being carsick.

The gustatory system is closely linked to the olfactory system. There are special receptors on different parts of the tongue that give us information about whether what we're tasting is salty, sour, bitter, sweet, or umami.

## THE THREE INTERNAL SENSES

The three body senses, not as familiar to most of us, give us information about our internal world: vestibular (movement/balance), proprioception (body awareness/body position), and interoception (internal body rhythms).

The vestibular system is housed in our inner ear. It senses changes in the position of our head in space, coordinates our head and eye movements, contributes to underlying muscle tone, and mediates our response to movement and gravity. The vestibular system gives us our ability to center and ground ourselves in relation to gravity, affects our spatial awareness, bilateral coordination, and postural activation, and is involved in our arousal levels, self-regulation capabilities, attention, and focus. When it's working well, we feel comfortable with normal movement. We know which direction we're moving in, how fast, and whether we're speeding up or slowing down. The vestibular system is intertwined with the other senses, particularly vision, hearing, and touch. Children who have difficulties with their vestibular system might be fearful of swings or slides or hate car seats or strollers. Or they might seem to be in constant motion. They often love to spin, enjoy fast rides, like being tossed in the air, and frequently jump and bounce. This system is often at play for our kiddos who have difficulty unwinding and settling to sleep.

The proprioception system works closely with the vestibular. The proprioceptors (the sensory receptors found in our muscles and joints) give us a sense of the position of our body in space and how our limbs are moving, which then gives us our sense of movement and spatial orientation. This is important for using our bodies skillfully with respect to body awareness and spatial processing. Difficulties in this area can appear as bumping into things or failing to notice obstacles in the environment, using too much or too little force (i.e., heavy feet), needing heavy blankets to sleep, and decreased body awareness, among other things.

For babies and toddlers, the proprioceptive and vestibular senses are essential for moving through developmental patterns to arrive at a sitting and eventually standing position. And then of course for learning to walk, run, climb ladders and stairs at the playground, and more.

The interoception system receives information through our internal organs and tells us about our comfort level and needs regarding hunger, thirst, digestion, temperature, elimination, and feelings of tiredness or alertness.

All eight of these systems work together to provide us with the ability to perceive, process, and react to sensory stimuli, but three senses (vestibular, proprioceptive, and tactile) are our foundational senses. They help regulate our nervous system. We cannot achieve higher levels of learning, such as self-regulation, or skills such as reading and writing, without a solid foundation in these three foundational senses.

Sensory processing issues can mean everyday activities are more difficult, require more effort, and are achieved with less success and satisfaction. In more significant cases, these difficulties can be signs of a sensory processing disorder, which I'll touch on in a bit.

## IT ALL STARTS IN THE WOMB

Sensory processing starts in the womb, with the senses of touch and vestibular. Touch is the first sense to develop, early during gestation. There is no light touch in the womb, only deep-pressure touch, providing the baby with what feels like an all-day hug or massage. As the baby moves against resistance in this small space, especially as they grow bigger, they receive a lot of feedback from their muscles about their body's position (i.e., proprioception). Touch continues to be important once a baby is born (cuddling, holding, hugging, massaging, and even swaddling).

The vestibular sense begins to function at five months and is well developed at birth but will only fully mature in adolescence. In the womb, baby is floating in amniotic fluid, which decreases the effects of gravity by about fifty times, [10] so you can imagine what they feel in life outside the womb. Mostly babies feel a rocking sensation, and this is why many moms notice that when they're active, the baby doesn't move as much—their movement is essentially rocking the baby to sleep. When the mom stops moving, the baby becomes more active. It's all tied to the vestibular system. By the third trimester, babies are ideally in a head-down position, preparing for birth, which gives them intense vestibular input, which is also important for baby's developing muscle tone. If baby presents as breech, they don't get this same vestibular input. And then there's all that nice tactile, vestibular, and proprioceptive input that baby gets as they come down the birth canal—which is something that babies born via C-section don't get. This is important to understand if your baby is born prematurely and perhaps didn't get as much time to develop their sensory systems.

Interventions—such as inductions with Pitocin, epidurals, or forceps or vacuums—can also have an effect on babies, their sensory systems, and their bodies. It's important to understand this and get the appropriate support to help them function at their best. If you sense that something is amiss with your baby or toddler, trust those mama instincts and seek additional support from bodywork professionals, such as craniosacral therapists, osteopaths, pediatric chiropractors, and professionals well versed in infant development, such as pediatric occupational, physical, or speech therapists.

## AFTER BIRTH—SENSORY PROCESSING ON THE OUTSIDE

Though a baby's sensory system is quite developed inside the womb, most of the input is calming and often dampened by mom's body. As mentioned, birth is a big transition for babies. They're immediately bombarded with sensory information. If you had a C-section, the sensory overload might be even more drastic because there would have been no warning that things were changing.

Because their brains are immature, babies aren't able to habituate to, process, or filter, the sensory input as well as we can. Before we're even conscious of the sensory information received, our brain determines whether it's important or not. If it isn't, the brain inhibits it (or filters it out). This is called habituation and it's vital—it ensures we aren't focused on things such as the feeling of our clothes on our body and that we can focus on important information without becoming overstimulated.

Habituation takes time, and experience, to occur. For babies, especially in that fourth trimester, it hasn't occurred yet, so their brains perceive all new sensory information as important, and they'll respond. This response may be emotional, such as crying, or physical, such as turning toward the breast for feeding.

What all this means is that babies and toddlers can become overstimulated easily. It's our job as parents to filter out excessive sensory input to help them avoid sensory overload (as much as possible). How do we do this? You guessed it: we tune in to our babies—and ourselves. We get curious about their cues. We pay attention to those signs of dysregulation that I mentioned earlier. Are their eyes glazing over because they're overstimulated or tired? Are they looking away or crying because they need a break? Once we get to know our baby's unique cues, we become better detectives. If your baby does get overstimulated, you can snuggle them, nurse them (I'll go deeper into this shortly; it can be very organizing and regulating), or perhaps dim the lights, slow your voice, and just hang out together in the quiet. A walk in fresh air can also do wonders.

This also means that you don't need to be on the go all the time, or buying the shiniest toys on the market. Phew. Doesn't that make you feel a little more relaxed and take away some of the "mom guilt" we all experience at times? I know you might sometimes feel pressure to attend all the classes, do all the things, be social, stimulate and play with your baby, and somehow teach them everything, but here's your permission (not that you need it) to just stop! Follow your instincts, tune in to what you really want, and rest in knowing that you are your baby's most favorite toy and place to be, especially in that first year. Just be!

Again, my goal with this book is to empower you to trust yourself, your mama instincts—and also to trust that your baby will develop and grow just fine (and yes, they will eventually sleep through the night) even if you do nothing but bask in the joy of being with and watching your baby. I promise you, if you slow down and tune in to how you're feeling, what you really want, and what feels light and right, the stress, the worry, and overwhelm will start to melt away. So take the money you were thinking of spending on those baby gadgets and put it in your child's college fund instead.

I know this is hard. I'm a type A recovering perfectionist (okay, working on the recovering part). But your baby needs you to have quiet times and even whole days throughout the week so that they can decompress, regroup, and reset. This is what will help them develop!

## SENSORY THRESHOLDS

Every individual is unique. Each of us has things that calm us, alert us, and overwhelm us. We all have different sleep patterns and developmental trajectories. So of course, we all filter or habituate sensory information in unique ways.

Some of us become stressed out, anxious, and irritated by a busy, noisy, and cluttered environment. This indicates a low sensory-stimulation threshold. We function best in quiet, calm, predictable environments. Other people need more sensory input to feel good. They thrive in busy, active environments and can tolerate plenty of stimulation. They have a high sensory-stimulation threshold.

Each of our senses functions in a unique way, and there's a specific threshold for each one. And, you guessed it, everyone has a different combination of thresholds. A baby may have a low threshold in one sensory system but a high one in another. For example, a baby may get easily overwhelmed with loud noises and crowds but may never sit still when they are at home. Babies who filter sensory information more effectively tend to be calmer and more settled. Babies who are sensitive to changes in their world are usually more alert and may be unsettled more often. Learning to recognize your child's individual sensory thresholds and being aware of their sensory needs and preferences will give you a far greater understanding of them. It will enable you to parent with compassion, sensitivity, and confidence.

I believe that how we process and integrate sensory information underlies our temperament, but I invite you to ponder this when we discuss temperament later in this book.

If your child's sensory thresholds and preferences begin to negatively affect their life, an assessment will be needed. These are often completed by occupational therapists with specific training in sensory processing and integration.

## SENSORY PROCESSING DISORDER

Maybe you've heard this term and it scares you a little. Or perhaps you've noticed that your child is extremely sensitive and you're wondering whether they have sensory processing disorder but aren't sure where to start.

Let's start here. "Sensory processing disorder (SPD) is a condition in which the brain has trouble receiving and responding to information that comes in through the senses."[11] The brain can be either under- or over-registering the sensory input, and this affects daily functioning.

Some children don't integrate sensory input adequately. This can lead to extreme fussing, poor sleep habits, feeding problems, and emotional irritability. Babies with sensory processing differences might not roll over, crawl, sit, stand, or even walk within typical time frames. Rolling and crawling in particular provide a wealth of touch input, so babies who dislike touch or are very sensitive to it (i.e., tactile defensive) might try to avoid doing these things. Perhaps your child throws a fit every time you try to get them dressed, brush their teeth, or put sunscreen on them. Maybe they don't want to be held or have difficulty falling or staying asleep, or maybe they sleep restlessly. They may be sensitive to loud noises that don't seem to bother other babies, or have difficulty transitioning to solids. Or maybe they're always on the move and don't want to be contained in a car seat or stroller.

Then there are babies who have difficulty calming down once upset (even when held by a loving caregiver) and frequently require extreme efforts and a long period of time to calm down. Yes, I'm talking about colic, which is often due to digestive issues but can also be due to body tightness (from in utero and birth experiences) or sensory processing differences.

As your baby becomes a toddler and then a preschool-age child, they may not move easily or gracefully. Running may be awkward. They may have trouble learning to tie their shoes or ride a bike without training wheels. They may seem clumsy.

## SENSORY PROCESSING RED FLAGS IN BABIES/TODDLERS

In general, if a baby is only exhibiting 1-2 of these, or if they are not affecting function, then there is generally no cause for concern. It is when these things are affecting a baby's or child's functioning in their everyday life, and that can include their relationship with others (i.e., caregivers or siblings), that is when these should be further assessed by an occupational therapist or another professional trained in sensory processing and sensory integration.

*(Note: This is NOT an exhaustive list, just a few ideas to get you started thinking about these issues. Go ahead and complete this for your baby.)*

### SENSORY PROCESSING RED FLAGS IN BABIES/TODDLERS, CONT'D

**Tactile Input:**

- ☐ Resists cuddling, pulls away, or arches
- ☐ Resists being swaddled
- ☐ Distressed at having face/hair washed
- ☐ Distressed by being dressed or undressed (may prefer being naked or with layers of warm clothes on)
- ☐ Distressed being strapped into car seat or stroller
- ☐ Avoids touching certain textures or getting hands messy

**Movement (Vestibular) Input:**

- ☐ Distressed when swinging or involved in boisterous play
- ☐ Resists being placed in certain positions (i.e., on stomach/back)
- ☐ Doesn't roll, creep, sit, crawl, stand, or walk in normal ranges
- ☐ Clumsy, awkward movements—falling, bumping into things (>~18 months)

**Sight (Vision):**

- ☐ Sensitive to bright lights—cries or closes eyes
- ☐ Avoids eye contact and turns away from people's faces
- ☐ Becomes overly excited in noisy, bustling settings (i.e., crowded grocery store or restaurant)

**Hearing (Auditory):**

- ☐ Is startled or distressed by loud sounds (such as doorbell or barking dog)
- ☐ No (or very little) babbling or vocalizing

**Distress with Transitions or Changes in Routines:**

- ☐ Baby becomes very disorganized if normal daily routine is disrupted or by transitions from one activity to the next
- ☐ Extreme reaction such as prolonged crying or fussing (i.e., 5+ minutes) and occurs frequently throughout the day

SENSORY PROCESSING RED FLAGS IN BABIES/TODDLERS, CONT'D

### Emotional Instability/Difficulty Self-Calming:

- [ ] Generally fussy, irritable, unhappy and tends to change rapidly from contented to distressed without any apparent reason
- [ ] Not initiating interaction with primary caregiver at 9+ months
- [ ] Not able to calm by bringing hands to mouth, looking at calming images, listening to calming voices or sounds, or being held by a trusted caregiver
- [ ] Requires extreme efforts to calm down

### Feeding Challenges:

- [ ] Difficulty latching as a newborn (not due to tongue- or lip-tie or malpositioning)
- [ ] Does not tolerate change from breast to nipple of bottle
- [ ] Does not have an established, regular feeding schedule (even babies that are fed on demand tend to have a somewhat regular schedule)
- [ ] Distress around intro to solids, with regurgitation and spitting out of food (particularly textured or lumpy foods)
- [ ] Extremely fussy about texture, often only preferring smooth foods, bland foods, or the "white/beige" diet
- [ ] Dislikes toothbrushing
- [ ] Refuses to put utensils in mouth
- [ ] Will not touch certain foods or put certain foods in mouth
- [ ] Avoids mixed-texture food or foods of certain tastes or temperatures
- [ ] Offended by smells or sights of foods
- [ ] Dislikes being messy (i.e., hands/mouth/face)
- [ ] Over-responsive gag reflex
- [ ] Refuses new foods—even when presented a few times
- [ ] Messy eating, overstuffing mouth, difficulty sequencing tongue and lip movements necessary for eating

SENSORY PROCESSING RED FLAGS IN BABIES/TODDLERS, CONT'D

**Sleep Difficulties:**

☐ Persistent problem in regulation of sleep-wake cycles or difficulty falling asleep and staying asleep, which are not associated with other issues (i.e., sleep disorders such as apnea, mouth breathing, latch or tongue-/lip-tie, vitamin/mineral deficiencies) or conditions

☐ Takes over 30 minutes to fall asleep, even after calming techniques and bedtime routine have been implemented

☐ Wakes frequently during the night for reasons other than age-appropriate night feeds

As you can see, a lot of these behaviors are typical for babies and toddlers. If your child is exhibiting only one or two of these, or if they aren't affecting their daily functioning, there's generally no cause for concern. But if they're affecting their daily functioning (or the family's), there might be something more going on. They may have SPD and require an assessment and intervention designed by a health-care professional trained in sensory processing and integration.

# CALMING STRATEGIES

Remember, every child is unique, as is every family, so each child and family will need slightly different strategies and tools. That said, here are some general strategies to help with calming throughout the day. These work for both babies and children who have SPD and those who don't.

## DEEP PRESSURE

Pressure on the body increases the production of serotonin, which helps produce melatonin (one of the sleep hormones, which we'll discuss in more depth later). One of the first things we're taught as new parents is how to swaddle our baby. Swaddling provides calming tactile and proprioceptive input, making the child feel safe and secure. Here are a few other ways to offer deep pressure:

- Bear hugs (firm hugs that encompass the arms and legs)
- Arm and leg massages with firm pressure (with or without lotion)
- Pillow squishes (offering resistive input with a pillow against the body)
- "Kiddo burritos" (wrapping them snugly in a blanket and then rolling them out)
- Weighted blankets or stuffies, or a weighed-down sleep sack (or one filled with little stuffed animals to provide that "hugging" sensation)

## MIDLINE ACTIVITIES

Activities that involve the midline of the body are soothing and organizing. This is often why older babies and toddlers nurse for hours and throughout the night and can't calm without it. Usually by about twelve to eighteen months of age, your baby is nursing more as a soothing mechanism than for nutrition. Doing heavy work (any activity that requires you to put pressure on your muscles and joints as they're moving) through the mouth calms the nervous system. Here are some ways your baby can get this input:

- Sucking on a pacifier
- Chewing on something
- Drinking through the straw of a water bottle or cup
- Blowing party favors, whistles, or bubbles through a straw

## VESTIBULAR INPUT (MOVEMENT)

Baby swings, bouncy chairs, and rocking chairs soothe our babies. The repetitive, gentle, linear, and rhythmic motions provide calming vestibular input to the nervous system and help our babies relax. Here are a couple of ways to provide this input:

- Slowly rock your child over an exercise ball (either sitting up or on their tummy) for a few minutes before bed.
- Read books to them or nurse them in a rocking chair as part of the bedtime routine.

## HEAVY WORK (PROPRIOCEPTION)

Get your child to do some heavy work that involves the joints and muscles. Pushing and pulling can have a calming, regulating, and organizing effect on the body. It also helps the body to feel grounded and centered. Here are a couple of ideas:

- Try having your baby or toddler push and pull things around—a ball, a toy with a string, or even a small pushcart.
- Activities such as crawling, rolling, tummy time on the floor, and downward-dog/upward-dog yoga poses will also activate the proprioceptive system.

## SOUND

As parents, we know that shushing noises or humming can help to calm our little ones. These repetitive, quiet sounds mimic the calming and reassuring sounds the baby heard when inside the womb (i.e., mom's heartbeat, her muffled voice, etc.). Here's another idea:

- White or pink noise (from a sound machine, a fan, a humidifier, or an app) can be calming for many children (and even adults) as they're trying to fall asleep and can also block out other sounds that might startle or wake them.

# A FEW OTHER STRATEGIES

Consider decreasing stimulation and focusing on quieter activities a few hours before bedtime. You could limit the use of toys that make noise or have bright lights, dim the lights in the room they're in, and play quiet music in the background (nature sounds, classical—think yoga-type music).

Children with sensory processing differences need an enriched diet of activities every single day, just as they need a diet full of nutritious food. The goal is to find the right combination of strategies for your child, knowing that it might change daily, depending on what has happened that day.

They typically do well when their foundational senses receive input—vestibular, proprioception, and tactile. Activities that involve these systems help their nervous systems maintain a more regulated state. Try some of the strategies listed above and know that it will take some trial and error. And try not to get discouraged if something doesn't work. What's most important is to be consistent when it comes to tuning in to your child and in terms of the tools or strategies you choose. Remember, it takes our brain a while before something moves from new and unfamiliar (aka scary) to familiar and predictable (aka safe)!

# Chapter Three

# ATTACHMENT

*Attachment* is a buzzword these days, and in the parenting world, there's much more focus on prioritizing attachment.

Attachments are emotional bonds. We all need strong attachments to others, regardless of age—they aren't just something that forms between parent and child.

A healthy attachment provides a sense of security, of safety—of knowing that you can rely on someone for comfort and to help you in times of distress. A baby must obtain this sense of security from you, their parent. As we looked at in Chapter One, when your baby is distressed, they need you to tune in to their needs and signals and help them to calm down through co-regulation. Co-regulation allows them to begin trusting you and attaching to you. When you co-regulate with them consistently and predictably, you create feelings of safety and comfort and help build that secure-attachment relationship.

Attachment starts in the womb. You set the foundation by bonding with your unborn child—you might talk to your baby, rub your belly, and send loving energy to them. They may share your feelings of excitement and perhaps nervousness. When you connect with your baby for the first time after the birth, that bond is strengthened and attachment begins to form. This is part of the reason why skin-to-skin contact is so important following the birth. If it isn't possible, you may feel a strange sense of detachment from your baby initially.

## THE MAGIC OF OXYTOCIN

Time to get a little nerdy (again) and talk about the brain chemistry that triggers this initial connection and the beginning stages of attachment. When moms give birth, oxytocin (the love hormone) is coursing through their bodies. It's released at birth, during an orgasm, and any time you're feeling deeply connected to someone and oh so good. In ideal circumstances, mamas and babies have an excess of this hormone flooding them during and after birth, essentially causing them to fall in love with each other. But oxytocin is also released when the right orbito frontal cortex (ROFC) is activated which can happen through the eye contact that moms and babies share.

The ROFC is located behind the right eye and is essentially like the CEO of the brain. It's very important for, and grows stronger with, attachment. It has many jobs, but some of the more important ones are regulating heart rate and hormones and controlling the autonomic nervous system (remember those three branches—sympathetic, parasympathetic, and social engagement). It's also involved in our emotions and attention span. The ROFC tells the amygdala (the part of our brain that is in charge of keeping us safe) to calm down when it notices we're dysregulated.

Kim Barthel, a well-known occupational therapist in the world of attachment, talks a lot about the role of oxytocin in attachment and bonding between mom (or primary caregiver) and baby. She often refers to the activation of the ROFC as "gleaming and beaming,"[12,13] which sounds so magical. So next time you're holding your baby for what seems like the millionth time that day, or perhaps they're comfort nursing yet again, or maybe you're on the floor with them while they're playing in tummy time, take a moment to gaze into their eyes. This simple gesture is one of the building blocks of a secure attachment, and it also sends loving energy to your baby. Notice how you feel. Pretty magical, right?

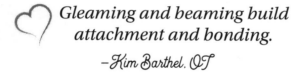

*Gleaming and beaming build attachment and bonding.*

*–Kim Barthel, OT*

Eye contact with loving intent (the intent is a key part here) is just one of the ways that attachment is strengthened. Touch is another fantastic way, as it also stimulates oxytocin release in both caregiver and baby. So give your baby massages, let them lie on your chest, wear them in a carrier or sling, and in general hold them close, knowing that all of this closeness is exactly what they need to develop that strong and secure attachment that will lead them through life. Oh, and another little nerdy tidbit: oxytocin helps to counteract the effects of cortisol (the stress hormone), which we'll talk more about in the sleep section of this book.

# BUILDING A SECURE ATTACHMENT

You can see how attachment underlies how we interact with our children and how we build loving and secure relationships from which they can develop and grow to be amazing humans. And it's also the first step in their journey to becoming independent! Now you might be wondering about how exactly, besides the gleaming and beaming and the use of touch, to build that secure attachment.

Before we get to that, let's look at the concept of independence. We're so focused on it in Western culture, almost from the moment our children are born.

A lot of our stress and overwhelm as parents (which often comes from the comparison game) stems from this idea that we must teach independence. Think about it. From the moment you give birth, you're bombarded with *usually* well-meaning advice about how not to create bad habits, how to prevent babies from becoming too dependent, and how to promote independence from an early age. "Drowsy but awake" sound familiar? As a result, we parents have taken it upon ourselves to teach our children how to sit, stand, and walk. How to read (are Baby Einstein or flash cards still a thing?), talk, eat, pee, and poo (usually on our timeline rather than theirs), and how to fall asleep on their own and get back to sleep without us. Phew—that's a lot of work!

But what if we didn't need to focus on teaching independence? What if we could just trust our babies and children, trust evolution, and rest in knowing that just by having the right opportunities to explore, move, experience, try, and fail, they'd learn these things on their own? What if just being present with our children, talking to them, loving them, comforting them, and getting to know them as the unique people they are, quirks and all, was enough?

Sound too good to be true?

Nope. A secure attachment promotes said autonomy and independence. Think about toddlers learning to walk. Initially they crawl or toddle away from us just a little bit to explore the environment, but they're always looking back to make sure we're still there. When parent and child bond, tune in to each other, and develop a secure attachment, a strong base is created. It's only when a child feels safe and secure that their independence can be fostered. Which means that we don't have to teach independence—but we can set the stage for it by cultivating a secure attachment and providing an optimal environment for exploring and learning.[14] And this sets the stage for lifelong patterns of self-regulation, a positive sense of self, and the ability to participate in meaningful relationships, roles, and activities.[15] Isn't that what we want for our children?

You can start to build attachment in the early days through simple things: gleaming and beaming through loving eye contact, holding them in a loving manner, rocking or swaying them, providing warmth and comforting words/ sounds, and responding in a timely and consistent way. And I'm going to bet that you're already doing these things without thinking about them. You're doing them because they feel good, they feel easy, and they're instinctual. You're trusting your instincts!

## TYPES OF ATTACHMENT

Secure attachment is what we should all strive for. But there are other, less-desirable types of attachment that can form, often without conscious intent. I want to bring your awareness to them so that you can consciously make parenting decisions from a place of knowledge rather than pressure. So that you can lean in to your instincts and trust that responsiveness, support, and comfort are the exact things your baby needs for optimal growth and development. If you identify with one of the other types of attachment, that's okay. Once you're aware of it, you can change your ways, if you want.

There are four main attachment styles—secure attachment and three types of insecure styles. These styles are more like patterns of behavior between a child and their primary caregiver but can be influenced by more than one caregiver. A child can also have different attachment styles with different caregivers.[16] In fact, most people have a mix of styles. Think back to your childhood and early life experiences and how you were parented. All of these things are part of you and likely play into how you parent your own child, how you show up in your other relationships, and what triggers you.

Secure attachment essentially means that your child is confident that their needs will be met and that when they're distressed, ill, or threatened, you'll be reasonably available and responsive emotionally. It's the confidence in the relationship that makes for security.

Insecure attachments form when your child isn't confident that you'll be there for them. This happens when caregivers are consistently insensitive or unresponsive to a baby's cues. It's often difficult for people with insecure attachments to learn self-regulation later in life.[17,18] There are three sub-types of insecure attachment: insecure-avoidant, insecure-ambivalent, and insecure-disorganized.

> **Insecure-avoidant** happens when the child becomes too independent because their needs are rarely or never met by their caregiver. They learn that when they signal their caregiver, they'll be ignored. These parents usually meet their child's physical needs but may come across as indifferent or insensitive to their emotional needs, often sending the message that they're happy to be with the child but not when they're crying. The child learns that their parent isn't interested in their distress and that they'll get a better response— or will simply conserve their energy—if they just don't show that

they're upset. This, in a sense, is what happens with more traditional sleep-training approaches based on behavioral and separation techniques.[19]

**Insecure-ambivalent**, on the other hand, is when the child is too dependent and clings to the caregiver. The baby's needs are met but in an unreliable and unpredictable way, which leads to the baby not knowing when or if their needs will be met. As a result, the child becomes hypervigilant and isn't easily soothed. Often these babies spend more time watching their caregiver and less time exploring their environment.

**Insecure-disorganized** is the style often involved in abuse and neglect, when the caregiver is scary. As a result, the child becomes unsure of how to approach them. They'll fight an internal battle when distressed, not knowing whether to approach or avoid their caregiver. These children often grow up with dysregulated stress systems, personality disorders, and anxiety and/or depression.

Please don't go down the rabbit hole of worrying whether you're inadvertently ruining your child if you're not the epitome of a perfect securely attached parent. There's no such thing as the perfect parent! Sorry to burst that bubble. Go ahead and breathe a sigh of relief. Let some of that stress go. It's not about perfection but about how you connect. And when you react in a less-than-perfect way (trust me, this will happen, possibly many times in a day), it becomes about how you repair the situation.

It's important to realize that how we attached to our primary caregivers influences how we show up as parents (sometimes on a subconscious level). With this awareness, we can make the best choices moving forward when raising our babies. We've all been there, setting the intention to "never be like my mom" or "not do that like my dad." I know you know what I'm talking about! While I was pregnant, I had clear ideas of how I wanted to parent, what I didn't want to do as a parent, and how I wanted my children to feel. These came from my childhood experiences, and I can tell you that as much as I've consciously tried to be different in certain areas, there are plenty of moments when something escapes my lips that I swore I'd never say to my children, or moments of frustration or anger that trigger a childhood memory. But you know what? That's okay! I'm not a perfect parent, but I am aware of my reactions and also my intentions when it comes to the type of parent I want to be. I hold these intentions in my mind when I make amends and apologize for my outbursts.

In case you need a reminder, remember what Maya Angelou said: "Do the best you can until you know better. Then when you know better, do better." And remember—a baby can relate in a securely attached way to one parent and an insecure way to another and *still* reap the benefits that come with a secure attachment. Attachment can also change over time. We need to continuously work on our relationships not just with others but also ourselves.

The goal is to be consistent when we respond to our babies, our children, our teenagers, and all the other people in our lives. Be consistent in how you connect, how you comfort. Be consistent in your responsiveness. And remember, you can't spoil a baby by holding them too much or by picking them up when they cry. Loving attention, soothing voices, comforting touches, eye contact, and physical closeness are exactly what our babies need when they're in a state of distress or a reactive state where their body is out of control (hello, tantrums, I'm looking at you).

Through co-regulation, you help your child move from dependence to independence, when they're ready. No matter what our Western culture says, what you hear from your pediatrician, what you see on social media, or what you read in books, we can't force independence. We need to spend less time worrying about independence and more time focusing on attachment.

A quick note about attachment parenting.[20,21] This approach aligns with what I believe in, practice, and teach, but it's often misunderstood and taken to the extreme, causing more stress for parents than it should. Some parents think that practicing attachment parenting means they should never let their child cry. And that if their child cries, they, the parents, are failing. This is so far from the truth!

## ATTACHMENT PARENTING

There are 8 main tenets of attachment parenting. I have taken the main principles from Attachment Parenting International and have slightly adapted them to be more inclusive to modern parenting, and my own beliefs.

### 1. Prepare for pregnancy, birth & parenting

Educate yourself around birth options and create a plan that works for you. Focus on promoting the bonding between you and baby as soon as possible after birth.

### 2. Feed with love and respect

Feed on demand (vs. on a schedule) and respect your baby's hunger cues. Breastfeed if possible, even past one year of age. If bottle-feeding, do it in a responsive and attentive way (hold baby close, feed on demand, make eye contact, practice paced bottle feeding). Offer healthy foods and model healthy eating behaviors.

### 3. Respond with sensitivity

Timely response by a nurturing caregiver (i.e., respond to your baby when they cry), as this creates the strong attachment and trust between parent and baby. Babies are initially unable to soothe themselves and need us, their caregivers, to co-regulate. Attachment Parenting International actually goes further and says that "baby-training systems, such as the commonly referred-to 'cry it out,' are inconsistent with this principle."

### 4. Use nurturing touch

Holding, wearing, and comforting your baby, as well as any form of touch through nursing, bathing, and massaging, are the fundamental components of this principle. This nurturing touch meets your baby's need for affection and contact and is so important for physical, emotional, and cognitive development.

### 5. Ensure safe sleep, physically & emotionally

While many parents who follow attachment parenting choose to bed-share (taking appropriate safety guidelines into consideration) or at least room-share well beyond the first year, the point is not the sleeping surface but that parents remain responsive to their children during sleep. Babies initially spend a lot of their 24-hour day sleeping, and their needs do not stop just because they are sleeping or it is bedtime.

### 6. Provide consistent and loving care

Secure attachment is built with even just one primary caregiver offering consistent and loving care, both day and night, but this does not mean it only has to be you! If you are not able to take care of your child (i.e., if you work during the day), then make sure to put thought into who will care for your child and whether they align with your values. You should also set the stage to make sure your child is comfortable with this new caregiver beforehand, something that Dr. Deborah Macnamara calls "matchmaking."

ATTACHMENT PARENTING, CONT'D

## 7. Practice positive discipline

There is always a reason for behavior, as it is a way of communicating something, and we as parents need to get curious about the why. Positive discipline encourages empathy rather than shaming, guilt, or time-outs. It encourages parents to teach by example using problem-solving, playful parenting, substitution, and even distraction at times. The aim is for parents to be coaches and cheerleaders for their child, but also to be mindful of setting their child up for success (i.e., consciously choosing toys, environments, and people their child can handle, and making sure basic needs are met, such as feeding and rest).

## 8. Strive for balance in personal and family life

Parenting is hard work and exhausting, especially in the first few years and in our Western culture where we have moved away from the village mentality and more into the nuclear family, where we are alone with very little support. We need to support and care for ourselves, so that we can have the energy and motivation to care for our children and parent the way that we want without being a martyr for the sake of our children. By taking care of our own needs, we lead by example and help our children build healthy relationships with themselves as well.

 *You do the best you can until you know better. And when you know better, you can do better!*

*—Maya Angelou*

Ultimately, building a secure attachment with your child starts with responding to their needs, soothing and comforting them when they cry (and allowing those tears to flow), holding them when they're upset, showing your love through physical affection and words of affirmation, and being consistent in your approach and actions—day *and* night. And it's worth repeating: Being consistent is *not* the same as being perfect. There's no such thing as perfection.

# TEARS AND BOUNDARIES

### TEARS ARE TRIGGERING

I'll bet that when your child cries you have a strong urge to stop those tears immediately, and this is totally natural. But crying is a normal part of the human experience, and it's not necessarily our job to stop the tears or prevent them in the first place.

Stay with me here! I'm not telling you to leave your children to cry unsupported.

Tears trigger something that's hardwired in you. In Chapter One, we looked at how parents' brains are chemically altered to respond to their babies' cries to protect them and ensure their survival. Tears are triggering on a physiological level but also on a deeper-rooted emotional level based on our own life experiences. We have an innate desire to respond to tears and prevent them. Though this sounds good, it can send the message that it isn't okay to cry. Crying is linked to emotions, so trying to prevent tears sends a message that emotions associated with tears aren't okay.

I'm not saying you shouldn't respond to your child's crying. Hug them and hold them. Meet their needs. Love them and show them you'll always be there for them. What I'm encouraging you to do is to become comfortable with the tears. Allow them to flow while you meet your child's needs and support them through those emotions.

 **Fact:** Babies and young children cry. They cry because it's their only way to communicate with you initially. They're not crying to annoy or manipulate you.

## CRYING AND STRESS

Crying releases cortisol. And we want this cortisol to be released so that it's not coursing through our bodies (or our children's bodies), as this hormone can affect our well-being in so many ways, as we discussed in Chapter One. We also release stress through screaming, raging, repeatedly talking about the hurt, shaking, laughing, perspiring, and yawning.[22]

*Tears release pain and stress.*
*—Pam Leo, Connection Parenting*

While crying is normal, crying unsupported and alone sends babies and young children into a fight-or-flight state in which cortisol is increased instead of released. Even if you can't stop your little one's tears (e.g., if they're in pain or discomfort and you can't "fix" that immediately), your support helps keep the cortisol levels lower. Responding with loving intention and offering physical or emotional support is what counts!

Sometimes this is easier said than done. Sometimes your child wants nothing to do with you when they're upset. In this case, you can simply remain present. Stay close by and offer help when they're ready, so that they know they're not alone in their emotional distress. I do this with my children (currently four and seven years old). When they're melting down and don't want to be held, I carry them to their room and sit inside it with them, with my back against the door (so they can't get out). I sit quietly (or sometimes hum) and let them do what they need to do—cry, scream, throw toys, etc. Eventually they come and sit in my lap and we have a big long hug and then we talk about what happened.

## SETTING APPROPRIATE BOUNDARIES

Just as we shouldn't let our babies cry in an effort to "teach independence" or "let them exercise their lungs" or some other nonsense you read in a book or heard from a well-meaning mother-in-law, we shouldn't contrive situations to prevent the crying. As mentioned, many parents who subscribe to the attachment parenting philosophy have come to understand it as a no-cry approach. This leads to not setting appropriate boundaries, which in turn can lead to parents' losing their role as leader.

Attachment is meant to be hierarchical, in a sense. In a secure-attachment relationship, there's a dependent and there's a leader (or "alpha"). In a parent-child relationship, the parent should always be the leader (the provider) and the child the dependent (the seeker). This doesn't mean that you're the "boss" (though initially you sort of are). Rather, you're there to care for your child, protect them, meet their needs, lead and guide them, and show them they can depend on you. Your child can then trust in you, look for guidance from you, feel as if they belong, and rest in the knowing that they'll be taken care of.[23]

You're allowed to put boundaries in place. In fact, it's one of your important roles as a leader. Some boundaries (or rules) such as "wear your seatbelt in the car" and "hold hands when crossing the street" are obvious. But you're also allowed to say no to your child if they're climbing on the furniture, putting their fingers in the electrical sockets, or pulling your shirt down and grabbing your boobs all day long. If something is no longer working for you or your child, it's okay to put a boundary in place around it. Maybe you read only two books at bedtime, or you nurse your sixteen-month-old only once during the night.

You might be thinking, "Well of course I have these boundaries." While they do seem like common sense, I often see a lot of issues around sleep and behavior as a result of boundaries not being set or adhered to. If you aren't setting boundaries with your older baby or toddler, you're sending the message that they're running the show and can do whatever they want. If they take on the leader (or alpha) role, they'll become more assertive, bossy, controlling, and demanding. They'll need to be center stage all the time, and they might be described as "strong-willed." Bedtime and meal-time battles, not listening to or following directions, and frequent tantrums could all be signs that your child has started to attach in the alpha role. As parents, we often think our children behave like this on purpose, leading us to get frustrated and try various approaches to discipline. In general, we may feel lost as to how to parent them. And this feeling feeds into our losing control of the leadership role. It's a vicious cycle.

I'm not going to sugarcoat it: putting loving boundaries in place isn't an easy feat but an important one. They can be necessary as early as at nine months, when babies typically start to develop a sense of agency. It's usually easier to put daytime boundaries in place first and work toward nighttime boundaries. The important thing when it comes to putting loving boundaries in place is to be consistent and hold the boundary.

This will take time, and there may be days when it's harder than others. Emotions may run high, and your child may hit, grab, run away, and scream. These are all normal reactions. With time and consistency, the boundaries will become easier to maintain. Your toddler will have expressed their emotions as they let go of the status quo (which our brain views as safe), and they'll start to become used to the new (which, with time, becomes more familiar and therefore safe).

There may be days or nights where the boundary just isn't working, or you're utterly exhausted and just need sleep. It's okay to put the boundary aside at times and try again the next day. The important thing is to keep trying if the boundary still feels right in your heart. Ultimately, you get to decide.

The key difference between setting loving boundaries and letting your child "just figure it out" is that in setting boundaries, you're supporting and responding to the emotions being expressed. You're there, in their presence, lovingly holding space, while they experience their emotions. We have to be allowed to express and move through emotions to get to the other side. And on that other side is relief, usually a big inhale and exhale, and calm. Dr. Gordon Neufeld calls these the "tears of futility."[24] You've likely felt immense peace and calmness after a "good cry," and that's because you were allowed to move through the emotion. Yet for some reason we've come to accept the idea that it's awful to let our children cry.

Imagine if you were sad, angry, hurt, or scared and just needed to feel safe and secure and your partner ignored you or told you to "stop right now," "calm down," or "there's no need to cry."

You'd be enraged! You'd feel unsupported—and maybe even unloved. Would you trust your partner fully? Nope? Me neither.

This is exactly what is going on with our children. Let's remember that they're doing their best. They communicate with us not just through words, but also through tears and actions. For this reason, we want to allow (and get comfortable with) tears, day *and* night instead of trying to prevent them. By allowing the tears to flow and supporting those emotions, we give our children the permission to become comfortable with *all* emotions, not just the happy ones. We also teach them through experience that we don't have control over everything in our lives and that's okay.

By consistently responding to a child's attempt to communicate their needs, we help them to become confident that their needs will be met, and their bodies and brains can develop the independence necessary for them to be able to calm themselves. We help them develop the foundation for emotional regulation and resiliency. That's ultimately what we want, right? To support our children to be happy, secure, resilient, compassionate, and fulfilled contributors to society.

# THE INTERPLAY BETWEEN CONNECTION AND SEPARATION

## BEING PRESENT

Now that you know some of the basics about attachment, how babies and toddlers attach and why attachment is so important, I hope that you've gleaned that attachment involves consistently paying attention to and addressing our children's needs, comforting them when they're in distress, allowing and supporting tears and emotions, and ultimately spending time with and connecting with them.

As humans we thrive on connection. Our children need us, no matter how old. One of the best ways to connect with children is through play. Play is the language of children. It's a powerful way to connect with them and fill their love cup.[25] This doesn't mean that you need to be your child's entertainer 24/7, nor that you need to be buying all the brightest, trendiest things to help your child grow and develop. Just the opposite, actually. Playing can be as easy and inexpensive as just showing up.

Showing up means being physically and emotionally present for your kids. It's about quality time. When we show up for our kids, we bring our whole being, our attention and awareness. You can show up for them throughout the day by meeting their needs (e.g., changing their diaper, bathing them, feeding them), expressing your love for them, laughing with them, and even setting boundaries. Remember, you don't have to be perfect. You just have to show up. Let out another sigh of relief!

In *The Power of Showing Up*, authors Dan Siegel and Tina Payne Bryson discuss how when kids feel safe (they're taken care of physically and emotionally), seen (their thoughts and emotions count), and soothed (they know you'll be there when they're hurting), they'll develop a secure attachment to their caregivers. I also love their acronym PEACE—a great reminder of *how* we can connect.[26]

| | |
|---|---|
| **PRESENCE** | When your kid is hurting, be there for them. Show up and do something. |
| **ENGAGEMENT** | Actively listen, make eye contact, give them a hug, and use other nonverbal communication to express how important your child is to you. |
| **AFFECTION** | Use your words and actions to communicate how much you love your child and want to help them. |
| **CALM** | Remain calm by regulating yourself, your emotions, and your nervous system first. |
| **EMPATHY** | Feel their experience. |

Connecting with your child is even a great way to reduce some of the daily battles (such as bedtime). I like the saying "connect before you direct." All too often when we want our children to do something, we immediately give them a command: "Get your shoes on," "Clean up," "Eat your dinner," "Brush your teeth and then to bed." And we end up frustrated when our children seemingly ignore said command and we hear ourselves on repeat.

Sound familiar? In my house, commands are often met with a big fat no or a full-blown screaming fit—and I study this topic and consciously practice it!

We're all humans, living the human experience. As parents we try our best to teach our children manners and set boundaries and limits, with the intention to help our children become independent, successful contributors to society. But when they meet our attempts to do so with defiance and resistance, life becomes very stressful. The strategy of collecting or connecting *before* you direct is so helpful!

Collecting a child involves getting down to their level, getting them to look at you (this may involve a physical cue, such as touching their shoulder), and eliciting a smile or a head nod from them.[27-29] We get their attention, often by joining in their current activity (e.g., commenting on the game they're playing) or validating their feelings ("I know how much fun you're having building with Legos"), and then we make our request ("It's time to eat dinner now"). This may seem counterintuitive, but you'll meet less defiance if you do it. I don't always remember this, but when I do, the results are incredible.

Though connecting and being present is inexpensive, it can also be exhausting for us parents, which is why it's so important for us to meet our own needs as well. You can't fill a child's love cup if yours is empty. This goes back to the importance of self-care—take care of yourself, take time alone, take time to rest, take time to do things that bring you joy and that don't necessarily involve your kids!

## BEDTIME CONNECTION

Children tend to need connection the most in the morning, when we first get home in the evening, and at bedtime. A lot of sleep challenges (bedtime battles, middle-of-the-night visits, etc.), especially for toddlers and preschoolers, are actually relationship issues (once everything medical and feeding related has been ruled out). It's as difficult for children to fall asleep when they're emotionally hungry as it is for them to fall asleep physically hungry. One of the biggest reasons children resist going to bed is that it's their last chance of the day for connection. Nighttime is the biggest separation. Separation threatens the attachment system, and so it's perceived as a threat and triggers a strong alarm response.[30-32] Add the scariness of the darkness to this separation and the stress is doubled.

The comforting presence of an attachment figure deactivates the stress system. So the next time your little one is "giving you a hard time" at bedtime, wanting that extra book or for you to lie with them while they fall asleep, remember that this transition from being with you during the day, attaching and connecting, to being separated from you is a big one. Reframe it as "they're having a hard time." This relationship between connection and separation is important to remember day *and* night.

As we've explored, it's not our job to teach our babies how to separate and be independent. It *is* our job to make separation easier for them. To give them something to hold on to in our absence. We do this by consistently responding to them and meeting their needs. When we let our babies and young children rest in the knowing that they're loved, no matter what, we help them better face and accept separation, whether that involves going to sleep or to school. We can also ease the separation by focusing on the next connection.[33] At night you might say, "Maybe we'll see each other in our dreams," or talk about the fun things you'll do together tomorrow. Another cute idea is to hang a bag on their door and tell them that you'll put a heart in it every time you check on them. You can return every couple of minutes with a heart until they fall asleep (and then fill the bag). You can also do things like set the table together before bed, so it's ready for breakfast the next morning.

> *A child needs five to six years of strong, reliable, generous care given by an adult in order to grow into a separate self.*
> —Dr. Deborah Macnamara, macnamara.ca

Another thing I hear often from parents is that their children hate the crib, so they resort to bed-sharing when they don't want to, or to having the baby sleep on them while they're sleeping in an armchair or on the couch (not safe). Truth is, it is likely less about the crib than it is about the separation. For babies, you can help to bridge this separation or make them more comfortable in their sleep spaces by giving them something to hold on to the connection with (e.g., a shirt that smells like you—the more breast-milk stained, the better). Pop it under the fitted sheet of the crib or lay it on the mattress during the bedtime routine and remove it when you lay baby down. You could also sleep with their fitted sheet for a few days, or wear a special high-grade essential oil all the time so that it becomes a familiar and soothing scent for baby. I did this with my daughter, my "oily" baby (she's been exposed to oils since my pregnancy). I rubbed an essential oil blend called Gentle Baby on my pregnant belly and then wore it on my neck after she was born. I even put it on her lovey when she was old enough for that. Eventually, I started to rub it right on her fitted sheets and pajamas. It was so soothing.

If your child can handle bedtime, it means you've given them enough to hold on to from an attachment and connection perspective during the days. If they have difficulty with bedtime and overnight, especially as they get older, focus on connecting more during the day and especially before bedtime, and make sure to bridge the separation and focus on the upcoming connection.

*Stop looking at all the things you are not doing and see all the things that you are! Your child does not need a perfect parent. They need you, just the way you are, to love them.*

*—Kaili Ets*

# Chapter Four

# DEVELOPMENT BASICS

When I had my son, I attended all the mom-and-baby classes—music, yoga, sign language. But for me, something was missing. There wasn't a class where I could learn to play with my baby. And the comparison game was in full force! I remember sitting in a class comparing my five-month-old who wasn't yet rolling (totally normal, by the way) to one who was already sitting. I questioned my baby and his development. *Should I be doing something different? Maybe I'm not doing enough?* I was exhausted. I was confused. I was stressed out. I was overwhelmed. And the mom guilt crept in. Maybe you've felt this way too.

The thing is, I should have known better, given my years of experience as a pediatric occupational therapist. I knew what was typical for infant and child development, but in those moments I wasn't using my "therapy brain." Instead, I was consumed by my mama heart and feelings. This is why I initially started running my Babies @ Play mom-and-baby classes, which focus on infant development. I figured that if I was confused and overwhelmed, other mamas had to be feeling this way too.

The more I researched, the more I realized that "normal" infant development isn't talked about much. I'd fill in some checkboxes at each baby wellness appointment and that was about it. Our society is so focused on catching atypical development and intervening that we've fallen short when it comes to supporting mamas in the postpartum period in so many ways, including education around what's biologically normal or developmentally appropriate for babies at each age.

There were once villages of elders and other mamas—people who would band together to teach new moms. Now we're essentially isolated, in our nuclear families, with extended family often miles away. We rely on Dr. Google and random social media groups and accounts. It's not good enough. In fact, rather than helping, it often causes moms a lot of stress (and contributes to the dreaded comparison game). There's so much misinformation being shared, some by well-trained health-care professionals. Luckily, I've started to see a shift. There are some amazing professionals doing great work around infant development, infant sleep, and postpartum support for mamas worldwide. You can find a few of my favorites at www.kailiets. com/favorites. My goal is to become a part of your "village" and to reduce your overwhelm by arming you with knowledge of what's normal for your baby in the first two years of life. And if you're looking for some fun ways to play and encourage development for your baby without needing a lot of equipment, join me for a Babies @ Play class, either in person or online.

Before we get started, come in close, Mama, and read carefully.

You don't have to teach your baby ALL.THE.THINGS! Nope. You don't have to teach them how to roll, crawl, stand, walk, hold their toys, babble, play, eat, and so on. Human babies are quite amazing and will learn to do all these things on their own.

Here's the catch, though:

It IS your job to set them up for success. To give them the right opportunities and environments in which to learn. For babies this means lots of freedom to explore and move—*on their own*! Babies develop best when they're unrestricted. Get them out of those expensive containers, set up a safe section in your house where they can explore, then sit back and watch what happens. Watch them and see all the little mini-milestones they hit. Babies are curious. They'll explore, fail, fall, adjust, get back up, and try again in a different way.

One of my clients struggled with sleep and had a bit of anxious energy to her. When I dug a little deeper, she admitted that she felt she had to be on the heels of her eight-month-old to prevent him from falling and hurting himself. This fear of her baby hurting himself was causing her so much stress, and guess what? Her baby was feeling all that energy too, and feeding off it—he was fussy, clinging, and battling sleep.

I'm here to tell you, Mama, that you DO NOT NEED to teach your baby all the skills. Enjoy watching them evolve with little effort on your part. This is the miracle and beauty of being human. Our bodies know what to do and how to flourish when given the right opportunities and support.

Did you know that typical development is measured in an age range and not by specific ages? That said, development does progress in a set pattern, with one skill being mastered before the next.

For example, the average age range for rolling is four to six months, but one baby might roll at three and a half months whereas others (ahem, my two children) will roll closer to seven months. With my firstborn, I was so worried about this. We practiced rolling for hours, and then one day, he just did it and kept doing it. Realistically, he probably would have done it all on his own. I could have saved myself hours of worry and practice had I known that this was totally normal!

## MOTOR MILESTONE DEVELOPMENTAL PROGRESSIONS

| | |
|---|---|
| 4-6 months | rolling |
| 6-9 months | crawling |
| 8-10 months | sitting independently, pulling to stand |
| 12-18 months | walking |
| 18 months+ | running |

Every baby has their own timelines. As long as they're within normal ranges, give or take a few weeks or even a month, it's fine. As long as they're progressing in their skills each week, even just in new little skills, what I like to call mini-milestones, it's fine (usually). Of course, there are red flags to be aware of, which we'll discuss. If you see any of them, please reach out to a pediatric physical or occupational therapist.

Let's start from the beginning. I'll take you through how development works, from the moment your baby is born all the way to the point where they're walking. Ready?

## SPINAL CURVES

We can't talk about developmental milestones without first talking about spinal curves, the "backbone" of development. Adult spines have an S shape, with curves at the neck (cervical curve), midback (thoracic curve), low back (lumbar curve), and sacrum or tailbone (sacral curve). These curves allow us to walk in an upright position, against gravity, and they help spread the gravitational load of pressure in our bodies. Newborns are born with C-shaped spines from being curled and scrunched in utero. Their spines start to stretch out after birth, but this happens over time and with lots of movement experiences. Until these various curves start to develop, a baby won't be able to move much on their own.

You may be thinking, "If this is true, why does my baby move their legs as if they want to walk when I hold them upright?" Because of the stepping reflex. When their feet touch a surface, this primitive reflex kicks into action. It's similar to the rooting reflex—when babies' cheeks are stroked, they turn toward the breast. It's a survival reflex.

 **A note about reflexes.** A baby's brain grows and develops through rhythmic movements, such as those stimulated by the baby being touched and rocked by their parents and by those the baby makes on their own. Reflexes are rhythmical movements that occur without conscious control (they're controlled by the brain stem). There are two types of reflexes: primitive and postural. Primitive reflexes develop before or shortly after birth, within the first year, to equip a baby with automatic movements. In the beginning these movements are awkward, but after some practice the baby becomes more accomplished in them. When a baby makes spontaneous rhythmic movements, the primitive reflexes are activated and then integrated (moved past), one after the other. Postural reflexes help us with our posture, movement, and body stability. These reflexes provide the framework for other parts of the nervous system to function effectively.

Sometimes reflexes fail to develop and/or integrate (meaning the reflex is still active). This can be related to heredity issues (e.g., genetic conditions, developmental delays, etc.), disease, lack of movement experiences or not enough of these experiences as a baby, physical or psychological trauma, toxicity, and/or prematurity and C-section delivery. If primitive reflexes aren't integrated, the child's nervous system will be immature and a number of things could be affected in terms of their functioning and/or behavior.

Okay, back to spinal curves. These form through the development of movement patterns. It is through movement patterns, as well as experiencing and integrating the primitive reflexes, that babies reach their motor milestones. Their spines start to straighten out of the C curve and develop the other curves as they get stronger in tummy time, twist their bodies while rolling, get on to hands and knees for crawling, and eventually push and pull themselves into sitting and standing positions.

# DEVELOPMENTAL MOVEMENT PATTERNS

There are four main developmental movement patterns that babies progress through in their first year and that stay with them throughout life.

1. **Navel radiation**. When baby is born, movement is centered around the belly button (the navel). Navel radiation is not only important for breathing but also for strengthening the diaphragm.

2. **Homologous**. This is head-to-tail movement, and baby develops this when they push through their arms and hands to lift their head and chest in tummy time, lift their bum (tail) in the air, and eventually grab hold of their tiny little feet (happy baby pose) and try to bring them to their mouths! Does your baby do any of these?

Each of these movements is a mini-milestone. Even a seemingly tiny action, such as getting into happy baby pose, helps your baby learn and grow stronger. In happy baby, they find their feet (yay—they eventually need those to help them move!) while working on fine motor (hand) muscles through grabbing and holding. Baby's core and leg muscles also get quite the workout—it takes effort to get those feet up against gravity (though easier for them than for us!). All these mini-skills will eventually help with rolling. You might see them shift side to side. I encourage you to sit back and let them do that, even if they rock all the way over to one side (at which point they might need some help).

3.  **Homolateral**. This refers to same (homo) side (lateral) movements. You might see baby getting one foot to their mouth while in happy baby pose, or perhaps they start to reach with one arm while in tummy time. Then comes the one-sided army crawl, which is often one of the first mini-milestones in crawling.

4.  **Contralateral**. In this movement pattern, opposite (contra) sides (lateral) work together and in opposition. This is the pattern that allows our babies to crawl and eventually walk. It also allows them to cross the middle of their bodies (i.e., the midline) and touch their opposite foot with their hand.

## SPINAL CURVE DEVELOPMENT

It's important to note that movement patterns and spinal curves develop at the same time, one affecting the other, which then affect the integration of primitive reflexes and the development of motor milestones.

The first curve to develop is the cervical curve (in the neck). It develops through tummy time (either on the floor or on you), when your baby is strengthening those neck muscles by moving their head side to side and eventually lifting it higher.

Rolling starts to develop the ability to rotate the trunk, which will help to strengthen the thoracic curve (middle back) and the beginnings of the lumbar curve (low back), which continues to develop as baby explores their world from the hands-and-knees position. The lumbar curve and all the muscles of the trunk and core (back, sides, and front) aren't fully formed and strong enough to support an upright vertical position until baby has gotten into a sitting position on their own (yes, this is key—*on their own*). The independent sitting milestone is a baby's first true vertical and what allows them to sit and move without falling over, as well as stand and eventually walk.

Isn't it cool how intricate our bodies are?

By understanding *how* their development happens, we can better support our babies while they're exploring movement patterns, developing their spinal curves, and lengthening and strengthening their muscles through pushing, pulling, and reaching. Perhaps it didn't occur to you just how much development is happening through simple activities, such as being on the floor. Your little one doesn't need a lot of fancy toys. All they need is an open space and perhaps one or two household items. That blue cup you have in the cupboard is great. A water bottle, a pot, a wooden spoon, or even balled-up socks (a favorite in my house) will do too! And of course, YOU are their most favorite thing in the first few months!

Again, don't feel as if you need to be entertaining or playing with your baby all the time. Put them on the ground, let them move and explore their bodies and environment, and watch their physical, cognitive, and emotional development unfold before your eyes.

# MOVEMENT TRANSITIONS

You're probably eagerly waiting for the discussion on motor milestones, but bear with me a bit longer. I'll get to them, I promise!

Movement patterns, spinal curve development, and muscle strengthening through pushing, pulling, and reaching are building blocks for motor milestones. Movement transitions make up another important building block.

Time and time again, parents "help" their babies with various skills under the false impression that doing so will teach their children these skills. Please don't feel bad if you've done this. Have you ruined your baby? Most likely not! And you know what? I did it too—I "walked" my first baby by holding his hands well before he could take a single step on his own!

Once again, do the best you can. When you know better, you do better! Okay?

It's just as important for your baby to learn how to transition between positions and milestones as it is for them to meet those milestones. For example, it's just as important, if not more so, for a baby to learn *how* to get into and out of a sitting position as it is for them to be able to sit upright without falling over. Otherwise, they'll have no clue how they got from one position to the other.

I talk a lot about movement transitions in my Babies @ Play classes and one-to-one support sessions. As parents, we're so used to just picking baby up and changing their position for them, but we're doing them a disservice. During movement transitions, babies are pushing, pulling, and reaching to lengthen and strengthen their muscles. They're learning about weight shifting and balance while also working all their little stabilizing muscles. They're learning about their bodies and how to interact with their environment. If we do it for them, they miss out on all the amazing learning. So I invite you to sit back and WATCH your baby and allow them to figure it out. Learning takes place in the doing!

Yes, babies may get tired in one position, just as we do, and if they can't quite figure out how to move out of it they may get frustrated. But it's important that we don't make up our baby's mind about what they like. Babies change and grow constantly. Give them a chance to keep trying on the floor. If they seem tired or fussy, instead of just picking them up, try rolling them over (see how we're helping them move through the transition?) to change their position, or even pick them up for a little snuggle and a change of environment before putting them down again.

## BABY DEVICES

In general, I don't like baby containers, such as jumping, sitting, or standing devices. Babies are often put into them long before they're ready. Many of these containers even state that they're appropriate for babies as young as four months! I definitely don't recommend this. If we put babies into positions (and devices) that they can't get into, they don't have the proper postural control muscles developed for that position, which can lead to pressure on the spine, joints, and muscles and impede their development later on.

In our society, we've come to rely on the convenience of these containers, which means that babies are spending *a lot* of time on their backs, or in positions that don't support their development or allow them to move and strengthen their muscles. A baby could spend the whole day on their back. Maybe you put them in the bouncy chair, and then they nap in the swing (not safe, by the way). Next, you run some errands and put them in the car seat, which transfers to the stroller. Back home, they have another swing nap and then go back into the bouncy chair while you cook dinner. This is the unfortunate reality of our world today, and it means that as your baby grows, they not only may be at risk for plagiocephaly (flat head), but also may skip milestones, not fully integrate primitive reflexes, and have weaker cores and reduced postural control. Later on, they may be unable to sit still and have difficulty focusing in class. They could have trouble writing, or copying from the board. They could struggle with visual motor integration. And so much more.

If you've been using all these devices, you *have not* ruined your baby. You can change the process today! And yes, you can still use them *in moderation* when you need a safe place for baby—maybe when you're making dinner, or having a shower, or need ten minutes to drink your coffee while it's hot. And of course, the car seat is a must in a moving vehicle and the highchair is the safest place for baby to explore solids. Just don't make these containers the primary place your baby plays and make sure to give them lots and lots of floor time.

*Chapter Five*

# MOTOR MILESTONES MADE EASY

As mentioned, there are ranges for each milestone, and these should be used as guides rather than hard-and-fast rules. Some babies develop outside the ranges, and that's okay, within a month or so. Of course, anything far outside the ranges warrants further investigation.

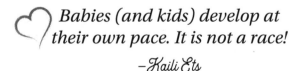

*Babies (and kids) develop at their own pace. It is not a race!*

*–Kaili Ets*

In this chapter I'm going to cover developmental milestones from birth to twenty-four months, including physical, cognitive, language, and emotional milestones. This coverage is by no means exhaustive but includes the main important milestones to be aware of.

These developmental milestones can often affect sleep, which I'll touch on again in Chapter Sixteen. We consolidate what we've learned during the day at night, and babies will often practice their new skills at night and then get stuck and need your support to get back to sleep.

> *Give your baby lots of opportunities to move and help them practice the movement transitions throughout the day, so they don't have to practice as much at night.*
>
> *– Kaili Ets*

Milestones shouldn't be a mystery! Let's unravel them now.

## DEVELOPMENT IN THE ZERO- TO THREE-MONTH-OLD

The fourth trimester is a huge time of experiencing in a baby's life. It's a time of learning to exist outside the womb. This is an important time to rest and heal your body and to bond with your baby, knowing that they need to be close to you in order to co-regulate. Embrace the closeness, know that you're supporting their development, and don't feel as if you're creating bad habits (you're not!). This isn't the time to worry about playing with your baby or teaching them skills.

# YOUR 0- TO 3-MONTH-OLD BABY'S SKILLS
## DURING THE FIRST 3 MONTHS, IT IS NORMAL FOR NEWBORNS TO . . .

- Tolerate being on tummy for short periods of time (2-5 min). At the beginning they may only be able to lift their head up briefly enough to switch sides. As they get toward the end of the fourth trimester, they should be able to start pushing up onto their arms in tummy time.
- Roll onto back when placed in side-lying—this is more to do with gravity pulling down that heavy head of theirs
- Start to open/close their fists voluntarily
- Notice hands and bring them to their mouth
- See and follow sounds and objects that are about 15–30 cm from face
- Prefer black-and-white contrasts
- Have a strong grasp reflex— aka the death grip
- Sustain brief alert periods where they show interest in their environment
- Begin to understand cause and effect (i.e., quiets more quickly when cuddled close or swaddled)
- Use thumb-sucking, pacifier, or sucking on nipple (of breast or bottle) to organize and calm/regulate
- Engage in eye contact for short periods
- Start to smile purposefully (not to be confused with the smile when they are working on a diaper explosion)
- Prefer contact with people rather than objects
- Cry to get attention and communicate if hungry, upset, tired (may have different cries emerging for hunger vs. upset vs. tired)
- Stop crying when picked up
- Coo when relaxed and happy

# REFLEXES

In these first few months, you'll see many of their primitive reflexes, such as rooting (to get food), grasping (holding on for dear life), and stepping (they might look as if they're practicing walking when their feet touch a surface). The Babinski reflex is what keeps their precious little toes curled in these first few months, and it also helps them figure out crawling. It remains active for the first one or two years of life. The tonic labyrinthine reflex (TLR) forward is what allows baby to be scrunched up inside the womb, and the TLR backward starts to develop as your newborn stretches out their little body. You'll eventually see them start to "swim" while on their tummies, which is called the landau reflex. There's also the classic "fencing position" (on their backs and looking in one direction)—the asymmetric tonic neck reflex (ATNR). This is the reflex that will help them start to roll, and it's usually integrated between four and seven months.

Then of course you have the Moro reflex. As parents, we've all seen it (and probably worried about it). Your baby gets startled and flails their arms and legs. This is your baby's initial fight-or-flight reaction and is usually integrated around four months and replaced by an adult "startle" reflex. When the Moro reflex isn't fully integrated it can lead to hyperactivity; impulsivity; sensitivity to movement, noise, and light; sleep challenges; food sensitivities; emotional and social immaturity; and overreactions to any type of stimuli. It overrides the higher-decision-making center of the brain. The Moro reflex and the Fear Paralysis Reflex (FPR) are closely linked to our limbic system and therefore our emotional health. The FPR serves as a protective mechanism. If it isn't integrated, it can lead to issues such as anxiety, poor self-esteem, sleep/eating disorders, aggression, fear of failure or embarrassment, and/or phobias.

These primitive reflexes are closely linked to the development of spinal curves and motor milestones.

> ## RED FLAGS FOR BABIES 0–3 MONTHS
>
> - Consistent irritability
> - Feeding difficulties
> - Unusual floppiness
> - Born with or develops a flat spot on head (brachycephaly, plagiocephaly, scaphocephaly)
> - Tight, turned, or twisted neck; only wanting to turn head/feed on one side
> - Unresponsive to sound or light
> - Breathing problems (including snoring and open-mouth breathing)
> - Poor color (i.e., gray/blue around lips or nose)

# TUMMY TIME

So many parents have questions about tummy time: "When?" "How, and for how long?" "Why does it feel like a torturous task on the mama to-do list?" I love to chat about tummy time and help babies and parents feel better about it, so I hope this section supports you and your little one.

Tummy time became a much-talked-about concept in response to the Back to Sleep program (now called Safe Sleep) to prevent SIDS in 1994. Today, tummy time is becoming even more important because we also have the baby market bombarding us with the newest, shiniest, most developmentally appropriate gadget to help our babies sleep, eat, play, and develop. This is becoming a big problem. Babies and young children are becoming weaker overall and delayed in their development as compared to children born in the eighties and early nineties. We're also seeing an increase in plagiocephaly (flat-head syndrome).[34]

In theory, tummy time may seem like a simple concept. You place your baby on their belly so they can wiggle and play on the floor. But then you try it . . . and you find out that it isn't as fun as it sounds.

Do any of these sound familiar to you?

- "My baby hates tummy time!"
- "I try and they just cry."
- "She fusses and seems unhappy on her belly."
- "His face is always smooshed into the floor and he just looks uncomfortable."

I hear these comments all the time from the lovely mamas I serve, and I've personally gone through the tummy-time stage twice, so believe me when I say I totally get this, Mama! I struggled to implement tummy time with my son. I knew it was important, but he seemed to hate it—and I hated to hear him cry. I had to take a step back and put my clinician hat on. After I invested a lot of time researching both the theory and the practical implementation of tummy time, it all started to make a lot more sense to me. Tummy time felt like a breeze the second time around, so I hope I can make it easier for you too!

Many babies struggle and fuss during early sessions of tummy time. A dear colleague, teacher, and mentor of mine, Ellynne Skove, calls tummy time on the floor, in that cobra yoga pose, Olympic Level Tummy Time. I fell in love with this term. It takes a lot of work, dedication, and practice to lengthen and strengthen the muscles, develop that cervical spinal curve in the neck, and support that heavy head! In fact, it takes months of practice for this Olympic Level Tummy Time to get comfortable. But that's no reason to stop doing it! If you were training for the Olympics, you wouldn't give up just because things got tough, right?

Here are a few reasons why it might initially be hard.

1. Consider that your baby spent the first nine months of their life enveloped in warm amniotic fluid. The world of gravity is a real surprise after a life of floating![35]

2. During infancy, the head is the biggest and heaviest part of a baby's body.[36] It's bigger than their bottom. Imagine if your head was bigger than your bottom. It would be a struggle to lift your head too, wouldn't it?

3. A baby's spine has minimal curves. Developmental movement patterns, along with tummy time, help to develop those curves. This creates the foundation and architecture for the body to stand.

4. The anxiety we parents bring to tummy time rubs off on our babies. If we're worried about it, the baby thinks they need to worry too—and starts fussing. Remember that concept of co-regulation?

5. Think about what it's like to hit the gym after a long period of not working out. Afterwards, our bodies ache, and during the exercise, we feel the stretch of extending our body's limits. We often need a push to stick with it. It's the same for babies.

These are good reasons for some fussing, don't you think? But I've got some good ideas to help you help your baby. It's important to note that without tummy time, some babies don't crawl at all. As we'll talk about later in this chapter, this isn't something we want our babies to skip. And according to researchers, babies who spend virtually no time on their tummies may experience developmental delays. In fact, did you know that an estimated one in forty babies is diagnosed with early motor delays?[37]

Tummy time is about more than just strengthening the baby's neck, back, and shoulders. Being on the floor helps your baby to trust, explore, and learn about their surroundings. They learn how to work with the surface that supports us our entire lives. They practice how to move with and against gravity—a skill we take for granted as adults. Early positioning on their tummies, even for brief periods, also helps with respiratory expansion, swallowing and breathing patterns, upper-body strength, depth perception, and spine and hip strength.

The good news is that it's easy to begin with a small amount of tummy time at a young age. You can place your baby on their belly from day one. And what if I told you that tummy time doesn't have to take place on the floor? Are you surprised? I was too!

Tummy time in those early months can happen in a variety of ways, many of which you're likely doing anyway. Babies in the fourth trimester crave closeness, and these tummy-time positions will help you achieve that too!

## TUMMY-TIME POSITIONS

### Holding Upright
When burping or carrying your baby.

### Lying Chest to Chest
When you are hanging out with baby, or they are napping on your chest.

### Baby-Wearing Facing In
Such a great place for baby to be, and it allows you to be hands free!

### Baby Across Lap
While you are chatting with friends, or catching up on Netflix, either over one knee or both knees. If you are sitting on the floor with baby over one knee, you can rock or do a little bounce to help elongate time in tummy time.

TUMMY-TIME POSITIONS, CONT'D

**Football Hold (Tummy Down)**

Another great way to get tummy time in while you transition your baby between various positions.

**Side-Lying**

Great place to play, as it still allows them time off their backs and works a variety of different muscles.

As you can see, you're likely already getting in more tummy time than you thought. Feel free to take a big breath in and let out that sigh of relief. Phew! Now, even though your baby is getting lots of awesome tummy-time practice, it's still really important to practice tummy time on a firm surface, such as the floor. In those first few months, while baby is still working on getting stronger and being able to lift their head, feel free to support them using various props (e.g., rolled-up yoga mat, firm towel, even your nursing pillow) under their chest and arms for added comfort and support and to eliminate the pull of gravity on their heavy head. And no, using props isn't considered "cheating" (that thought crossed my mind with my first). Your baby is still receiving all the benefits of tummy time.

Here are my favorite tips for a successful tummy-time experience for you and your little one—because hey, if you're going to be doing tummy time multiple times a day, you might as well enjoy it, right?

## TIPS FOR A SUCCESSFUL TUMMY TIME

1. **Add some entertainment**

   Feel free to talk, sing, and play with your baby. This can be a great time to bond. Use toys, scarves, and instruments to help. In my Babies @ Play classes, we practice tummy time every week with the zero- to six-month group and have a special tummy-time song to keep things fun!

2. **Respond to your baby's limits**

Don't overdo it in one go. Try a little at a time and keep building gradually. Even a few seconds in tummy time will help your baby get used to this position (and get stronger). Remember, babies change and grow constantly. Give your baby a chance to keep trying, but don't push it too far. Take note of what your baby's learning edge is and then stop. If they fuss or cry, roll them out of tummy time, pick them up, and soothe them. Once they're calm again, you can put them back down and roll them back into tummy time for another short period, or just try again later.

3. **Build it into your routine**

Diaper changes are a great opportunity to incorporate some tummy time. I also recommend scheduling it in throughout the day. Even ten to fifteen minutes of rolling your baby in and out of tummy time, a few times a day, can do magical things for their development.

4. **Prepare your baby with relaxing activities**

Massaging your baby's tummy amid diaper changing or after a bath is a wonderful way to prepare them for a relaxing and soothing tummy-time experience. Singing favorite lullabies or other gentle songs while doing this is beneficial for both mom and baby. And then get down on your tummy on the floor with your baby and look at them. They love this!

5. **Remove the clothing**

Babies love being naked because human skin has tons of sensory receptors. Try tummy time with less clothing, or even naked, without a diaper, on a mat. This will help them feel their body as well as the surfaces around them more easily. Think of the difference between being barefoot and wearing socks. Which experience offers you more input? It's the same for babies!

6.    **Switch it up**

As mamas, our initial reaction is to swoop in and save baby when they're fussing. Our protective mama bear instincts are a good thing when there's real danger, but when your baby fusses in tummy time, they aren't in danger or even really in distress. They're likely tired (tummy time is hard work, remember!). Or they might just be bored—really, how long can you look at the floor or the same toy? I encourage you to not be so quick to assume your baby hates tummy time when they fuss. I'm not saying leave them there to cry. Rather, get their attention, change the toys in the area, or slowly change their position. You can also "extend" tummy time by switching into a different form of tummy time, lessening the level of difficulty, or adding a prop.

A positive tummy-time experience is about helping your baby to trust the world around them—to discover that the world is safe, supportive, and endlessly fascinating. Fun tummy-time experiences also mean your baby won't need to spend as much time in containers such as bouncers and swings—a great win for development and also in terms of keeping your baby happy without having to hold them all day (trust me, I know those arms get tired and you want some personal space too).

Don't forget to be aware of your emotions and responses during tummy time. This is especially true when your baby fusses during the initial tummy-time experience. Babies are intelligent and pick up everything you do and say. You don't want to inadvertently establish a negative emotion around tummy time. Instead, encourage your baby, sing songs, or change the activity.

You might be wondering just how much tummy time your baby should be getting. Perhaps you've heard the popular recommendation—having baby spend forty-five to sixty minutes in tummy time daily by the time they're three months old. Pediatricians and other health-care professionals have adopted this idea. But looking at this through my occupational therapy lens and based on my knowledge of development and sensory processing, I recommend ensuring baby spends as much time on their tummies as on their backs.

I realize that this might sound like a lot, but think about all the tummy-time positions outlined in the chart earlier in this section. Also, tummy time includes side-lying. Even having baby play on the floor on their back promotes unrestricted movement, exploration of their body, and strengthening of their muscles. Push, pull, and reach! These are key. What we really want to limit is the amount of time baby spends confined to devices. Allow them lots of time to be on the floor, in your arms, or worn.

## DEVELOPMENT IN THE FOUR- TO SEVEN-MONTH-OLD

Yay, you survived the newborn period! Congrats, Mama! Your baby is becoming more alert and responsive. It's almost as if they're waking up to the world. This is often the stage when you'll start to see them craving more social interaction (and looking at everything). They may also become more distracted while feeding during the day (and make up for it by waking more at night to eat when it's dark, calm, and quiet).

# YOUR 4- TO 7-MONTH-OLD BABY'S SKILLS
## DURING THIS 4- TO 7-MONTH PERIOD, YOU WANT TO SEE YOUR BABY STARTING SOME OF THE FOLLOWING SKILLS . . .

- More comfortable in "Olympic level" tummy time
- Stronger head control
- Reaching with both hands to grab their toes (while lying on their backs)
- Rolling from back to tummy and tummy to back
- Reaching for toys while on their tummy
- Able to hold toy in their hand and voluntarily release it
- More aware of toys and trying to purposefully play with them
- Transferring toy from one hand to the other
- Bringing toys/objects to their mouth for exploration (yes, this may make you squirm, but it is a good thing and how they initially learn about the properties of the object!)
- Following moving objects with their eyes
- Recognizing familiar faces, voices, and smells
- Expressing basic emotions—happy, angry, sad, distress, surprise
- Smiling when socially stimulated (i.e., imitating your smile or when their favorite song is heard
- Laughing, chuckling, and yes even squealing (you might hear the squeals turn into high-pitched screams at times too—usually nothing to worry about, as they are finding, exploring, practicing, and strengthening their vocal cords)
- Babbling sounds—often starting with b, p, m and then eventually to ba, ma, and da
- Starting to understand more (up to ~100 words)
- Entertaining self by playing with hands or toys
- Starting to enjoy bathing and other caring/grooming activities
- Making sucking noises and "blowing bubbles" with their saliva (oh what fun that is to experience for the first time!)

---

YOUR 4- TO 7-MONTH-OLD BABY'S SKILLS, CONTD

- Starting solids closer to 6 months (initially more exploratory phase vs. eating for nutrition)
- Sleeping changes—stop pooping at night, sleep cycles lengthen and deepen, and sleep may be disrupted due to developmental milestones

- Teething may start around this time, which can affect overall well-being and sleep

---

# REFLEXES

The primitive reflexes in the four- to seven-month range include the asymmetric tonic neck reflex, which helps with rolling and integrates around this time, and the symmetric tonic neck reflex, which develops around six to nine months and integrates between nine to eleven months. It's involved in your baby being able to sit up and also get into a hands-and-knees position. The Spinal Galant reflex develops in utero and integrates sometime between three and nine months of age. This one is important in helping the baby wiggle and move down the birth canal as well as in the development of the vestibular system (our movement/balance system). If the Spinal Galant reflex isn't integrated, it can lead to clumsiness in the lower part of the body, tension in the legs, restlessness and hyperactivity, a preference for loose clothing, and a dislike of wearing anything around their waist (e.g., diaper, underwear, pants, etc.).

# STOP THE COMPARISONS

Remember, these are all ranges of typical development, but anything a little outside these ranges is usually nothing to worry about. It's really important to internalize this. I say this from experience. I had a serious case of comparison and the resulting stress and worry that comes with it when my first was around five months old and we were attending all the mom-and-baby groups. When he wasn't yet rolling at six months, I really started worrying (unnecessarily, as it turned out—he started rolling at seven months). I also noticed that when he did the army-crawl movement, one of his legs always lagged behind. My OT brain went into high gear to figure out what the heck this meant, and I had to work hard to not get stressed out or anxious about this. What did I do? I reached out to a trusted physical therapist to get her input. She said that most likely it was normal and nothing to worry about and gave me a few tips to try.

So, Mamas, stop stressing, stop comparing! But do get your babies out of the containers and onto the floor. Let them move and explore on their own. This is the best way they can learn to move! If you want to help them, roll your baby into and out of tummy time, help them transition from their hands and knees back into sitting, and from sitting back into tummy time on the floor. Remember that transitioning between positions is so important for babies—they learn what the movement *feels* like and can then imitate it another time.

## RED FLAGS FOR BABIES 4–7 MONTHS

- Poor head control
- Consistent irritability
- Floppiness
- Not smiling or making eye contact
- Asymmetric movements (i.e., movements are not the same on each side)
- Tightly fisted hands (this is more of a newborn posture)

# DEVELOPMENT IN THE EIGHT- TO TWELVE-MONTH-OLD

This is such a fun age, albeit a much busier one. Your baby is likely on the move, more active, and getting into everything! If you haven't already babyproofed, now is the time—and this doesn't have to be overwhelming! We put away the breakables, covered the outlets, and baby-gated the stairs. That's it! We didn't worry about installing all the contraptions to lock the drawers or padding on all the corners.

A lot of noticeable development happens in this age range—physical, cognitive, social emotional, and language. Remember this, because it might mean that baby is waking more frequently, is clingier, or is doing something else out of the ordinary. Of course, if something doesn't feel right, get support and ask questions!

# YOUR 8- TO 12-MONTH-OLD BABY'S SKILLS
## THE 8- TO 12-MONTH DEVELOPMENTAL PERIOD INCLUDES . . .

- Consistently rolling from back to tummy and tummy to back
- Moving in/out of sitting on their own
- Able to sit unsupported and reach for toys without falling over
- Turning head to visually track objects while sitting
- Getting into a hands-and-knees position for crawling
- Pulling up to stand with support; may stand unsupported for a few seconds
- Cruising along furniture and may take a few steps unassisted
- Feeding self using hands; starting to pick up small objects/food with pincer grasp (thumb and index finger)
- Sipping from an open cup (with assistance to hold and tilt the cup initially)
- Transfering small objects from one hand to the other without dropping
- Continuing to explore objects by mouth
- Purposefully reaching, grasping, and releasing objects into containers
- Throwing and dropping objects (best game ever for them is to throw things off the highchair and you pick it up only to have them throw it again . . . yup, all part of development!)
- Clapping hands
- Turning pages in a book
- Enjoying cause-and-effect toys, and looking at self in mirror
- Object/person permanence is established and they will search for the missing person/object (peekaboo becomes really fun at this age)
- Can focus on a toy or person for at least 2 minutes
- Imitating others (spinning toys, pushing, pulling, clapping, waving, and sticking tongue out, coughing, etc.)
- Crying in response to another baby's cries

---

### YOUR 8- TO 12-MONTH-OLD BABY'S SKILLS, CONT'D

- Knowing difference between familiar and unfamiliar people and has a clear preference for 1-2 adults
- Seeking parental proximity when approached by a stranger (quick to comfort with familiar person)
- Shouting for attention
- More babbling sounds—da, dee, ma, ba, goo; saying mama or dada by 12 months
- Responding to name by turning head or shifting gaze
- Understanding "no" but does not comply; can shake head for "no"

---

Phew, that's a lot, and there are many other mini-milestones in this period, but these are the main ones.

Now let's chat more specifically about sitting, crawling, standing, and separation anxiety, mainly because these things are often misunderstood, cause unnecessary worry, and may affect sleep (it might seem as if everything can affect sleep, and trust me, I know it's frustrating, but it's also quite typical).

## SITTING

Sitting is a milestone that many people think happens much earlier than developmentally appropriate. Independent sitting is a baby's first true vertical. And until they can get into a sitting position *on their own*, they aren't ready. Many physical therapists recommend sitting your baby up or propping them in a tripod position, but most of the babies they see have some sort of developmental delay, weakness, or condition that requires different positions. Your baby will reach this milestone when they're ready—when their spinal curves have formed enough to support vertical positions and their muscles are strong enough. Remember, if we put babies into positions they're not ready for, we actually impede their development because they don't know how they got into that position and can't get out. Focus on the transitions between positions as much as the milestones themselves.

You might be thinking, "But what about the highchair when my baby starts solids?" As with most things, there's an exception to the rule! Though I'm a *huge* advocate for floor play and truly believe the floor is the best place for baby to be for most of the day (safely of course), sometimes it's okay for baby to sit before they can do so on their own. A highchair is the safest and best place for baby to eat because it allows them to be upright and supported, which helps them breathe, chew, and swallow safely. If your baby isn't quite sturdy in a highchair, you can hold them upright in your lap for those first few weeks or months of introducing solids. Similarly, the car seat is the safest place for your baby when your car is moving. But there's no reason it should come out of the car and into the stroller and then out of the stroller and onto the floor. It's all about moderation! Finally, your lap can be another occasional exception. It's a great place for baby to play, learn, and bond as well. In your lap, ideally their back is right up against your body. This way, their spines are better supported and they're getting feedback from your movements (your body is unconsciously moving to support theirs).

## CRAWLING

Perhaps you've heard that crawling isn't that important. I hear doctors say this all the time to mamas, but I'm here to tell you that crawling *is* important! And it's *not* something you want your child to skip. Crawling leads to so many developmental skills. It strengthens the core, arms, and hands, improves postural control and bilateral coordination (learning to use the two sides of their body together and in opposition), and helps near and far vision develop. These are all skills that a baby doesn't get to practice or develop with just walking. Skipping crawling, or any milestone for that matter, isn't great for your baby's development and can potentially lead to various difficulties and even delays later in life. They might have trouble handwriting/printing, sitting upright in a chair with good control (not wiggling or sliding), copying from the board, coordinating their body, and more.

I *always* recommend that parents promote crawling in their babies and children, even if they walk first! I know how hard it is to get a toddler back on the ground once they're up. One of my favorite ways to encourage crawling is to get an inexpensive tunnel (the Ikea ones are great) and chase them through it. You can also create an obstacle course, put puzzle pieces at one end of the tunnel and the puzzle board at the other, or roll some balls through it. So many play opportunities to be had with a tunnel, and really only one way through it—on hands and knees or pulling yourself on your belly (both develop the crawling skills). Another way to get some crawling in is to crawl UP the stairs (which can be done with babies as early as about seven or eight months) or climb the ladders (or slide) at the playground. You'll initially have to help them, but this is a great way to develop all the same skills that crawling does.

Like many other motor milestones, crawling includes some mini-milestones that you can look for before your baby gets into the traditional hands-and-knees crawling (which doesn't typically happen until about nine months).

## CRAWLING MINI-MILESTONES

- pushing self backwards
- turning in a 360 circle
- pulling self forward with both hands (sometimes feet help)
- pulling self forward with one hand and pushing with one leg (think army crawl)
- getting on hands and knees briefly
- rocking on hands and knees
- crawling on hands and knees

## STANDING

I know how enticing it can be to stand your baby by holding their hands in the air and walking with them. But we don't actually walk with our hands in the air, so this doesn't teach a child to walk normally, and again, it's always better to wait until baby can pull themselves into the standing position (or at the very least has been able to get into a sitting position on their own) before we move on to this next vertical position. Once you see baby trying to pull themselves to stand, here are some things to do to encourage and practice this milestone:

- Have baby stand and play using the outside of a container for support (instead of sitting in the contraption).
- Place favorite toys on the couch, chairs, and coffee table so that baby needs to stand to access them.
- Get them to crawl up the stairs (with your help initially)—this is great for core and leg strength, both needed for standing.

Oh, and one more thing. Babies are designed to handle bumps and bruises. Generally, if baby falls from their own height, there's nothing to worry about. It might be uncomfortable for us to see them let go and fall on their bum, or bonk their head, but your baby has more cushioning (from cartilage and softer bones) than you do. So you don't need to follow them around, ready to jump into action, to prevent the fall or bump, okay?

## SEPARATION ANXIETY

Babies need a caregiver to survive, and many child-development professionals who specialize in attachment believe that separation anxiety (during the day and night) is a survival mechanism.[38] Separation anxiety happens because your baby believes that if you disappear, you may not come back and they'll never see you again. I know this sounds dramatic, but remember, your baby's brain isn't fully formed yet. They don't understand that you're coming back, and they'll constantly check that you're still around (yes, at night too).

> *Babies are designed to be in close proximity to their caregivers, both during the day and the night. We are meant to be there for support.*
>
> *–Kaili Ets*

Separation anxiety seems to peak when a baby begins to learn locomotion skills—usually around six to nine months, with the crawling phase, and may intensify within the twelve- to eighteen-month range, when they learn to walk. There's often another peak of separation anxiety around the age of two as well, which is tied more to language development. The theory is that the anxiety is a safety check when your baby has the motor ability to move away from you but not the mental capabilities to handle the separation.[39] I know it can be hard when your baby seems attached to you at the hip (literally) or cries whenever you put them down and go into the next room, but what they're experiencing is normal, healthy behavior, and is often a measure of how secure a baby's attachment is. The presence of a strong attachment figure, usually you or another primary caregiver, acts as a coach of sorts, to give your baby the go-ahead to explore further.

So what can you do about separation anxiety besides wait for it to pass?

## GENERAL TIPS FOR SEPARATION ANXIETY

1. **Be aware of your energy during separation**
   If you project feelings of strength and calm, your baby will start to feel that this separation is safe.

2. **Use voice contact**
   Talking to your baby while you are out of sight can reassure your baby and stimulates your baby's ability to associate your voice with a mental image of you, which over time can help prevent the separation anxiety.

3. **Be consistent with limits**
   You do not have to have your baby glued to your hip. You are allowed to shower, to nap, to go for a walk without baby, and that doesn't make you any less of a mother.

4. **Validate their feelings**
   Allow the tears and the emotions. Validate and talk about them. Comfort and connect with your child when you return.

5. **Prepare for the separation**
   Let your baby know that you will be leaving, tell them who they will be staying with and when you will be back. (i.e., "After you wake up from your nap, Grandma will feed you a snack, and then I will be home.")

## GENERAL TIPS FOR SEPARATION ANXIETY, CONT'D

6. **Fill their "love cup" before the separation and when you get home**

   Take 10-15 minutes to spend some quality time being present with your little one before you leave and when you get home.

7. **Practice leaving your baby with familiar people**

   This will allow your baby to practice with other people and help you to build your village. If you are the only one who can care for your baby and the only one who can put your baby to sleep, then you may experience burnout.

8. **Do not sneak away!**

   Make sure you say a short goodbye so that your baby understands they are safe and you are confident about the separation.

9. **Practice safe separations at home**

   Make sure your baby is safe, then tell them you are going to get the laundry, to the bathroom, or to get a sip of water, then come right back.

10. **Get your partner involved**

    Have them do bathtime, or naptime, or a portion of bedtime, and then you can start leaving the room and eventually have them take over.

11. **Allow the separation**

    If your baby moves away from you, let them, and watch your reaction if they get upset realizing that they are no longer close. Calmly talk to them or go get them rather than "swooping in to save the day."

12. **Build the attachment to a lovey**

    When your baby has something that smells like you and reminds them of that comfort, even when you are not around, it will ease that separation. You can place the lovey between you and your baby when you are nursing or wear it in your shirt so that it smells like you.

Know that separation anxiety and even the clinginess that comes with it is normal, that it is a phase, and that with the right response, you can continue to build that attachment and connection, which will be critical for fostering independence down the road. Your baby is not manipulating you but rather understanding and practicing independence and interdependence for the first time. And it isn't until about two years of age that a baby will develop the object/person permanence that allows them to have the brain capability to understand and move more easily from the familiar to unfamiliar.

## RED FLAGS FOR BABIES 8–12 MONTHS

- Not sitting independently by 10 months
- Not weight-bearing on legs during supported standing
- No babbling or vocalizations
- Not passing objects from one hand to the other
- Refusing foods, gagging, choking, or vomiting (closer to the 12-month mark)

# DEVELOPMENT IN THE THIRTEEN- TO EIGHTEEN-MONTH-OLD

You've officially made it through the baby stage and have a toddler! "How in the world did that happen?" you might be wondering (as I was). I relished the first year of my son's life (minus the sleepless nights) and really noticed all his milestones. With my second, well, let's just say that I blinked and she was a toddler and now I've blinked again and she's off to kindergarten. I found that entry into the toddler stage, with each of my children, came with a bit of sadness. My "little baby" wasn't so little anymore.

One of the main milestones that we associate toddlerhood with is walking. For some reason our society has decided that walking must happen around your baby's first birthday. So if your toddler isn't walking, the worry might creep in and the comparison game might come into play in full force. But the typical range for walking is twelve to eighteen months! Yup, you read that right. It's totally normal if your toddler doesn't start walking until they're eighteen months. My son started walking around fourteen and a half months and my daughter didn't start until she was seventeen and a half months. Sometimes babies walk before twelve months, but often this means they've skipped the crawling stage (and by now you know how important that is and why we don't want to skip it).

Walking is a huge milestone developmentally. It means that baby's spine has developed into more of the S shape that we have as adults, and that they have also developed enough core stability for postural control in the upright vertical position. Initially their walking might look awkward and jerky, and they might wobble and waddle, but smoothness and coordination come with practice. Now is definitely the time to babyproof your home if you haven't done so already.

Here are some other developmental skills your toddler is learning in the thirteen- to eighteen-month range.

---

## YOUR 13- TO 18-MONTH-OLD TODDLER'S SKILLS

### IN THE 13- TO 18-MONTH DEVELOPMENTAL PERIOD, YOUR TODDLER IS LEARNING . . .

- Cruising around furniture
- Walking with "flat feet"
- Squatting to pick up toys; bending over to pick up toys without falling
- Walking up/down stairs while holding on to railing or parent hand
- May try to walk backwards

## YOUR 13- TO 18-MONTH-OLD TODDLER'S SKILLS, CONT'D

- Likes to practice sitting in chairs; climbing on furniture
- Dancing and moving to music
- Pushing/pulling wheeled toys
- Putting toys away (this is a great time to start practicing "cleaning up" at the end of your playtime)
- Drinking from an open cup more independently
- Using spoon and maybe fork (though messy)
- Assisting in self-care activities (grooming—hello toothbrushing, washing face and hands, dressing)
- Pulling off their clothes, socks, etc.
- Using pincer grasp for smaller items
- Scribbling with larger crayons on paper
- Building a tower with 3 blocks
- Holding 2 objects at a time
- Starting to put simple shapes (i.e., circle) into a puzzle board
- Dropping and throwing things
- Turning pages in a book, knobs, etc.
- Imitating cause-and-effect toys (i.e., placing ball into tunnel to watch it roll)
- Beginning signs of symbolic play (i.e., "pretend to read a book")
- Starting to understand rules and limits and complying about 50% of time
- Upleveling their peekaboo play and starting to hide
- Starting to demonstrate assertiveness
- Using objects to soothe (i.e., lovey, blanket, toy, water bottle, etc.)
- Babbling and jabbering to get attention
- Asking for what they want by pointing (or sign language if you have been practicing this)
- Having about 7–20 words (approximations of the word count)—dada, mama, nana, up, no, yum, uh-oh, ba (for bottle), etc.
- Understanding simple, one-step commands/directions (i.e., sit on chair, get your shoes)
- Enjoying rhythm and singing games
- Imitation and copying are still big and fun ways for learning
- May still need 1–2 night feeds and wake-ups for connection

## RED FLAGS FOR TODDLERS 13–18 MONTHS

- Not speaking 10-15 words (approximations like "ba" for ball count) by 18 months
- Not using single words like mama, dada
- Does not know the function of common household objects (i.e., brush, telephone, fork, spoon)
- Does not point to show things to others
- Does not follow simple commands
- Does not notice or mind when their primary caregiver leaves or returns
- Wakes up frequently at night (i.e., every 1-2 hours)

# DEVELOPMENT IN THE NINETEEN- TO TWENTY-FOUR-MONTH-OLD

This is the age where all the skills that developed in the first half year of toddlerhood get more refined and less awkward, and perhaps your life gets even busier!

## YOUR 19- TO 24-MONTH-OLD TODDLER'S SKILLS
### IN THE 19- TO 24-MONTH DEVELOPMENTAL PERIOD, YOUR TODDLER IS . . .

- Walking up/down stairs with assistance
- Climbing—furniture, crib, playground equipment, etc.
- Walking backwards
- Sitting in a child-sized chair independently
- Starting to try running, jumping—may be awkward
- Enjoying going down the slide, swinging on swings

### YOUR 19- TO 24-MONTH-OLD TODDLER'S SKILLS CONT'D

- Pushing and pulling toys
- Fussiness with eating is common during this time, as is deciding they don't like something they used to love
- Stringing large beads
- Helping with getting dressed and undressed
- Starting to show a hand preference during certain tasks (i.e., scribbling with the left, feeding with the right)
- Exploring opening/closing scissors
- Doing simple 3-shape puzzles
- Enjoying playing with sensory play—playdoh, paints, etc.
- Playing independently for a few minutes
- Exerting their independence
- Starting to recognize self in mirror
- May have increased fears and anxiety around certain things (i.e., scared of the dark)
- Matching sounds to animals, objects to pictures
- Becoming more aware of soiled diapers and may show interest in potty training (still unreliable)
- Following parent around the house
- Wanting constant attention; may be resentful of attention shown to other children/siblings
- Continuing to increase in words (may still be unintelligible)
- Starting to join 2 or more words into a sentence (closer to 24 months)
- Enjoying being read to and stories
- Sleeping may still be disrupted due to all the development happening

> # RED FLAGS FOR TODDLERS 19–24 MONTHS
>
> - Not walking
> - Poor hand control (i.e., dropping things, no pincer grasp, etc.)
> - Poor balance, stiffness, or rigidity
> - Toe walking (if it is on a consistent basis, though isn't usually a problem until after 2 years)
> - No pretend play
> - No first words; not interacting with caregivers or others
> - Food refusals, gagging, choking

## WATCH, WAIT, AND WONDER

I hope that this section has eased your mind and clarified a few things. When we know what "normal" is, we don't get as overwhelmed. We don't worry or compare as much. We can trust our baby and ourselves. Trust that they will develop "typically," even if it's on their own timeline, as long as we give them the right opportunities and environment. Trust that you will know, in your heart, if there is something that needs further assessment and support.

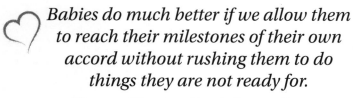

*Babies do much better if we allow them to reach their milestones of their own accord without rushing them to do things they are not ready for.*

—Marianne Hermsen-Van Wanrooy, Babymoves

There's no need to rush your baby into sitting, crawling, standing, walking, sleeping through the night, eating solids, and being fully independent. Evolution has designed us humans pretty well. Given the right opportunities to play and discover, we learn these skills on our own. Ultimately, letting babies explore their environment and move their bodies is what will help them develop, not teaching, pushing, or buying the latest and greatest device. I love the mantra *watch, wait, and wonder*.

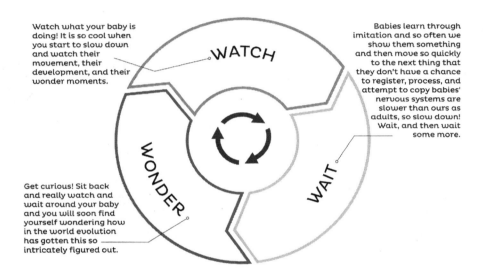

Watch what your baby is doing! It is so cool when you start to slow down and watch their movement, their development, and their wonder moments.

Babies learn through imitation and so often we show them something and then move so quickly to the next thing that they don't have a chance to register, process, and attempt to copy babies' nervous systems are slower than ours as adults, so slow down! Wait, and then wait some more.

Get curious! Sit back and really watch and wait around your baby and you will soon find yourself wondering how in the world evolution has gotten this so intricately figured out.

I challenge you to sit back and watch, wait, and wonder how your baby is doing exactly what they should be doing at the exact right time for them. Relax, slow down, put your baby on the floor, and just watch them! Doesn't that sound easy?

As long as you're seeing little changes and new skills each week (mini-milestones), whether physical, cognitive, or even social emotional, your baby is likely developing just right. Which means that you can stop the comparison game, okay? Your baby is unique, just like you are, just like I am. Keep an eye on these mini-milestones and enjoy the moment! Enjoy the new. Enjoy the smiles and giggles when they accomplish something they've been working at.

Use this section as a guide and get in touch if you have any questions or concerns, or need some extra reassurance!

# Chapter Six

# BODYWORK

Babies do all sorts of funny things in utero, and sometimes they can become twisted in suboptimal positioning, stuck in a specific place (like under your ribs—ouch!), or squished due to lack of space (multiples and/or low amniotic fluid). Then they twist and rotate as they make their way through the birth canal, where they sometimes get stuck and need assistance from forceps, a vacuum, hands, or even a C-section. All the twisting, rotating, and general stuckness can lead to straining and tightening of the fascia, a thin but strong layer of tissue that forms a network that surrounds and protects our entire body—muscles, organs, brain and spinal cord, and nerves. We're connected from the tip of our tongue to the tips of our toes with this fascial network.

This fascia is really good at protecting and will tighten quite easily but isn't so great at stretching or releasing on its own. Tight fascia pulls on everything below it and can cause tightness in the tongue (e.g., tongue-ties, poor latch), tightness in the neck (e.g., torticollis), or anywhere in the body, really. This tightness can pull bones out of alignment and compress nerves, which can lead to pain, stiffness, discomfort, and more.

During birth, there's also a certain amount of molding of the cranial bones as they move over top of each other to make the baby's head capable of fitting through the tight birth canal. While this molding is normal and often resolves on its own, sometimes it doesn't. Extended suboptimal positioning and birth interventions, which can include manually turning and manipulating the baby on the way out, can cause excessive molding and compressions of the cranial bones and nerves, which can lead to weak suck, constipation, digestive difficulties, reflux, gas, flat head (plagiocephaly and brachycephaly), and overall fussiness due to pain and discomfort, to name a few issues.

The beautiful thing is that with the appropriate bodywork, whether it's craniosacral therapy, osteopathy, or chiropractic care, much of this body tightness and compression can be resolved. In particular, I love craniosacral therapy as it can help release fascial tension and gently move the cranial bones back into place while relieving the compression of the cranial nerves, making more space within the cranium, and ultimately restoring the flow of the cerebrospinal fluid and the body's internal craniosacral rhythm.

I was living in NYC when Kristjan was born, and I'd recently become interested in various alternative and complementary therapies. I'd gone to acupuncture for the first time while my husband and I were trying to conceive, and kept going throughout my pregnancy. I was doing yoga, meditating, and had started to explore the magical world of energy healing. When my son was born via C-section, I knew, from my years of experience as a pediatric occupational therapist, that he'd missed out on a lot of sensory input and stimulation of primitive reflexes, and that this might lead to various issues in development.

I asked a mentor for some recommendations, and she mentioned craniosacral therapy. That first session in our tiny NYC apartment bedroom was the start of my love affair with craniosacral therapy and osteopathy. I knew it was magical even though my son cried for almost the entire treatment—which I was told was normal, as he relived his birth experience and the shock of being born. Since then, I've regularly been taking both of my children to an osteopath who primarily treats children with craniosacral therapy. It changed my life and my career trajectory. I'm now a certified infant craniosacral therapist.

Every single baby (and mama) should get at least one to three craniosacral therapy treatments, or some other type of bodywork, done after birth. The ideal time is within the first few days and weeks, but it's never too late. I recommend bodywork to every single family I work with, whether we're addressing sleep, reflux, or even sensory processing differences. I truly believe in the magic of craniosacral therapy, not just for babies and mamas, but for everyone.

## WHAT IS CRANIOSACRAL THERAPY?

Craniosacral therapy is a noninvasive, hands-on technique that uses a very light touch (about the pressure with which you would touch your eyelid), to determine where energy is blocked. It can be used as a stand-alone therapy or in combination with other methods. I blend craniosacral therapy with my expertise in infant/child development, sleep, reflux, and sensory processing. The term *craniosacral* is a combination of *cranium* (the head) and *sacrum* (the base of the spine). The focus is on releasing fascial restrictions, bringing space to compressed cranial bones or nerves, and creating a better flow to the fluid in the body. Once the restrictions have been eased and the flow has improved, the body can self-regulate and heal as it was meant to do.

Before you start thinking "this is too woo-woo for me" and stop reading, take a breath, be conscious of your mindset, and intentionally become curious and keep an open mind. I promise it will be worth it.

The human body is an amazing and complex system, and it's really good at self-healing and self-regulating. At night when we sleep, our bodies regenerate themselves. But living can be exhausting at times (especially if you have little ones), and stress, including labor, can put a little wrench in this repair system, meaning the body may start to work less effectively. This is where craniosacral therapy comes into play. Those places where the energy is blocked, the muscles are tight, or perhaps there's a misalignment or asymmetry are the places that have been influenced by stress. The craniosacral rhythm is a strong pumping system for cerebrospinal fluid through the brain and spinal cord. If there's any compression of this space, the fluid cannot flow properly. The better the flow of this fluid, the stronger the rhythm and the more life energy can fill this space, allowing the brain to grow and do its job. The task of the craniosacral therapist is to give back the space the body needs to do its job.

Babies are fully clothed for their sessions and are often treated in the parent's arms (sometimes even while the baby is nursing or feeding), in the therapist's arms (if baby allows), or lying on a table in various positions (back, tummy, and side). This technique is a holistic treatment that works slowly, gently, and deeply and therefore may take a few hours or days to settle in. Craniosacral therapy is a safe and often very effective treatment that can be used right from birth, and you usually only need a few sessions to see amazing results. I highly recommend trialing this magical treatment.

*Section Two*

# FEEDING YOUR BABY

I breast-fed both my children, but it definitely wasn't easy, at least with my first. Kristjan was born via C-section, and our bodies weren't in sync to start the whole cascade of hormones needed not only for labor and birth, but also for milk production. I got about two hours of sleep in the thirty-six hours I was at the hospital after delivering Kristjan. I spent each waking moment hand-expressing colostrum, trying to pump what I could and stimulate my breasts to get even a little milk flowing, and finally resorting to spoon-feeding my son the small amount that I got. I was determined, and we managed, but not without my mama bear claws coming out.

When we got home, where it was less stressful and we weren't being bothered every two hours, we managed to latch and feed just fine. Or so I thought. Then came the painful and cracked nipples, the latching and unlatching, the eating every hour, the constant spit-up . . .

I remember crying every time he latched and then sitting at the kitchen table trying to soak my breasts in warm bowls of salt water to heal them (something I'd read about in one of my middle-of-the-night Dr. Google searches).

I asked for help from a lactation consultant and found myself sitting in a tiny little office (more like a converted closet). It was hot and I was sweating from the stale air, my anxiety, and trying to find a comfortable, laid-back feeding position in the rickety armchair without falling over backward. It was an awful and highly unproductive first visit, and I wish someone had told me to get a second opinion. But I didn't. I should've listened to my gut and searched for someone who made me feel supported and comfortable while we worked through the challenges.

I'm proud to say that my son and I managed. I was determined, I persevered, I researched a ton, and we managed. Was it easy? Nope! But it gave me a great experience to draw from. And now I can help mamas like you.

Luckily, things were much easier with my daughter, since I knew what to look for and what to try. Were things perfect? Again, nope! She still had some fussy periods, and there was about a week where I couldn't figure out why she was crying and crying, but we found a great nursing position (football hold), I was calmer, there was no pain, and we didn't have any spit-up. To me that felt glorious and helped me get through the rough patches (there will always be some bumps along the journey).

This section is for all mamas. It's for the new ones who are still learning, the ones who are feeding during a growth spurt, those who have overcome struggles, those who are exhausted, those who have twins and are working double-time to reach their breast-feeding goals, those who wanted to breast-feed but couldn't, those who don't want to, those who breast-fed for one day or many years, and those who don't but support mamas who do. Feeding your baby is such an important part of your daily life. Breast milk is important and wonderful for many reasons, but sometimes formula is the right choice. Regardless of how you choose to feed your baby, I see you, Mama! You're doing a great job.

Did you know that feeding has milestones too? I didn't! When I started to research and learn more about feeding, I realized just how intricate it really is. Digestion, colic, and reflux—it all starts with the mouth. And as you'll learn, so do many other development milestones, as well as things such as body tightness (think torticollis) and even head molding (think plagiocephaly and brachycephaly). Everything is connected, and the tongue and mouth are the foundation of feeding as well as motor development.

Here are a few things I want you to remember as we go through this section.

## FEEDING TIPS TO REMEMBER

1. Feeding has milestones too!
2. Babies bellies are initially very tiny and they need to eat frequently because their bellies can only hold so much—as they grow, their bellies grow, and they start to be able to do longer stretches of sleep because they can fill those bellies more!
3. Human breastmilk has less fat than breastmilk of other mammals; therefore, it gets digested more quickly (and more quickly than formula too. But don't be fooled into thinking formula will make your baby sleep longer!).
4. Tongue-ties, lip-ties, buccal (cheek) ties, can impact feeding and therefore sleep.
5. Food intolerances/allergies can impact digestion, which can impact feeding, comfort level, and yes, even sleep (same for when you initially introduce solid foods).

# Chapter Seven

# BREAST-FEEDING

Over the years, Western society has taken many different views regarding what's best for feeding our babies. It was once considered best to breast-feed your own children. Then came the era, around the sixteenth to eighteenth centuries but even before that, in Ancient Rome, where it was a sign of wealth to have a wet nurse,[1] followed by the period where formula was invented and touted as having additional benefits. In the 1970s and 1980s, formula was the recommendation for new mothers, and hospitals were giving out free formula as you left the hospital. We've now come full circle and breast-feeding is again being encouraged whenever possible, although I've noticed an upswing in formula-feeding again with the COVID-19 pandemic.

The fact is that human babies are meant to drink human milk, just as calves are meant to drink their mothers' milk (cow's milk) and other animal babies their mothers' milk. On a purely biological and evolutionary level, it doesn't make sense to feed our babies milk from another species. And when we do—there's often cow's milk or goat's milk in formulas—it can lead to sensitivities and digestive issues because it's pretty heavily processed to make it more digestible for humans.[2] I know that feeding your baby breast milk isn't always possible for various reasons and choices, but it's something to keep in mind because it's easy to think, for example, "If I just feed my baby formula, they'll sleep better." Breast milk is a living substance, and as a baby's needs change, so does the milk composition, to meet those needs. The composition of breast milk actually changes over the course of a day in response to your baby, and also in response to your circadian rhythm, which isn't something that formula can mimic.

As mamas, most of us know the benefits of breast-feeding for both mom and baby, and we likely initially have the goal to breast-feed our babies. We often prepare for and look forward to it under the assumption that it's natural and easy. But for many women it can be a major challenge. It's a topic that comes up again and again in my Babies @ Play classes. And when breast-feeding is a challenge and feels like a full-time job, it can leave you feeling frustrated, guilty, or inadequate.

Yes, breast-feeding can be hard, but it doesn't have to be. Finding the root of breast-feeding challenges, or feeding challenges in general, is so important when it comes to feeling supported. Seeking the right help is key. I've heard all sorts of things from hospital nurses, the mamas in my classes, and in various mommy groups on Facebook. Things such as "Your nipples have to toughen up," or "The first few weeks are painful and then you'll get used to it." The truth is, breast-feeding should *not* hurt or pinch. It may feel a bit strange at first, but it should *not* be painful. Nipples should *not* blister or bleed. If any of this is happening, I urge you to see an international board-certified lactation consultant (IBCLC) and/or a pediatric dentist with extra training in tethered oral tissues (TOTs) to have a full assessment done, which should include an actual look (ideally with a headlight) *and* feel inside your baby's mouth to check the appearance *and* function of the tongue. Tongue-ties, lip-ties, cheek-ties, tongue function, body tightness, and/or pain can all affect breast-feeding. In addition to a full mouth assessment, I also highly recommend getting bodywork (either craniosacral therapy, osteopathy, or chiropractic care) done for your baby.

## THE FIRST FEW WEEKS OF BREAST-FEEDING

A woman's body starts to produce colostrum when she's about sixteen weeks pregnant. This is the first milk baby will receive when they're born. Around forty-eight to seventy-two hours after your baby is born, or longer if baby is induced or born via a C-section, you'll begin to produce transitional milk and then mature milk by one week. For the first six to eight weeks, hormones are helping to maintain your milk supply. During this time, it's important that baby is breast-fed on demand, and often, to ensure your supply becomes well established. After that, your breasts begin to work more on a feedback system, meaning that if your baby empties the breast, your body knows to make more milk. If your baby doesn't empty the breast, this signals your body to stop producing more milk. This is why it's important to feed on demand instead of on a schedule.

I get it—feeding on demand might be a new concept for you. Perhaps a well-meaning mother-in-law or nurse told you that you should have your baby on a schedule and only feed every three or four hours. Some sleep trainers also tout this nonsense. When it comes to breast-feeding, a schedule isn't ideal unless it's needed for medical reasons. Think about it: Do you eat on a rigid schedule and only every three or four hours? Probably not! You likely eat and drink (breast milk and formula are your baby's only means of hydrating in the early months) when you're hungry and thirsty. So go ahead and nurse your baby whenever they indicate that they're hungry (it may happen often in the early months!). This will help you establish and maintain your supply. By offering to nurse whenever you notice baby's hunger cues, you'll prevent them from getting worked up due to hunger and have better latching success overall—and a calmer baby. Nursing in the evening and overnight increases the melatonin available for your baby, which can help them sleep more restfully. And it's totally normal for your baby to nurse more frequently during periods of increased development and/or growth spurts, which we'll talk about shortly.

## THE LATCH

It's so important to get the latch right. A poor latch is often the cause of many breast-feeding difficulties, including pain, blistered/bleeding nipples, increased air and resulting discomfort in your baby's tummy, reflux, low milk supply, mastitis, and more. And a poor latch can be caused by issues such as poor positioning while feeding, TOTs (we'll talk more about these in a bit), and body tightness. Get help if you and your baby are having trouble, ideally from an IBCLC.

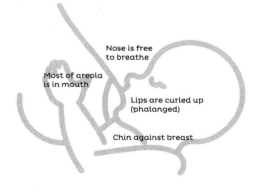

Nose is free to breathe

Most of areola is in mouth

Lips are curled up (phalanged)

Chin against breast

Getting a correct latch might require some effort initially—remember, this is new for you and your baby. But with practice it should come more easily until one day you won't even think about it. One way to set yourself up for a good latch is to put your nipple right under baby's nose, which will result in them tilting their head up and opening their mouth to take in a large portion of your breast. The second way is to lie on your back and place your baby on your belly near your boob. Let them find it with that instinctual "crawl" up your body. Do *not* put the nipple in your baby's mouth. Let them find it!

You also want to support your baby's neck at the *base* of their head, instead of holding or cupping their head directly. I know that might sound weird, but when you hold baby's head, you'll likely cause their head to tilt downward a bit, almost restricting their range of motion rather than allowing them to tilt their head up to really get a good open mouth and a deep latch. To get a better understanding of this, look at the floor and open your mouth. Now look at the ceiling and open your mouth. Babies need to be able to tilt their heads back to get a good latch.

## BREAST-FEEDING POSITIONS

When I had my first, I didn't know about all the different feeding positions. I probably learned about them in my prenatal class, but when push came to shove, the only one I could remember when I first held my son was the cradle hold. It's the one that most people think of—the one you typically see in pictures, on social media, and out and about in the world. But there are actually at least five different breast-feeding positions! These five are the ones most often recommended and discussed in the lactation world. I highly recommend that you try these various positions as your baby grows and develops. You may have different favorites throughout your breast-feeding journey.

# BREAST-FEEDING POSITIONS

### Cross Cradle

Great for the fourth trimester.

Baby is positioned across your body (supported by a pillow is great) and your hand is supporting their neck/base of head to promote a good latch.

### Football Hold

Great for babies 0-6 months. Good if you have larger breasts or faster flow (with you leaning back). Best to support baby's body with a pillow so your hands are free to support back of neck to get a good latch.

### Laid Back

Great for babies of all ages, but especially in the fourth trimester. Often the first feeding position you do right after birth. Get yourself comfortable—in bed, lying back with pillows supporting your back and arms. Baby is belly to belly with you. You can allow your baby to breast crawl to latch.

### Cradle

Good for babies 4-5+ months. Baby's neck is often supported in the crook of your arm, which doesn't give you good access to promote a good latch, so your baby needs to do more of the work. Easier if you are out and about.

### Upright

Good for babies 6+ months with good head and trunk control. Baby can be sitting in your lap, facing you, or supported in a carrier. Helpful for babies with reflux, stuffy nose, or ear infections because gravity is helping.

### Side-lying

Good for babies 3-5+ months. Takes some practice to find the best position for you and baby with the right supports. Keep trying, as this can be a great position overnight.

# TYPICAL FEEDING CUES

I talk to a lot of mamas about the concept of tuning in to your baby and their cues. Here are some feeding cues to look out for. You may only see one or two of them, or you may see them all. Tune in and when in doubt, offer a feed (your baby will let you know if they don't want it—trust them)!

## FEEDING CUES

### EARLY CUES

- Stirring
- Mouth opening
- Turning head
- Seeking
- Rooting (nuzzling your breasts)
- Licking lips
- Sticking tongue out

### MIDDLE CUES

- Stretching
- Increasing physical movement
- Hand to mouth (i.e., eating hands–up to 4 months)
- Lip smacking

### LATE CUES

- Crying
- Agitated body movements, turning red

Do your best to feed your baby when you see the early or middle cues, but if you find yourself with an agitated baby, calm them first, then feed. You can calm them with cuddling, skin-to-skin contact, singing, shushing, bouncing, rocking, swaying, baby-wearing, or even swaddling for the deep pressure that's often calming (just make sure to unswaddle before they latch and during feeding).

# CLUSTER FEEDING

As if breast-feeding and learning to deal with sleep exhaustion weren't enough, now there's cluster feeding, where your baby is attached to you for what seems like, well, ALL.THE.TIME! Cluster feeding is when your baby wants to nurse almost constantly, sometimes with only ten to thirty minutes in between. These cluster-feeding periods—yes, they're a phase and *will* pass (I promise)—were the hardest for me. I got absolutely zero time for myself in the evenings, which was a hard pill to swallow. In the early days with my first, I'd put him down in his crib after nursing and bouncing him for hours only to have him wake up five or ten minutes later wanting to eat again. It was back and forth for weeks, and I was so tired, emotionally drained, frustrated, and at my wits' end. All I wanted was some time without this little baby attached to me or needing me. It was hard. And then it passed and he got older, bigger, and stronger. Our feeding journey got more manageable and I could relax.

It was much easier with my daughter because I knew what to expect. Instead of trying to feed and put her to sleep in the evenings, I'd settle in to watch a show or movie with my husband and have my daughter sleep on my chest. This way, I could nurse her during those cluster feeds without feeling as if I needed to put her down afterward, to teach her to sleep, and without getting frustrated. After the show, I'd be ready for bed and we'd all just go up, which made the wakes more manageable.

It can happen for you too, Mama!

Cluster feeding, which tends to happen between 5:00 p.m. and 8:00 p.m. (coinciding nicely with the "witching hour" . . . sigh), is a normal and developmentally appropriate phenomenon. Your milk-production hormones are at their lowest in the evening, so baby cluster feeds to tank up before bed. Cluster feeding also increases your supply to keep up with your baby's needs as they grow. The more baby nurses, the more milk they extract, which signals to your body that it needs to make more, and thus your supply increases. You might think, "How could there possibly be more milk in there" after the second or third nursing session in an hour, but trust me, even if your breasts feel empty and deflated, they're never truly empty. Your baby is likely still getting milk even on the third or fourth let-down, even if you no longer feel that tingly sensation.

During these cluster-feeding periods, it's easy to think that your baby is feeding so frequently because they aren't getting enough milk and that your supply is low. It can be tempting to supplement because you a) feel touched out and frustrated with baby on the boob nonstop, b) think baby needs it, and c) think that supplementing with formula will "fill baby" more and help them sleep longer because it takes longer to digest. But supplementing during these cluster-feeding phases can actually lower your supply. Remember, there's a supply-and-demand feedback loop. Baby needs more milk because they're physically growing and expending more energy. Your body senses this and makes more milk. If you supplement, your body doesn't get the same feedback and won't make as much milk.

Don't let cluster feeding and even extreme fussiness in the evening shake your confidence. If baby is gaining weight and having plenty of wet (and dirty) diapers, you're good! Go ahead and tell your partner about this (or have them read this section) so that they understand this phenomenon as well and can be helpful (e.g., bring you water and snacks, make sure you're comfortable where you're feeding baby, put on your favorite Netflix show) while also reminding you that this is normal, rather than adding to your worries and stress.

# BREAST-FEEDING CHALLENGES OR OBSTACLES

I often hear about various things that mamas are worried about when it comes to breast-feeding. I'll address some of them here.

## EFFICIENT EATERS

Babies can take in a lot of milk in a short period. In a five-minute nursing session, an efficient eater can consume more than five ounces of milk. This was my firstborn—classic five-minute feeder, especially as he got older. It was quite rare that he'd be on for much longer than that actively sucking and eating.

So if your baby starts to have shorter nursing sessions as they grow, it might be because they've become more efficient, assuming that they're not popping off due to distractions (a common thing too!). It's normal for babies to stop having lengthy nursing sessions as they grow. The key is to remember that this doesn't necessarily mean that your milk supply is decreasing. Tune in to your baby. Are they producing wet and dirty diapers regularly (they should be pooping at least once a day)? Are they happy after a feed? Are they distracted and popping off during nursing sessions? All these things can give you clues as to whether your baby is getting enough milk.

## FORCEFUL LET-DOWN

Ever had your milk squirt out all over the place as you pull your breast free to feed your baby? It can't just be me! With my son, I'd squirt milk every-where—on baby, on my clothes, sometimes across the room—almost every time I went to feed him. Sometimes it even got right in his eye as I was trying to latch him (poor guy). Forceful let-down is a thing, and often a huge annoyance for us mamas who are graced with an abundant milk supply.

Though most babies will eventually be able to manage whatever let-down and flow you have, initially, your milk may flow at a rate faster than your baby can keep up with. Your baby may gag or choke while trying to feed, especially in the first few minutes, or maybe they pull off or clamp down (ouch!) on the nipple to control the flow. They may fight nursing and rarely settle in and fall asleep at the breast. They may be gassier and spit up after almost every feed (more on reflux soon). These may all be signs that you have a forceful let-down. But they could also be signs that there are other things at play, such as TOTs, cranial molding, or nerve compression, affecting baby's ability to suck, swallow, and breathe in synchrony (we'll get to that in a bit).

Changing your feeding position to either laid-back breast-feeding (either on your bed or in a chair) or side-lying can help baby to manage the flow a little better if you have a forceful let-down. You can also try hand-expressing the initial let-down into a towel, a breast pad, or, if you really want to save every last drop, into milk-saver shells. I had a shell on hand every time I fed my first and was usually able to catch a few ounces of extra milk from my let-down and also from my other breast, which would drip as I nursed. Sigh. The joys of motherhood, right?

## BITING

Ouch! This is a big fear that mamas have once their baby starts teething, but the good news is that it's often short-lived. This is one of the reasons mamas give up breast-feeding early. I like to get curious and put myself in a baby's shoes, and I encourage you to do this too! Your baby isn't biting you with bad intentions, despite what you might hear on the Internet. Babies often bite because the pressure against their gums feels good, calming, and organizing. Remember the proprioceptive input we talked about in the chapter on sensory processing?

There are a lot of proprioceptors in the muscles and joints in the mouth, tongue, cheeks, and jaw. When activated, they release hormones (serotonin and dopamine) that help us to feel good and calm and help us regulate. This is why baby may bite when comfort-sucking rather than actively drinking milk. The pressure from biting can also be soothing to gums that are sore from teething. Of course, your baby could have TOTs, which produce more of a munching or chomping pattern than a sucking pattern, which turns into more biting once they get teeth. Everything is connected.

Just because it's normal doesn't mean you have to suffer, though. When baby bites you, gently put your finger in their mouth and slowly pull your nipple out (your instinct will be to pull it out fast, but sometimes this can hurt even more). Then say something such as, "Ouch, that really hurt Mommy. I don't like the biting." Wait a few seconds, and if your baby shows you signs that they want more milk, you can latch them again. Repeat whenever your baby bites. I also highly recommend getting your baby's latch checked and a thorough assessment of your baby's tongue, lip, and cheek function done to rule out possible TOTs (a quick look inside your baby's mouth while they cry isn't good enough).

## PERIODS AND BREAST MILK

Your breast milk changes in composition and flavor depending on what you eat, how you're feeling, and whether you're on your period (yes, you can get your period back while you're breast-feeding—if it hasn't happened to you, consider yourself lucky!).

Some babies don't like the different flavor during menstruation. Common sense tells us that if your baby doesn't like this new, different taste, they likely won't nurse as often or as well for a few days. Which means that your supply might dip for a little. But keep offering—the stimulation and saliva from baby's mouth on your nipple will continue to alert your body that baby still needs milk. If you have some pumped milk stashed away, now would be a good time to use it for some of the feeds (you may still need to pump to keep up your milk supply).

## LOW MILK SUPPLY

Very few women can't produce enough milk for their babies, and for those who can't, it's often due to medical reasons. What? Yes, I know this probably isn't what you're used to hearing. It seems as though every other mother thinks they don't have enough milk for their baby.

Based on research on breast-feeding and body tightness and conversations with multiple IBCLCs, the consensus is that it's not about not being able to make enough milk. Something else is usually affecting the milk supply, such as not eating enough calories or drinking enough water during the day, not nursing frequently enough (ahem, feeding schedules, I'm looking at you!), or feeding your baby bottles (of breast milk or formula) and not pumping during that time. Or perhaps the baby can't latch and suckle the milk out efficiently due to body tightness, TOTs, compressed cranial bones and/or nerves, or even undiagnosed food allergies/intolerances.

If this is the first time you're hearing about how these things can impact milk production, you might be frustrated, and I understand. Unfortunately, our society doesn't do a great job supporting and educating new moms about all these things related to feeding and more. I'm trying to change that!

## DISTRACTED FEEDERS

Oh, the joy. Your baby starts to twist and turn at every sound or movement while they're feeding, leading them to pop (or pull—ouch!) off the breast. Distracted eating generally starts to happen around four or five months, and getting your baby to focus for a full feed can be quite challenging. Gone are the lazy days of nursing for twenty to forty minutes. Once babies become more alert and "wake up" to the world, they start to notice every little thing in their environment, which means that you need to work extra hard to get those feeds in! This is normal, and there are a few things that you can try to help.

A quiet, dark, distraction-free room can definitely work, but in reality, who has the time or desire to always be looking for this elusive room, especially if you're out of the house? My favorite option for feeding a distracted baby when I'm out is to use the carrier. Just loosen the straps, lower the baby so their nose is to your nipple, and you're good to go. The carrier prevents them from being able to wiggle and turn too much, blocks out at least some of the exciting things happening around them, holds them close (their favorite place), and also "contains" your wiggly baby a bit more. Feeding in the carrier requires a bit of practice, and your baby should have somewhat good head control, but usually around the time they become more alert, they're also strong in tummy time and their head is more stable.

It's also important to know that teething babies' feeds may be smaller, shorter, and more frequent because of the soreness in their gums. They may even go on nursing strikes for a few days. Try some of the teething tips and tricks in Chapter Twenty-Three before feeding to see if they help. As well, babies often become more frequent feeders if they're experiencing separation anxiety. They essentially use the breast for comfort and closeness.

Feed your baby more frequently during the day during these periods of distraction, teething, and separation anxiety because often, they'll start to wake more frequently at night, when it's dark, quiet, and distraction free, to make up for any missed calories during the day.

## GROWTH SPURTS

During a growth spurt, your baby will likely nurse more often than usual. Growth spurts can last for two or three days, and sometimes for up to a week.

Remember, if you're nursing on demand, your supply will increase to meet your baby's demand. Growth spurts happen around seven to ten days, two to three weeks, three months, four months, six months, and nine months.

## BURPING

Mamas are often worried about not burping their babies before putting them into their sleep space when they nurse their babies to sleep. Burping a baby helps bring up air that has been swallowed while nursing. In those first few weeks and months, it's good practice to burp your baby between sides and after every feeding mainly because you're both working on getting a good, deep latch and there will likely be more air getting in while you figure things out.

Many breast-fed babies learn to control their mother's milk flow and don't need to be burped as regularly as bottle-fed babies, and after those first few weeks or months, if your baby is content and no air comes up when you attempt to burp them, then there probably wasn't any trapped air and not burping is fine. If your baby is fussy, has a painful look on their face, or is refusing to latch, continue attempting to help them bring up air or burp. As time goes on, trust that you'll learn your baby's unique burping needs.

I mentioned that air can come in from a poor latch, which may be due to a tongue-tie, but it can also come from poor positioning while feeding or body tightness that prevents the baby from getting comfortable during feeding. A baby can also take in more air if they're popping on/off the breast or bottle, arching away from you during a feed, or even crying a lot before or after a feed. Increased air in the belly can also be due to intolerances to something in your diet—your baby may not be able to digest something properly and so it sits undigested or partially digested in their bellies, causing more gas as a byproduct.

# Chapter Eight

# BOTTLE-FEEDING

Whether you're exclusively bottle-feeding or doing a combination of breast-feeding and bottle-feeding, know that there's no shame in any of it. Nothing in this section on feeding is meant to be a judgment about your feeding choices, or to make you feel bad for choosing one over the other.

Many of the mamas I work with start out with the goal of exclusively breast-feeding and then, for various reasons—excruciating pain, perceived low milk supply, allergies and intolerances, or too much work in their situation—decide to get in extra pumping sessions, supplement, or move exclusively to formula-feeding. This decision often comes with a lot of guilt and perhaps even feelings of failure. If this is you, I want you to know that any amount of breast milk you were able to provide your baby, whether it was your own or a donor's, provided your baby with the many benefits of breast milk. And if you're still offering some breast milk to your baby, whether from your breast or a bottle, your baby is still getting those benefits. This is your permission to stop feeling guilty. Stop worrying that you aren't doing enough for your baby. You are! Your baby is fed, and hopefully growing and thriving, and that's what's most important.

## OVERFEEDING

It's much easier to overfeed a baby with a bottle than at the breast, whether it's breast milk or formula in that bottle. Overfeeding your baby can lead to spitting up, can increase the air in their bellies, which can lead to discomfort or reflux, and can potentially confuse your baby's understanding of their hunger needs. If you primarily breast-feed, giving baby formula so you can get a break is actually counterproductive. Each formula-feeding tells your body that your baby needs one less breast-milk feeding. As discussed, your body will start producing less milk thinking your baby needs less, and this can create a vicious cycle. If you desperately need a break and want to give a bottle of breast milk or formula, one or two bottles won't make a big impact, but if it's a regular occurrence, I recommend pumping (or hand-expressing) at least a bit so that your body thinks your baby still needs the milk.

## PACED FEEDING

When bottle-feeding, it's important to understand the concept of paced feeding. A quick Google search will bring up some great YouTube videos demonstrating paced bottle-feeding. Essentially, you lower the bottle angle after every few suck-swallow-breathe rounds. This allows your baby to have a break from the milk/formula and will also allow them to signal when they're finished with the feed, just as a breast-fed baby would stop sucking on their mother's nipple or pull off from the breast when finished. If the feeding isn't paced, your baby won't have much control over the milk flow. It will continue to dribble from the bottle nipple whether they're sucking on it or not. Paced feeding allows you to tune in to your baby, follow their lead, and give them more control, and it can prevent overfeeding.

I'm not a lactation consultant, nutritionist, dietician, or naturopath, so I haven't included specific guidelines for the amount of formula or ounces of milk to feed your baby in a twenty-four-hour period. I will say that it will vary based on your baby and their age. Usually it will range from about eighteen to thirty-two ounces in a twenty-four-hour period, with the amount at each feed also varying based on the time of day. It's still so important to tune in to your baby's cues and feed them on demand (unless you've received explicit instructions from a feeding specialist to do otherwise) rather than follow some arbitrary (and usually rigid) schedule you found on the Internet.

## TO PUMP OR NOT TO PUMP (AND HOW MUCH)?

With both of my children, I was blessed with an abundance of milk—so much so that with my son, I'd leak right through all the nursing pads onto my shirt. Talk about embarrassing! I figured if I pumped things would get better (and I'd leak less). I often found myself pumping at 2:00 a.m. while my baby slept because my breasts were so full and engorged and I needed to relieve the pressure.

Little did I know that the more I pumped, the more milk my body made, which made things so much worse. And I had eight years of experience as a pediatric occupational therapist under my belt and had been a camp counselor and babysitter to countless babies and children. I definitely didn't know all the things. I struggled—hard! A reminder that we all do, even when it seems everyone else has their shit together on Instagram, or even in real life. Everyone has their low points, their stress points, their worries. Everyone has felt the overwhelm at one point or another.

Back to pumping. You should discuss how frequently and how much you should be pumping with an IBCLC who has assessed you and understands your goals.

Pumping won't drain your breasts as well as your baby should, so it's normal to not pump the same amount that your baby takes on the breast. That said, if your baby isn't draining your breast well and is struggling to extract the breast milk, there's likely a reason and it should be investigated and ideally resolved as soon as possible.

And if you're pumping too much, as I did, your body will think that your baby needs that milk and will produce more, so it might cause an oversupply. But remember, if you're giving your baby expressed milk or formula at night and breast milk from the breast during the day, pump (or hand-express) a little bit at night to maintain your supply, at least in the first six or so months.

## BOTTLES AND BOTTLE NIPPLE FLOW

Go into any baby store and you'll see an assortment of bottles and bottle nipples, all touting something different. Maybe one mimics the shape and feel of the breast, or another reduces air intake to help with colic and reflux. So many choices can lead to a lot of confusion—you just want to know which is best for your baby! The reality is that this is simply good marketing. Believe me, I fell for it as well with my first, spending a good chunk of change on different types of bottles to find one that would miraculously work.

The truth is, it's less about the bottle type or the bottle nipple (though the ones with the longer nipples tend to work better, as they promote a better suck) than it is about the way you're offering the bottle. You essentially want to mimic breast-feeding. Follow your baby's feeding cues and offer the bottle in a calm, stress-free manner. Hold your baby close and comfortably and tickle their lips with the bottle nipple, allowing them to draw it into their mouth. Hold the bottle horizontally in line with their nose, to allow for a good latch. Tune in to your baby during the feed, and use paced feeding.

You may want to try two or three brands at first, to see which one is easiest for you and your baby to use, but once you pick a bottle brand, stick with it. If you're constantly trialing bottles and nipples, your baby won't have the chance to practice and become familiar and confident with one. As with everything, practice and consistency will allow for proper learning and eventual mastering of the skill.

Bottle nipples will inherently allow for a faster flow than a breast, which means that a baby won't need to suck with the same vigor as they do at the breast. But this also means that sometimes they'll get milk in faster than they can manage, which can cause gagging, coughing, and spitting up. Lactation consultants and feeding experts recommend using slow-flow or "newborn" nipples to help. The flow can also impact how your baby takes a breast versus a bottle. Since it's easier to get milk out of the bottle, your baby may tire easily at the breast if they're getting bottles regularly. Just keep trying and offering. Give your baby time. Remember to use paced bottle-feeding. And if you continue to have concerns about your baby's feeding experience, get a proper oral motor function assessment done to rule out TOTs and consider bodywork to release any body tightness.

## INTRODUCING A BOTTLE TO A BREAST-FED BABY

Introducing a bottle to a baby who's been exclusively breast-fed may be a more frustrating experience than you anticipate. With my first, I heard all sorts of things along the lines of "don't introduce it too early as it will cause nipple confusion," so I was terrified of introducing a bottle, and didn't—until one day I had to be out of the house for an appointment. I left Kristjan at home with my husband with a bottle and lots of pumped breast milk. Oh my goodness, what a disaster that was! The struggle, the tears, the frustration, the agitation. Eventually, my husband gave up on trying the bottle and just fed our baby some breast milk on a spoon, which worked but was definitely not efficient in terms of filling a little belly quickly. Needless to say, I came home to a *hangry* baby!

After that experience, I was determined to practice using bottles every now and then so that my son could learn. Was it easy? No! It took a lot of practice and patience, but eventually he did get the hang of it. He always preferred the breast, though, and if I was anywhere in the house, he'd refuse the bottle. In hindsight I wish I'd introduced the bottle when he was younger (and had that strong sucking reflex) and that we'd practiced with it more consistently before that fateful day.

I hear similar stories all the time from the mamas in my community, so I thought it might be helpful if I shared some tips to make introducing a bottle to your breast-fed baby easier.

## TIPS TO MAKE BOTTLE-FEEDING EASIER

1.  If you have the option, I suggest introducing a bottle to your baby early on, ideally in the first three or four months, when the sucking reflex is strong. Trust me, it gets so much harder later on.

    If your baby is older and you need them to start taking a bottle because you're returning to work or will be away, give yourself at least two to four weeks to introduce and practice with the bottle. Try to pick a consistent time of day to do so—and it's helpful if the person giving your baby the bottle isn't you! Your baby will likely put up a fight if you suddenly try to give them a bottle, as they're used to your breast, and you won't be the one to give them the bottle (the whole point is that you'll either be away or you need some extra sleep or time for YOU). It's also helpful to not be in the room when the other person is trying to feed with the bottle. Get your partner, family, or friends to help.

2.    Have something that smells like you. Ideally, it will have some leftover milk on it—an unwashed shirt or bra is a great option, but even a lovey that you hold while you nurse your baby is great.

3.    Get your baby to play with the bottle nipples while they're off the bottle. Pop it on your finger and engage in some oral motor play (in and around the mouth). Allow your baby to grab it, take it into their mouth, munch on it, pull it out, or even hold it, as they might do with a pacifier. This will help familiarize them with the bottle nipple.

4.    Change up the environment that you feed in—a different room, or go outside if weather permits. If baby is refusing the bottle, stop, walk around, and then try again in a different location. Remember that babies will be co-regulating. They can read our energy, so try to take deep breaths and watch your anxiety, frustration, and overall mood when trialing the bottle.

# Chapter Nine

# TETHERED ORAL TISSUES

When my kids were babies, I didn't know about tongue-ties. I vaguely remember my midwives telling me that each of them had a "mild" tongue-tie but that it was nothing to be concerned about. Since then, I've become more interested in tongue (lingual), lip (labial), and cheek (buccal) ties, which, if they're short, tight, or thick, are collectively referred to as tethered oral tissues, or TOTs. My interest stems from my passion for supporting infants with sleep, reflux, and body tightness—and lo and behold, TOTs play a pretty significant part in each of these areas.

Oral dysfunction, under which TOTs fall, is a big deal, and should be investigated and assessed in every single baby. TOTs can be the root cause of feeding issues (such as cracked and bleeding or painful nipples, clicking, milk dribbling from mouth, and more), reflux, colic, difficulties with solids, sleep challenges (frequent waking, restlessness, difficulty staying asleep), and communication and language issues later in life, and can even affect overall mouth and tooth structure, leading to more orthodontic requirements. Tongue-ties are also often related to head-shape issues, such as plagiocephaly or brachycephaly (flat head), as well as torticollis (tightness from neck to hip on one side). Often if there's a lip- or cheek-tie, there's also a tongue-tie.

The tongue is a complex organ comprised of eight muscles. These muscles are intricately involved in feeding, breathing, speaking, sleeping, posture, and many other functions. The tongue has often been referred to as the foundation of development, and low tongue mobility affects the whole body. If the tongue is restricted, then it does not have the full range of motion necessary to achieve proper tongue positioning in the mouth, often called oral rest posture, which is essentially the tongue resting on the roof of the mouth with the lips closed. This posture is necessary for optimal sucking and swallowing, as well as molding and growth of the palate and the dental arches and facial/airway development.

## WHAT ARE TOTS?

TOTs aren't new, or a fad—they've been around for thousands of years. They've been documented in historical texts, and midwives used to have one long, sharp fingernail to clip or slice the tight frenulum, the corded tissue under the tongue. There are various definitions of *tongue-tie*, but I like this simple one, which is the one agreed on by the International Affiliation of Tongue-tie Professionals: "An embryological remnant of tissue in the midline between the undersurface of the tongue and the floor of the mouth that restricts normal tongue movement."[3] The key is that these frena are *affecting function*. They prevent the tongue from lifting, the top lip from properly phalanging (folding upwards), or the cheeks from moving freely (as required for proper sucking and eventually chewing), thus preventing these structures from doing what they're supposed to do.

Tongue-ties, specifically, can be anteriorly attached, right at or near the tip of the tongue, but they can also be less apparent and present more posteriorly (closer to the back of the tongue), which means they can be seen only with a thorough oral assessment. This too thick, tight, or short frenulum means that your baby can't bring their tongue forward far enough to latch onto the breast, draw the nipple far enough back into their mouth, or lift their tongue high enough to the palate to create a vacuum for sucking, swallowing, and feeding well.

Lip-ties cause the lip to turn down rather than phalange up and out when feeding on the breast or bottle, which can affect latch and allow increased air to get in during feeds. A lip-tie can also prevent the lips from fully closing when the body and mouth are at rest and during sleep. And yes, the lips should be closed when at rest and when sleeping, to achieve the oral rest posture.

Cheek-ties are less common, but dimples usually mean that something is pulling on the other side, and these can affect your baby's ability to effectively suck.

## HOW TO CHECK FOR TOTS

Tongue-ties are often hereditary, so if either you or your partner have or had one, there is a good chance your baby does as well. You might even have one that's undiagnosed. You can usually tell whether something is going on with your baby's latch by the symptoms. Many latch issues, if not corrected through positioning, are a result of tongue- or lip-ties. Both make feeding very tiring for babies. Milk will often dribble from the side of the baby's mouth as they feed, or you may hear sucking or clicking noises while they eat. Babies who have latch issues due to TOTs will take in a lot of air while they feed, which can lead to reflux. So if your baby has reflux, this is definitely something that you should look to rule out.

You can also run your finger under your baby's tongue to see if you feel any resistance, something like a "speed bump" that prevents your finger from gliding smoothly from one side to the other. If there is, it could be a tongue-tie. For a lip-tie, try lifting your baby's upper lip to see if it can curl up and out (ideally to touch the nose), and pay attention to what your baby's top lip does while feeding—is it phalanged (this is what we want) or curled under?

Though this self-assessment is a good place to start, I always recommend an assessment by a qualified professional. More and more IBCLCs, speech-language therapists, occupational therapists, and dentists are becoming trained in tongue- and lip-ties, but make sure they have this additional training. Your regular doctor or dentist and even your midwives are usually *not* qualified to do a comprehensive assessment of tongue- and lip-ties. And remember, make sure that whoever is doing the assessment gets their fingers inside your baby's mouth to feel around. Just looking into a baby's mouth isn't enough!

## TOTS AND SLEEP

Many sleep disorders—such as sleep apnea, snoring, teeth grinding, and more—are related to the anatomy and function of the mouth, tongue, and upper airway. If a person goes to sleep and their airway is too small, the throat and mouth muscles will allow the tongue to obstruct the airway. And if the tongue is held down by a tongue-tie, it often falls backward during sleep and blocks the airway. This often leads to mouth breathing, which prevents the brain from experiencing the deepest levels of sleep. People who mouth-breathe often wake up not refreshed. Research shows that after tongue-tie releases, children consistently sleep more deeply, snore less, exhibit fewer movements, and feel more refreshed in the morning.[4]

# TETHERED ORAL TISSUES—SIGNS AND SYMPTOMS

## DO YOU (OR YOUR BABY) HAVE ANY OF THESE SYMPTOMS?

### FOR MOM

- [ ] Poor latch
- [ ] Poor breast drainage
- [ ] Plugged ducts, engorgement, mastitis
- [ ] Nipple thrush
- [ ] Feeling like feeding baby is a full-time job
- [ ] Painful nursing; cracked, creased, flattened, or bleeding nipples

### FOR BABY

- [ ] Falls asleep while feeding (after brief time ~5 min)
- [ ] Pops on/off breast or bottle
- [ ] Reflux or colic symptoms
- [ ] Clicking, smacking noises when eating
- [ ] Poor weight gain
- [ ] Biting/chewing nipple (from the beginning)
- [ ] Poor latch at breast or bottle
- [ ] Milk dribbling out of sides of mouth; coming out of nose
- [ ] Mouth breathing, snoring, noisy breathing

## WHAT TO DO IF YOUR BABY HAS TOTS

Tongue-ties and lip-ties can often be easily corrected by a qualified professional, who may cut the frenulum with scissors or use a laser (the $CO_2$ laser is currently the gold standard for TOT releases). You'll most likely be able to feed your baby straightaway, and you may be surprised by how much easier your baby feeds and sleeps after this procedure.

That said, the healing process can be tough on babies and parents. Both pre- and post-operative exercises are very important. Pre-operative stretches help you (and your baby) practice and get familiar with the wound-care stretches beforehand. Post-operative stretches (for the first three or four weeks) allow the wound to stay open and heal in a lengthened state (secondary healing) rather than heal back to its original position (primary healing). Other post-operative therapeutic exercises are important to retrain the tongue to do what it's meant to do—work on sucking, tongue lateralization (side to side), tongue extension (out), and tongue elevation (up). Please find a practitioner who not only releases the TOTs but also recommends these post-operative wound-care stretches for at least three to four weeks after the release, along with the therapeutic exercises to retrain the tongue.

# Chapter Ten

# NUTRITIONAL DEFICIENCIES

Nutritional imbalances or vitamin/mineral deficiencies are often a missing and overlooked piece of the puzzle when it comes to sleep disturbances, mood, behavior, gut health, and so much more.

Unfortunately, nutritional deficiencies are more common than you might think in our Western world, so it's always good to get blood work done to see where you stand. If you have low levels of something and are breast-feeding, it's highly likely that your baby also has low levels of this thing. (Even if your baby is on formula, look into possible nutritional imbalances if you're seeing issues that might warrant a closer look.)

## IRON

Many new mothers are iron deficient. If a woman starts her pregnancy with lower iron stores, these will be further reduced during the pregnancy, leaving her depleted after birth even if she has no excessive bleeding (more so if there was excessive bleeding). Iron is vital for cell growth and repair, energy, and cardiovascular function. Iron deficiency can cause symptoms that we often relate to tiredness from looking after a sleepless baby, and it's also linked to an increased risk of perinatal mood and anxiety disorders, lowered milk production, fatigue, exhaustion, and urinary tract infections. Iron deficiency is also associated with insomnia, weakness, certain parasomnias (i.e., periodic limb movement disorder), restless sleep and poor quality of sleep.

Iron is also important in our babies' development of sleep stages.[5] Have your baby's iron levels checked (or at least your own), as more iron might improve sleep, especially if you have a baby or toddler who seems restless before bed and during the night. Truthfully, most of us are deficient in iron, and if you had low iron or anemia before or during pregnancy, you most likely have low iron now. Your baby gets their iron stores from you in the first six to nine months, so if yours are low, so are theirs.

## MAGNESIUM

Another big one is magnesium deficiency. Magnesium is an essential micronutrient that supports deep, restorative sleep. It's also important for the development of sleep stages and circadian rhythm regulation. Low magnesium can lead to poor sleep quality and difficulty falling asleep or staying asleep. Magnesium is also involved in muscle contractions, especially of the sphincters, such as the lower esophageal sphincter. If this sphincter is loose or weak, it can cause reflux.[6] Low magnesium can also lead to constipation, irritability, grumpiness, anxiety, depression, muscle tension, cramps or spasms (especially in the eyelid), growing pains, restlessness, teeth grinding, and sensitivity to noise. Even headaches and migraines can be due to low magnesium.

Our body uses magnesium to deal with stress, so it's actually quite easy to become depleted of this nutrient. Magnesium is mainly found in unprocessed whole grains, legumes, seeds, nuts, and dark leafy greens. Most adults don't eat enough of these to meet our magnesium requirements—same for our kids. And it can be depleted when we eat dairy, sugary foods and refined carbohydrates, too much animal protein, and even caffeine. Um, hello, that was basically my entire diet as a new mama! Grab-and-go snacks and coffee were my staples in those first few months when I had a baby who wouldn't sleep and was always attached to the boob.

One of the great things about magnesium is that it's a safe supplement. Unlike many nutrients, magnesium is eliminated from the body daily—it needs to be replaced about every twelve hours. And our body has a failsafe mechanism: an excess of magnesium is excreted through the bowels, which is why many people experience diarrhea when they take too much magnesium at one time (I know, TMI!).

## VITAMIN D

Vitamin D regulates calcium and protects bone density. It also plays an important role in metabolic and immune functions. The American Academy of Pediatrics and the Canadian Paediatric Society say babies and children should get at least 400 to 600 IU of vitamin D per day. Most people, adults and children alike, don't get this much. Vitamin D deficiency is associated with an increased risk of diabetes, chronic pain, fatigue, and sleep problems, particularly difficulty falling asleep.[7,8,9] So remember to give your little one those vitamin D drops. (And hey, if you forget a few times, as I often did, it's all good—just try your best!)

## ZINC

Zinc is a mineral that can easily be low in babies, especially breast-fed babies. Low zinc can result in poor sleep quality and shortened sleep duration, reflux, and skin conditions such as eczema (especially if found around the mouth, bum area, and hands). Zinc is important for the immune system, wound healing, and normal growth and development, and zinc deficiency has been linked to decreased growth, increased colds and infections, impaired memory, learning disabilities, and poor attention span.[10]

Babies are at risk of low zinc largely due to their mothers having low zinc.[11] Pregnant women need more zinc than usual, as it helps the developing baby. Zinc deficiency can also happen if a person has difficulty absorbing nutrients due to poor gut health, low stomach acid, or a gastrointestinal disease.

Protein helps the body to absorb zinc, so vegetarians and vegans and people on long-term restricted diets who eat mainly grains and legumes may be more at risk of zinc deficiency and often need more zinc than people who eat meat.[12] Zinc is found in oysters, red meat, poultry, beans, nuts, crab, lobster, whole grains, breakfast cereals, and dairy products.

## VITAMIN B12

This vitamin is needed for healthy immune function and brain development, among other important functions. It's especially important for vegetarians and vegans to be aware of, in addition to folate and iron.[13] Vitamin B12 is needed to produce melatonin (the "sleep hormone"). Vitamin B12 deficiencies can cause insomnia, night sweats, and fatigue. It's involved in daytime fatigue, or that feeling of brain fog. When I remember to take my vitamin B complex supplement, I feel much more energized during the day (I'm going to go grab one right now!).

## CALCIUM

Calcium deficiency is another one associated with difficulty falling asleep and poor sleep quality. It's used to produce tryptophan, the precursor of melatonin (there's that sleep hormone again), which explains why a calcium deficiency can cause problems with falling asleep.

## SELENIUM

Selenium is important for immunity and regulating inflammation, and low levels of it are also associated with difficulty falling asleep. Selenium is found in meats, seafood, dairy products, nuts, and grains, so make sure to get plenty of those into your diet daily.[14]

## VITAMIN C

Finally, a vitamin C deficiency can cause many health problems, but specifically nonrestorative sleep problems. Vitamin C is found in fresh fruits and vegetables, though the longer the fruits and vegetables have been picked for, the more it decreases.

I don't want you to go out and start filling your cabinets with all kinds of supplements now. It can be hard to determine whether your baby/toddler has nutritional deficiencies as a blood test is required, and these are usually difficult to do on little ones (their veins are so small). And simply eating foods rich in these vitamins and minerals won't guarantee better sleep (I know that's what you were hoping, right?). But it can help! And whatever you do to help yourself will be passed to your baby if you're breast-feeding, and you'll see a ripple effect.

The most important thing I want you to take from this section is to eat a variety of foods and avoid consuming processed foods too often. Chat with a dietician, a naturopath, or your doctor if you suspect that nutrient deficiencies are at play in you or your child.

Also, be aware that not all supplements are created equally. Many have fillers and sugars that do nothing for your health and/or aren't properly absorbed into your body. Make sure you're using high-quality supplements. I love Young Living supplements because they're more bioavailable in our bodies due to the care and quality taken in creating them, and also because they're often infused with essential oils, which are close to human cells in composition.

*Chapter Eleven*

# REFLUX

Have you ever wondered, "How much spit-up is too much?" Or, "My baby seems to spit up *all the time*—is this normal?" Or perhaps you've wondered if your baby has reflux and your doctor told you there isn't much that can be done and they'll outgrow it? Or maybe you were offered medication for your teeny-tiny baby and something about that just didn't feel right?

Reflux is an important topic in the world of infants (and their parents) and can impact their overall functioning, from sleep to feeding to overall ability to be happy, thriving, and growing as they move and explore. It's vital to understand why reflux is happening because it's a symptom of something else. My aim with this chapter is to give you a basic understanding of what could be causing reflux and where you can get additional support to resolve the cause.

First, know that it's perfectly normal for babies to spit up after feedings or to vomit occasionally without apparent cause or warning. In fact, some babies spit up frequently and show no ill effects (this was my first—the only ill effect was my spit-up-stained clothing, even after they went through the wash).

## TYPES OF REFLUX

A baby's stomach is more horizontal than an adult's, their esophagus (the tube that carries food from their mouth to their stomach) is shorter, their lower esophageal sphincter (LES) is weaker, they lack core strength, and their digestive system isn't fully mature. So some of this spit-up is due to gravity and lack of development, which is generally the thinking behind the rationale that "they'll grow out of it."

Then there's the fact that sometimes babies consume a larger volume of milk than their small tummies can handle. This combined with a short esophagus means that some of the milk simply spills back out through the mouth after a feed.[15] This is likely a protective mechanism. This type of spitting up is physiological gastroesophageal reflux (GER)—*gastro* (from the stomach), *esophageal* (into the esophagus), *reflux* (involuntary regurgitation)—usually referred to as "reflux." It starts around two or three weeks, peaks around four or five months, and typically goes away by twelve months.[16,17] While all the extra laundry and cleanup is annoying, GER is usually nothing to worry about. Research shows that 41 percent of three- to four-month-olds spit up some portion of their feedings.[18]

This involuntary and effortless regurgitation is important for two reasons:

1.   It moderates the digestive system by removing air from the stomach before it goes into the intestines and causes further upset.

2.  It protects the body. The stomach and intestines are big parts of the immune system. There are little detectors in them that pick up on anything that might make us ill or that the body perceives as a threat, and they'll try to get rid of this threat. For example, when you get a stomach bug or food poisoning, your body vomits to get rid of pathogens. The goal is to prevent additional pain and distress to the body. This is why reflux can also be a symptom of allergies. The allergy is a protective mechanism and the reflux is a symptom of the allergy. So reflux in and of itself isn't a bad thing.

But when baby is spitting up a lot and/or with complications—such as pain, distress when they feed, arching or pushing away during feeds, constant discomfort, projectile vomiting, poor weight gain, or respiratory problems— it's another story. This type of reflux is called pathological gastroesophageal reflux disease (GERD), which is often also referred to as "reflux." Studies have shown that infants without GERD have an average of 1.5 reflux episodes per hour, but infants with clinical GERD average 6.7 episodes of reflux per hour.[19] That's a significant difference in both frequency and volume.

We don't want our babies in pain or discomfort for any longer than they already have been if we can help it, so the "wait it out" approach isn't good enough here. But as we'll look at in this chapter, the medication approach may not be appropriate either, so it's imperative that the cause of the GERD is found—because it's a symptom of something.

You may have also heard about silent reflux and wonder how it's different from GER and GERD. To put it simply, no spit-up or vomit comes out with silent reflux. Instead, regurgitated milk comes partway up the esophagus and into the back of the throat (laryngopharyngeal reflux, LPR) before returning to the stomach. Or it can come out through the nose (nasopharyngeal reflux, NPR). Silent reflux is often more concerning than regular reflux because the stomach acid goes up and down, over and over, and never leaves. This causes irritation and pain due to lesions and inflammation of the airway.

Again, reflux is normal and important to a certain extent. What isn't normal is pain, discomfort, or ongoing suffering or distress. Then the reflux *is* a problem. But there's a lot that can be done about it, which we'll look at shortly.

## WHAT CAUSES REFLUX?

According to most doctors and pediatricians, as well as many other health-care practitioners, reflux is caused only by a weakness in the LES, a ring of muscle around the base of the esophagus, where it meets the stomach. It's true that babies have natural weakness in all their muscles, including the sphincter muscles—their muscles haven't had time to strengthen or mature yet. Strengthening happens when they move their bodies against gravity. As well, in young babies, the stomach lies much more horizontally than vertically, which means the opening to the stomach from the esophagus and from the stomach to the intestine, at the other end, are almost on the same level. And yes, it's also true that babies will usually outgrow reflux by about twelve to eighteen months as they develop and move into upright positions because this helps their stomach become more vertical. Gravity can then help keep things down.[20,21]

But there are many other causes of reflux, and they're all relatively easy to investigate and potentially resolve, so why not try?

Keep in mind that these might also be the underlying reasons for GER. Families often reach out to me because they're concerned that their mostly happy baby is spitting up *a lot*, or at every feed. For these "happy spitters," as long as there's no marked distress and the reflux isn't affecting their functioning or weight gain, then there's usually nothing to worry about. If you want to explore the causes, though, the following section will help you.

## CAUSE #1: AEROPHAGIA/AIR INTAKE

This is the drinking or swallowing of air. When air is added to the milk/formula in the belly, it creates an explosive pressurized container of sorts. There are only two ways out—back up through the esophagus or down and out the back. This is why gravity is really important for babies who have reflux—it can allow for a natural flow of stomach contents. But assistance from gravity doesn't necessarily ease pain and discomfort, so it's only part of the solution.

There are various ways that air can get in. A poor latch is one way, so look at positioning while feeding. Tongue- and lip-ties, tongue mobility, and the ability to maintain a proper suck can also be factors, whether your baby is breast- or bottle-fed. And if you're bottle-feeding, are you doing paced bottle-feeding?

Crying could be another reason your baby is taking in more air, especially if they're crying a lot. They swallow air every time they gulp or gasp for a breath. If this is the case, consider why your baby is crying. Are they overstimulated, overtired, or in some kind of pain or discomfort? Do they have unmet needs (hunger, thirst, a soiled diaper, wanting to be held close, etc.)? The crying could even be a result of unprocessed birth trauma.

The sad reality is that sometimes babies are put on reflux medications because of regurgitation due to constant crying, but the crying is the result of something else, which means the medication is pointless.

## AIR INTAKE (AEROPHAGIA)—SYMPTOMS DURING FEEDS

- [ ] Frequent feeds (> 8 feeds/day under 6 mths)
- [ ] Short feeds (< 5 mins) or long feeds (30+ mins)
- [ ] Posseting (brings milk up and swallows again)
- [ ] Sputters, coughs, gags, or chokes during a feed
- [ ] Can hear milk sloshing in baby's tummy
- [ ] Makes clicking sound while feeding
- [ ] Claws own face or Mom's, at breast, and/or lashes out or swats to hit
- [ ] Gulps while feeding
- [ ] Milk bubbles at side of mouth or spills out
- [ ] Falls asleep during a feed
- [ ] Often refuses to feed
- [ ] Bobs on/off breast or bottle during a feed
- [ ] Feeds best when partially asleep
- [ ] Mom has flat, cracked, painful, bleeding nipples
- [ ] White tongue (i.e., coated with milk)
- [ ] Baby has high arched palate
- [ ] Baby has strong gag reflex
- [ ] Weak suck

## SYMPTOMS AFTER FEEDS

- [ ] Calluses or blisters on lips
- [ ] Projectile or frequent vomiting
- [ ] Green/yellow vomit
- [ ] Slow or poor weight gain
- [ ] Vomiting worse in mornings
- [ ] Chokes or blue spells (i.e., skin turns blue)
- [ ] Brings up food after several hours
- [ ] Squirms around or grunts
- [ ] Swallows constantly, even after a feed
- [ ] Bloated or swollen belly
- [ ] Milk comes back up through the nose
- [ ] Spits up frequently
- [ ] Appears to be in pain, discomfort, gassy, etc.
- [ ] Snoring, noisy breathing, or mouth breathing
- [ ] Mom—engorgement/mastitis/plugged ducts
- [ ] Difficulty burping
- [ ] Pulls knees up (frequently)
- [ ] Hard, rumbly tummy
- [ ] Lots of or painful gas
- [ ] Tender tummy

## CAUSE #2: DIGESTIVE ISSUES

Another major cause of reflux is digestion. Food allergies, intolerances, or sensitivities could be causing the regurgitation or projectile vomiting of stomach acid, discomfort, and/or pain. Remember, our bodies are smart. If the stomach senses that something might be dangerous to our health, it will get rid of it.

Another thing to consider is whether you took antibiotics during pregnancy or labor/delivery. Antibiotics wipe out your gut bacteria and therefore affect your baby's gut bacteria, which can affect your baby's ability to digest various foods and even make them more prone to allergies or intolerances. If your baby was born premature, with an even more immature digestive system, this can also affect the chance of developing reflux.

It's estimated that approximately 42 percent of children with reflux have a cow's milk protein sensitivity.[22] Other common foods that might trigger an allergic, intolerant, or sensitivity response in babies are eggs, dairy, soy, wheat, corn, rice, oats, tree nuts, and even some legumes and meats. Of course there are many other foods that your baby might be reacting to. If you're breast-feeding, your diet is very important to consider. If your baby is formula-fed, pay attention to the ingredients—many formulas are made with cow's milk protein or have lactose in them, and some are also made with egg or soy products as well as various sugars (not easily digested by babies) and additives, such as milk thickeners (e.g., maltodextrin or carob bean gum), which can also cause digestive issues. And often the ingredients of the powdered formula and the liquid counterpart of that brand of formula are different.

Also make sure you know the ingredients of any probiotics, supplements, and medications you or your baby are taking. Their digestive system is immature and doesn't have all the necessary enzymes to properly digest all foods. When food sits in the stomach undigested, it can lead to increased gas, constipation, bloating, and discomfort.

## DIGESTIVE SYMPTOMS

- ☐ Milk comes back up through the nose
- ☐ Spits up after feed—fresh or curdled
- ☐ Difficulty burping
- ☐ Projectile or frequent vomiting
- ☐ Tender tummy
- ☐ Pulls knees up (frequently)
- ☐ Bloated or swollen belly
- ☐ Rumbly, hard tummy
- ☐ Constipation
- ☐ Diarrhea (no fever)
- ☐ Rhinitis (runny nose, stuffy, or sneezing)

- ☐ Eczema or psoriasis
- ☐ Reaction to food (within 2 hrs)
- ☐ Hives or itchiness on skin
- ☐ Dark circles under eyes
- ☐ Coughing or congestion of nose, throat
- ☐ Lots of or painful gas/wind
- ☐ Bloody, green, black poo
- ☐ Excessive crying
- ☐ Acidic or smelly breath
- ☐ Mucus in poo

You may have noticed that some of the symptoms indicating digestive causes are the same as those indicating air intake. The trick is to deal with any air-intake issues first and then move on to other potential causes. Air intake is one of the most common reasons for reflux, and ruling out latch issues is often easier than investigating food allergies, intolerances, and more. However, there are very distinct symptoms indicative of digestive causes, so if your baby exhibits these then I suggest focusing on the digestive issues at the same time as ruling out air intake.

Digestive symptoms, skin symptoms, and behavioral symptoms are more indicative of food intolerances or allergies or high levels of sugar and refined carbohydrates (in the case of behavioral symptoms). In these instances, it would be best to make food changes with support from a naturopath, nutritionist, or dietician.

Since we're on the topic of gut health, this is a good place to mention that sometimes babies who've had reflux in the past may experience flare-ups with the introduction of foods. Usually it's because they're eating foods they cannot yet digest. (Babies who've been on or are currently taking gastric-acid-suppression medication may also experience reflux flare-ups when solids are introduced, as the medication changes their bodies' digestive and absorption abilities.)

Initially, babies mainly have the enzymes needed for breaking down healthy fats. Then they develop the enzymes needed for protein digestion, and finally comes the development or maturation of digestive enzymes needed to break down complex carbohydrates, starches, and grains. So get curious and watch for signs that certain foods aren't agreeing with your baby's tummy. I'll chat more about this in Chapter Twelve.

## CAUSE #3: PHYSICAL ISSUES

Pregnancy and birth can also factor into reflux—more specifically, the baby's position in utero and their birth experience might have affected whether they were able to complete various innate reflexive movements (cardinal movements). As well, babies' heads mold. Their cranial bones shift and overlap so the head can fit through the tight space of the pelvis and birth canal. Ideally, these bones move back into place a few days or even weeks after birth, often with the assistance of the strong and frequent sucking babies do.

But in many cases, especially for babies who weren't in an optimal position in utero or during the birthing process, or for those who had various interventions, the increased compression and molding of these cranial bones doesn't rectify itself. This can lead to whole-body tightness, head-shape discrepancies, and compression of cranial nerves, which can impact digestion and feeding functions, such as latch, sucking, and swallowing, and lead to a baby taking in more air, which can lead to reflux.

Various medical conditions (e.g., galactosaemia, lactose deficiency, cleft lip/palate, congenital lactase deficiency, laryngomalacia, stridor, enlarged adenoids, and more) can also make reflux more likely to occur. It's important to know that ruling out the other main causes of reflux (and getting support in reducing those symptoms) can offer a great deal of relief to babies, even if the reflux itself isn't fully resolved due to more structural issues.

## PHYSICAL SYMPTOMS

- [ ] Arching or stretching (a lot) during or after feed
- [ ] Throws self back very suddenly
- [ ] Difficulty burping
- [ ] Gassy
- [ ] Spits up after feed—fresh or curdled
- [ ] Excessive crying
- [ ] Torticollis (curved spine and/or tight neck)
- [ ] Plagiocephaly (flat head syndrome)
- [ ] Only likes to feed in a specific position or side
- [ ] Cleft lip or palate
- [ ] Enlarged adenoids or tonsils
- [ ] Baby pushes away from you during feeds
- [ ] Pulls knees up (frequently)
- [ ] Scrunches face (frequently)
- [ ] Sleeps with head in extended angle (90 degrees)
- [ ] Can't open mouth very wide for prolonged period
- [ ] Turns head away during feeds
- [ ] Ear infections (especially early on and/or a lot)
- [ ] Bulging fontanel
- [ ] Rapidly increasing head circumference (>1cm/wk)
- [ ] Palpable mass on stomach

## OTHER SYMPTOMS

Some respiratory symptoms might be indicative of reflux, especially silent reflux. If your baby has ongoing symptoms—such as a cough, a snotty or runny nose, acidic or smelly breath, or other sinusitis-type symptoms—they may have stomach acid coming up the back of the throat and even going to the nasal passages. The membranes of these parts of the body produce mucus to protect themselves and eradicate potential pathogens from the body. This can lead to a snotty nose, congestion, and coughing—the body's natural way to expel this mucus. If these symptoms are caused by reflux, they *will not* be accompanied by a fever.

## WHO CAN HELP WITH REFLUX?

While there likely won't be many health-care professionals who will fully understand all the components underlying your baby's reflux, many of them can help identify and resolve most causes. Here are some of my favorite and most frequently referred to professionals.

1.  IBCLCs help with latch, positioning while feeding, and trouble-shooting breast- or bottle-feeding difficulties, so an IBCLC should be one of the first professionals you seek support from if your baby is demonstrating any symptoms of air intake. Some of them also have additional training in TOTs.

2.  Bodyworkers are a huge piece of the puzzle and support team when it comes to supporting reflux. Craniosacral therapists, osteo-paths, and even pediatric chiropractors and physical therapists can all help with residual body tightness or compression from in utero positioning and birth experiences. And don't forget that the tongue is a group of muscles that can hold tension, so an osteopath or a craniosacral therapist who can work to release tension in the tongue can be helpful, especially before and after a frenectomy (tongue- or lip-tie release)—and may also prevent the need for one.

3.  Naturopaths or dieticians can help with digestive issues and gut
    health.

4.  Speech-language pathologists and occupational therapists with
    additional training in TOTs can help with the function of the
    tongue, cheeks, and lips, and pediatric dentists (again with spe-
    cialized training in TOTs) can release the frenulum as needed.

## REFLUX RELIEF STRATEGIES

Now that you know a little bit more about what reflux really is, when to be
concerned and look for further support, what types of issues can cause
reflux (remember, it's always a symptom of something else), and which
professionals to contact for additional help, here are a few strategies to help
relieve reflux symptoms and your baby's pain/discomfort.

### STRATEGIES TO HELP WHILE YOU RESOLVE THE CAUSE OF YOUR BABY'S REFLUX

1.  Reducing use of car seats as much as possible—this can
    exacerbate both GER and GERD because of the crunched
    position with legs bent into the tummy.
2.  Being held upright as much as possible after eating (at least
    20 minutes) with no stomach compression and no swinging
    or bouncing.
3.  Lying prone (i.e., on tummy) when they are awake—it
    seems counterintuitive, but lots of tummy time (supported
    as needed) can be great for babies with reflux and more
    comfortable than being on their backs (which can make
    reflux worse). Do not do this immediately after a feed.
4.  Changing diaper in side-lying position (or standing if they
    are old enough) instead of on their backs, which can make
    reflux worse.

---

STRATEGIES TO HELP WHILE YOU RESOLVE THE CAUSE
OF YOUR BABY'S REFLUX, CONT'D

5. Letting babies sleep on their sides or tummies (after about 4-6 months and once they roll onto their tummy on their own), if this is more comfortable for them, especially while they are being supervised (such as for naps or the beginning of the night, or if sleeping next to you).
6. Calming surroundings/environment—darkened, quiet room, consistent routines, calming music, having a favorite transitional object or developing a bond to a lovey.
7. Having a feeding schedule (vs. just feeding on demand)—basically in an effort to "prevent the binge" cycle by limiting volumes of milk/formula. This should always be done under the direction of a feeding specialist or doctor.
8. If your baby refuses to feed, take a break for 10 minutes, play, and then try again.
9. Sometimes rocking your baby so they are a little sleepy can help them relax enough to feed while partially asleep.

---

A quick word on reflux medication. Many babies are on it when the root of their discomfort is related to challenges with cranial-bone alignment, cranial-nerve compression, latch, tongue-ties, tongue function, crying from overstimulation or overtiredness, and/or food allergies or sensitivities. Medication won't resolve any of this. Sometimes medication is needed in the short term (not months on end) to mitigate the pain and the erosion of the esophagus, but there should always be someone investigating the *cause* of the reflux. Parents have told me that their babies were on medication for almost the entire first year! That is NOT okay! Many of these medications have their own side effects and can cause sleep issues and changes in babies' digestive systems, and might even lead to food sensitivities later on.

So if your baby is on reflux medication or has been prescribed it, I encourage you to go back to your doctor and ask for a review of your situation. Find out what the plan is for determining the cause of the reflux and weaning off the medication. You're now armed with more knowledge to make an informed decision. You have the ability to have a more effective conversation with your doctor, and hopefully you feel empowered to search for the underlying cause of your baby's reflux. It's okay to ask questions, to say no to medication if it doesn't feel right to you, or even to postpone starting the medication while consulting some of the other professionals I mentioned.

## WHAT ABOUT COLIC?

Colic is described as a period of irritability, fussing, or crying that begins and ends for no apparent reason. The rule of three tends to come into play: crying lasts at least three hours a day, at least three days a week, for at least three weeks in an infant about three or four months old. Unfortunately, our medical system essentially says that there's no true cause of colic, and a "wait and see if they outgrow it" approach is recommended. It's unfair to leave babies and parents in such a stressful situation when in reality, there's probably a reason for the colic. "Colicky" babies are in genuine pain or discomfort, very likely from many of the same causes of reflux—increased air intake, digestion issues, cranial-bone misalignment or compressed nerves, etc.

Another theory is that colic may be due to an imbalance of foremilk and hindmilk. During a feed, breast milk is somewhat watery at let-down and becomes thicker and fattier as the baby drains more from the breast. If your baby doesn't have a good latch, is popping on/off the breast, falls asleep quickly when feeding, and/or isn't draining milk from the breast efficiently, they may not be getting the fattier hindmilk. The watery foremilk is thirst quenching but high in lactose and low in protein. While it may temporarily fill the baby, it won't satisfy them for long and can also ferment in their gut and cause increased gas (air in belly) and its resulting pain. If your baby is getting more of the fattier hindmilk, they'll be more content. The shift from foremilk to hindmilk happens gradually. If your baby isn't feeding from one breast for very long, try offering the same breast again. If your baby objects, try the other breast. You'll know if your baby has had their fill of richer milk as they'll look "milk drunk" and they'll be satisfied—for at least a few hours.

We also need to remember that babies cry for all kinds of reasons but mostly to communicate a need. They might be hungry, tired, cold, lonely, or have a tummyache. They might feel unwell, be overstimulated, or be suffering from sensory overload. If they have sensitivities to sensory stimuli, irritation, or pain they can become easily stressed out. And then they cry—and they may cry until that stimulation or pain is removed. It may take hours and hours to figure out what it is.

Crying is also a way to release stress. An overstimulating day, frustration at learning new skills, or unprocessed trauma from birth can cause stress. This is yet another reason it's so important for you, as the parent, to really tune in to the baby in front of you. Get curious as to why they're crying, try holding them in different ways, take breaks and change the scenery, go outside—do whatever you need to do to get through, and most importantly, please ask for help (I know, easier said than done).

# Chapter Twelve

# INTRODUCTION TO SOLIDS

Oh the wonderful—ahem, the scary, fearful—time in your baby's life when you introduce them to solids! You, like every parent out there, want your baby to be a good eater, enjoy food, eat a nutritious diet, and for it all to be stress free! Unfortunately, there will likely be struggles along the way (have you figured out yet that this is a pattern of parenthood in general?). Struggles might involve spoon-feeding, coping with different textures, spitting out food, picky eating, and mealtime battles. Before you get even more stressed out considering all the possible struggles, please remember this: the goal of introducing solids (at least initially) is to play, explore, learn, strengthen skills, and, yes, get messy!

You might have heard the catchphrase "food before one is just for fun," and there's a lot of truth to it, but babies need the opportunity to explore foods without necessarily ingesting them. They need time with and exposure to different foods to get used to the taste, smell, sight, texture, and consistency of them. They need to practice manipulating the foods with their hands and their mouths while they start to develop the necessary oral motor skills required to eat more-solid foods. So in the first six months of introducing solids, the focus should be on enjoyment, exploration, and practice, NOT volume! Before a baby is twelve months old, solids are meant to be complementary—they don't take over from breast milk or formula but add to it, so that baby's diet gradually becomes more varied.

## SOLIDS READINESS

Just as babies reach their motor milestones in a somewhat set pattern, they learn feeding skills in a pattern. Some feeding skills develop gradually and some seem to appear overnight.

If given the chance, almost all babies will show their parents that they're ready for something other than milk simply by grabbing a piece of food and lifting it to their mouth. Yup! This might happen at five months, or maybe even closer to eight months. Babies don't need us to decide when to introduce solids to them, whether we spoon-feed or not. So even though the current guidelines indicate starting around the six-month mark, know that your baby might have a slightly different timeline and you can save yourself a lot of frustration and worry by following their cues.

That said, the six-month guideline is there for a reason. Introducing solids before that isn't generally recommended (even though some professionals still recommend starting at four months). One reason is that solid foods aren't as densely packed with nutrients and calories as breast milk and formula. Gasp! Shocking, right? This doesn't mean that solid foods aren't nutritious, but you need a larger volume of them to match the nutrients and calories found in breast milk or formula. And realistically, babies (and even toddlers) don't have the belly space (or the oral motor skills) for that volume just yet.

The other reason is that solid food isn't as easily digested by babies because their digestive system isn't working efficiently enough yet to get all the good nutrients out of the solid foods. The digestive system continues to mature well into the second year of life, once all the milk teeth come in. And constipation, gas, bloated tummies, and general tummy discomfort isn't fun for anyone, especially our little ones.

Before introducing solids to your baby, look for a few other key readiness signs. They should have good head and neck control and should be developing trunk control and be able to sit independently for about ten to thirty seconds. I often hear from the mamas in my community that their babies aren't sitting independently at six or seven months. They worry about starting solids and where they should sit their baby during meals. Mamas often recommend Bumbo chairs to each other. Cue the cringe face here. These types of chairs put your baby's body in a very unnatural position, with a tilted pelvis, which isn't good for trunk stability and eating.

In my work with mamas, I talk a lot about the importance of getting into a sitting position independently, which doesn't happen until around seven to nine months, depending on a baby's spinal curve development and the development/strength of their trunk muscles. But, as mentioned, mealtimes are an exception. A highchair is the safest place for a baby to eat and explore solids. They should be in it for only ten to twenty minutes at a time, though—it shouldn't be used as a place to play. If your baby isn't stable when sitting in the highchair (most highchairs are poorly designed and should have some kind of foot support to promote good posture) and they wobble all over the place, sitting them upright in your lap while you hold them against your body is likely a better, sturdier, and thus safer option.

Use your mama intuition! Follow your gut.

When it comes to starting solids, you can also let your baby lead. They'll start to watch you, reach for your food as you eat, want to hold your spoon, and perhaps even fuss until you hand them a piece of something. These are all signs that they're ready to start trying some on their own.

# HOW TO INTRODUCE SOLIDS

A lot of brain power tends to go into thinking about whether to feed your baby solids before or after a nursing session, how much time to leave between, if it's better to feed them solids once a day or multiple times, and whether it should be done at breakfast, lunch, or dinner. And then of course there's the question of whether to start with purees or go right to solid food using a baby-led weaning approach. And are you allowed to do both? And if you choose to offer solid foods, how big or small should they be? Do you cut them lengthwise or mush them slightly? Talk about choices that can lead to that "deer in the headlights" feeling of overwhelm! Trust me, I was there too, with my firstborn, and I *had* training and experience with feeding at that point. Motherhood is a steep learning curve, isn't it?

Let's tackle the whole "which method should I choose" question first. There are different schools of thought about introducing solids to your baby, namely the spoon-feeding purees approach and the baby-led weaning approach, sometimes called the baby-led feeding approach.

## SPOON-FEEDING

When it comes to a neurotypical baby (and yes, most babies will fall into this category), I don't recommend starting with spoon-feeding purees only, at least not for many months. Are there situations where this is the best approach? Yes. But for your average baby, I personally and professionally don't believe this is beneficial for development. This isn't to say that spoon-feeding is inherently bad, but we need to be aware of why and how we're going about it.

Imagine you're six months old. You enjoy imitating your family and want to grab the things they're holding to find out what they are. But instead of allowing you to join in, your parents insist on putting something mushy into your mouth with a spoon. Sometimes this spoon is a cold metal thing and sometimes it's room temperature and plastic. The mush on the spoon is usually the same consistency, but the taste seems to vary—sometimes it's nice, sometimes it's not. When you reach out to try to explore said mush, your parents might let you look at it but rarely let you touch it. And when they're feeding you, sometimes they seem to be in a hurry and other times you have to wait for the next mouthful. When you spit out the food because you weren't expecting it, your tongue is still learning how to manage it, or you just wanted to see what the food looked like, your parents scrape it up as quickly as they can, scraping your face with the spoon as they go, and poke it back into your mouth! That feels weird, so you turn your head away, and suddenly mealtime is over.

So many mamas in my community say that their babies hate spoon-feeding and as a result, the introduction to solids "isn't going well" or is "really stressful." They're often anxious and worried that their babies aren't eating properly and that this will affect their development. I love taking them through this analogy—putting yourself in your baby's shoes can help you understand why they may not "like" spoon-feeding!

Here are some of the reasons I don't recommend starting with spoon-feeding *only*:

- Purees are easy to suck off spoons and don't need to be chewed. Sounds great, right? Well, yes and no. If your baby isn't getting the chance to experiment with food that needs chewing, or at the very least manipulating in the mouth, then they aren't actually developing the oral motor skills that they'll need later on, when it's time to start the more-solid foods.

- Babies learn to cope with lumps better and more quickly if they're allowed to feed themselves because it's easier to manipulate and chew food when it starts off at the front of the mouth (near the tip of the tongue). When they suck it to the back (off of the spoon), they can't move it around as easily.

- When being spoon-fed, your baby isn't in control of how much or how quickly they eat. Often, babies will eat faster and more than they need when they're spoon-fed.

## BABY-LED WEANING

I love baby-led weaning, but more than that I love helping families find an approach (usually a combination) that works for them.

The baby-led weaning approach is one that many cultures around the world use when introducing solids to their babies. Quite simply, it's offering your baby whatever you're eating and watching to see what happens. Of course, you have to use common sense, but this approach doesn't have to be complicated. You don't need to make special meals for your baby or toddler, there's no specific program to follow, no stages to complete, no order of food or texture introduction. You can use this approach as the next step whether you're breast-feeding, formula-feeding, or doing a combination of both. It's safe, natural, and as easy as you make it. It can be as simple as making yourself lunch, sitting at the table with your baby, putting some of your lunch on your baby's highchair tray, and seeing what happens.

There are so many benefits to this! You're eating and engaging with your baby, sharing a meal and connecting. Your baby is watching you eat and learning through imitation while also exploring different food textures, tastes, shapes, and more. They're also learning to manipulate all these different foods with their hands, their lips, their tongue, and the inside of their mouth. So much learning happens, regardless of whether your baby is actually chewing and swallowing that food. In fact, as mentioned, chewing and swallowing isn't the expectation initially. Those are skills that emerge with time and practice.

Okay, Kaili, but can I really expect my six-month-old baby to start exploring pieces of food? Can they really do that? And what about choking?

Mama, I hear you, I see you, I was you! Stay with me here.

By the time babies are about six months old (as with other milestones, this is an average age), they're starting to reach for and grab objects (think hand sized), pick them up with their fists, and get them to their mouth, whether it's a balled-up sock, a rock from the garden, your keys, or a handful of sand. They love to put everything in their mouths around this age, and we should encourage this because it's how they learn about the properties of said object! They feel it with their mouth first; refinement of touch through their fingers comes much later.

Generally, offering a longer piece of food is better at this stage because children don't have the precise pincer-grasp ability or accurate hand-to-mouth aim, so longer pieces of food stand a better chance of being picked up and reaching their mouths. This is also usually the stage where they're exploring the food with their lips and tongue. Remember, "food before one is just for fun *and* exploring."

Between the ages of six and nine months, several new skills and abilities develop, one after the other. This is when your baby often manages to gnaw or bite off a small piece of food with their gums (and yes, these are strong—your baby doesn't need teeth to explore and eat solid foods). Soon after that, they learn how to keep the food in their mouths, for a while, and then eventually move it around (specifically, they need to learn to move it to the back molar area) and chew it. At this stage, it's still more likely to fall out of the mouth than get swallowed. The act of moving food to the back of the mouth happens after your baby has discovered the ability to bite and chew (and requires good tongue mobility). Around nine or ten months, your baby will develop the pincer grasp (using thumb and index finger) and be able to pick up smaller pieces of food. Before this, it will be difficult for them to pick up small pieces of food (think peas, blueberries, or Cheerios).

Holy cow! See how many steps there are to eating? Especially if you count the sensorial experiences of seeing, smelling, touching, and eventually tasting the food! So yeah, it takes babies a while before they "get it"—before we can expect them to be able to chew and swallow enough food to get the required nutrients from their solid food. This is why solid food is considered complementary to breast milk or formula between six and twelve months. Once your child is twelve months, the breast milk and formula become complementary to the solids because there's been about six months of practice with all those new skills. This is why this approach is called baby-led weaning. Your baby gradually weans themselves off breast milk or formula as their main source of nutrition.

It's important to be aware that babies who are spoon-fed for the first few months will still need to go through all the steps to develop the oral motor skills, so their ability to eat finger foods might develop slightly later in comparison to a baby who was introduced to solid foods from the beginning (because they didn't start practicing the necessary skills until later).

So which approach resonates with you the most? Really sit with this question and follow your heart. What feels light and easy? What feels right? And remember, you don't have to take an all-or-nothing approach (despite the fact that baby-led weaning communities can be a bit intimidating with their strong opinion that it's the only way). Both of my children enjoyed the baby-led weaning approach, but I also spoon-fed them purees on occasion, without issue. One thing I always did was watch their cues and follow their lead with the spoon—I'd either preload the spoon and hand it to them (you can also have more than one spoon for those times they don't want to give it up) or get down to eye level with them (it's hard to swallow when you're looking up), move the spoon close to their lips, and wait for them to lean forward slightly, open their lips, and stick out their tongue a bit in an effort to draw that spoon in. Then I'd gently move the spoon into the front of their mouth and see what they did with it, allowing them the time to figure out how to lick off the puree instead of just "dumping" it on their tongue.

The other thing my kids loved, which gave them more control and was more "fun," was using foods to deliver purees to their mouths. I'd give them a long raw carrot stick or celery stick, or something of that nature, which they could dip into their purees. You get way more bang for your buck with this "food delivery device." And it was still a way for me to allow the introduction of solids to be baby led.

Regardless of which approach you choose, initially the best time to schedule a solid foods introduction or exploration session is a time of day when your baby is their happiest, which is usually about an hour after a full breast-feeding or bottle-feeding. It's important that your baby isn't too hungry when you sit them down to explore food because in the early weeks of solids, mealtimes have nothing to do with nutrition and everything to do with play, exploring, and imitating others—we don't want our babies getting frustrated because they're actually hungry.

It's also important to *embrace the mess*. Place a splash mat or garbage bag under the highchair and dress your baby in a bib or even just a diaper. Be aware of your own sensory preferences and tune in to whether you're cleaning your baby's face after every bite, which can be invasive and irritating to your baby (especially if it's done with the tip of the spoon). It's best to save the cleanup for after the feed.

Before we talk about how much and what to feed your baby, I want to take a moment to discuss (and perhaps ease your mind about) the fear-of-choking part of solids introduction.

## CHOKING VERSUS GAGGING

Many parents are worried about their baby choking when introducing solids. But it may surprise you to learn that choking is no more likely with a baby doing a baby-led weaning approach than a baby being spoon-fed, provided they've demonstrated signs of readiness, are sitting upright, and are in control of any food that goes into their mouth.

Gagging is often confused with choking, and though these two mechanisms are related, they're not the same. Gagging is that retching or coughing movement that pushes food away from the airway if it's too big to be swallowed or not able to be properly managed. Sometimes the gagging can lead to vomiting a little, but it's usually over quickly and doesn't seem to bother babies who are feeding themselves. In adults, the gag reflex is triggered near the back of the tongue. But this reflex is triggered much farther forward on the tongue in a six-month-old and even a nine-month-old, so not only is it activated more easily in a baby than in an adult, it's also activated when the piece of food is much more forward in the mouth, and thus farther from the airway. When a six-month-old gags on food, it doesn't mean the food is too close to their airway. The gag reflex is actually a key part of babies' learning how to manage food safely and is a safety mechanism *against* choking. When a baby has triggered this reflex a few times, by putting too much food into their mouths or pushing it too far back, they learn not to do that again. As a baby gets older, the place where the reflex is triggered moves back along the tongue, so that gagging doesn't happen until food is nearer the back of their mouth. This happens whether or not they've experimented with self-feeding.

Choking, on the other hand, is a silent event (trouble breathing, possible changes in skin color, and often a look of terror)! Of course choking is scary and the thought of it is anxiety inducing. But understanding that gagging is a protective mechanism and also preparing yourself with infant CPR skills (just in case) will allow you to feel more comfortable and confident in introducing solids to your child. Make sure you're always with your child when they're eating, so that you can monitor and react as needed. If your child does start to gag, try hard not to intervene by sticking your finger in their mouth (this can make it worse). Best to allow them to get it unstuck while watching closely.

Be aware of your own reactions. Remember that our kids regulate through us, so if we're anxious or scared, these feelings will rub off on them. Similarly, if we're calm, they have a better chance of being calm. Try to keep that fear of them choking on the inside and maintain as calm a demeanor as possible. I'd sit in the kitchen with my kids during mealtimes. If they started to cough or gag on food, I'd reach into their highchair and unbuckle the seatbelt, with the intention that if I needed to pull them out I could do so more easily. Thankfully I never did need to pull them out due to a choking event, but this small act of reaching in and unbuckling that seatbelt helped me manage my fear and anxiety because it helped me feel prepared.

## FIRST FOODS

You now know about the two main approaches to introducing solids, but if you're anything like I was, you're probably still wondering how much and what to introduce first. As with everything from sleep to breast- versus formula-feeding, there are various recommendations. The old advice to start with solids once a day then progress to two and then three meals over a period of a few weeks was aimed at babies starting solids at three or four months of age, whose digestive systems are too immature for solids. Babies who are six months and older are less likely to react badly to new foods because their gut is already more mature. (And remember, your baby isn't usually actually ingesting a whole lot of food initially.)

What you feed your child in the first few months (as well as what you ate during pregnancy) will affect their food and taste preferences for the rest of their lives, as well as their gut bacteria and hormonal systems. You might already be thinking about what the most nutritious foods are for your baby and are likely aiming to feed them clean and perhaps even organic, grass-fed, pasture-raised foods whenever possible. If so, good for you! These may be more expensive, but the nutritional density and health benefits are worth it.

It's more important to focus on the quality of the food you're offering than the quantity, though it's so easy to focus on the latter. I often hear mamas describing their child's solid intake: "She ate three tablespoons of applesauce." But babies take in very little volume (of course there are exceptions). Another thing to consider is that many of the packaged "first foods" in grocery stores are low in nutrients and loaded with sugars and fillers. This doesn't mean you have to be Betty Crocker and make all your own purees or baby food. I definitely wasn't that mom—I had no interest in spending what precious time I had without my baby attached to me making extra food. But again, it's your choice. You get to choose how you do motherhood! Just know that you don't have to do things just because the mom down the street is.

Do your best to ensure that the little food your baby is consuming is chock-full of nutrients and energy. Less energy intake from food during the day can lead to more frequent night wakes for milk. You also want to make sure that your baby is eating foods they can easily digest. Remember that their digestive system is still maturing, and when you start offering solids, it has to work overtime to figure out how to digest all these new foods that are so different from breast milk or formula.

As long as solids haven't been started too early, most babies' digestive systems will cope well with solid foods. If your baby has a history of digestive upset, they may have more reactions to solids once they start. It's normal to see a thickening and slowing in frequency of bowel movements, at least initially. As your baby increases their food intake, their stool will become more formed, and typically more stinky! This isn't usually a cause for concern, but some babies can find this change uncomfortable.

As mentioned, not all the digestive enzymes are present at birth. If you feed your baby solids that they cannot digest properly, they won't actually get the nutritional benefits from them, and you also run the risk that they'll sit in the stomach, undigested, leading to various tummy troubles, potentially exacerbated reflux symptoms, and, ultimately, a fussier baby who doesn't sleep well.[23]

## FATS

One of the first digestive enzymes that babies have is lipase, which helps to digest healthy fats. A baby's brain is about 60 to 70 percent fat,[24] so healthy fats are an important part of your baby's diet, especially in the first two to three years, when rapid brain growth and development is happening.[25,26] Fats also have a high energy density, which can help you feel fuller for longer. If you're breast-feeding, know that your milk is made up of about 50 to 60 percent brain-building fats and cholesterol[27] (and the enzymes to properly digest it). So rest assured, if you continue to feed on demand while transitioning to solids, your baby will be getting plenty of these good fats into their system, regardless of the amount of solids they're ingesting initially.

Formula is a different story. Unfortunately, while some formulas have added these brain-building fats (such as DHA—docosahexaenoic acid), which is great, most commercial formulas are low in saturated fats and some (especially soy-based) formulas have no cholesterol, which means that you'll need to be more mindful about adding these healthy fats into your baby's diet once they start solids.

The best high-energy fats come from meat (especially organ meat) that is pasture-fed, fish, butter, eggs, and tropical oils, such as coconut, olive, and avocado oils. As a bonus, these foods also give your baby good doses of iron and zinc, both of which they start to need more of as they grow.

## PROTEINS

After fat digestion comes the ability to digest proteins. These are found in most foods to varying degrees and are essential for overall health, specifically growth, brain development, and milk production. Meats, eggs, nuts, and legumes are all high in protein, and again, quality matters. If you're providing your baby with a vegetarian or vegan diet, you'll need to make sure the diet contains a higher amount of fats, protein, iron, and zinc from other sources.

## CARBOHYDRATES

Carbohydrates are about half as energy dense as fats, so you need more of them to feel full. You can get all the carbohydrates your body needs just from fruits and vegetables. In fact, your baby's body doesn't start making the amylase digestive enzyme (needed to break down carbohydrates) until they're between eight and twelve months, though mom's breast milk will supply some of this amylase.[28] But babies aren't fully ready to digest grains until well into their second year.

All carbohydrates are broken down into sugar (glucose) in the body, and the more processed a food is (i.e., made with refined carbohydrates such as white sugar, white grains, white flour, etc.), the more sugar and fewer nutrients it has. Which means that rice cereal or even oatmeal isn't actually a great first food. Too much glucose in the body can lead to dysregulation in blood sugar, and in babies this can lead to various issues, such as waking for a feed well into the first two years; refusing proteins and fats and only wanting carbs (because our brains become addicted to sugar); mood swings and changes in behavior when hungry; gas and bloating; skin rashes (such as dermatitis and eczema); and a reduced ability to focus. In older children, sugar has also been associated with hyperactivity, behavioral issues, lack of concentration, and aggression. And if that weren't bad enough, refined sugars also wreak havoc on your gut, feeding the bad bacteria and potentially causing an overgrowth of it, which has been linked to food allergies, reflux, colic, and even poor sleep in babies.

Remember that I mentioned it can be quite easy for our babies to be deficient in vitamins and minerals? Some research shows low levels of zinc in diets that include a lot of whole grains (e.g., wheat, corn, rice, oatmeal) and legumes (e.g., soy).[29] This is due to phytic acid, which is found on the surface of all grains and blocks the absorption of most of their nutrients (including zinc, magnesium, iron, and calcium) while interfering with digestive enzymes. In some babies, phytic acid can even trigger an immune response, leading to allergies. Phytic acid can be somewhat removed by soaking the grains before cooking, making them easier to digest, but this may not eliminate all the digestive difficulty.[29,30] Bottom line: grains shouldn't be the first or main food source for your baby when they start solids and are perhaps better left until they're two years old.

## THE IDEAL DIET

So what is an ideal diet for your baby when they initially start solids? First foods that contain fat, cholesterol, protein, and lots of absorbable iron and zinc will mimic breast milk and be easiest for your baby to digest. All these things can be found in animal-source foods. Instead of focusing on the fruit and vegetable purees and baby cereals, you might consider puréed or softened meats, bone broth, and eggs from pasture-raised organic animals; coconut oil, high-quality olive oil, and cod liver oil; and organic bananas, avocados, and other fruits. You don't need to offer all these things in one meal at the beginning, though this will be the goal as your baby becomes a superstar at eating solids. In the beginning, try to offer foods that cover these main categories throughout the day or week. It's also a good idea to offer new foods earlier in the day, so that you can watch for a reaction before they go to bed.

## WATER

A final note. Many parents think about offering water when they start feeding their baby solids, but your baby doesn't need water in the first eight or nine months of life unless you live in a very hot climate. As long as you're nursing or bottle-feeding on demand, your baby should be getting enough fluids. With water, you risk filling up your baby without giving them nutrients. If you feel they need some hydration while eating a meal of solids, offering pumped milk or a little bit of watered-down formula in an open cup (versus a sippy cup, which isn't great for proper oral motor development) is a good idea. Your baby will get the added nutrition from the breast milk or formula while still exploring the solids, and the liquid can help digest the solids.

# Chapter Thirteen

# PICKY EATING

Picky eating is another hot topic. We all want our children to eat nutritious food from all the food groups as well as be adventurous eaters who eat pretty much anything we serve, right?

Picky eating tends to be misunderstood. We often label our kids as picky eaters even during times when reduced food choices are part of their development. That said, true picky eating, sometimes referred to as problem feeding, is serious and needs more specific interventions. It can be due to reduced oral motor skills and a resulting inability to manage and manipulate certain foods because of restrictions (e.g., TOTs or low tone). It can also be due to sensory processing differences and not liking the texture, taste, or smell of certain foods. Sometimes a combination of things is at play.

Let's start with this: *it's normal for babies to reject certain foods at certain times, and this often changes from day to day.* But we parents automatically see this as a rejection and therefore decide for our children that they don't like a food, so we don't prepare it or offer it again. It's important to be mindful of this because if we stop offering certain foods, this can lead to restricted food choices and picky eating down the road.

It takes our brains somewhere between fifteen to twenty-one trials of a particular food before we can accurately decide whether we like it. As well, our taste buds regenerate themselves every few weeks, which means that it's likely that your tastes will change as you grow. This is something to remember when offering and re-offering foods to our little ones. Eating, learning about, and enjoying foods involve so much more than just the acts of tasting, chewing, and swallowing. Meals are an important part of your child's day. They're rich in sensory and social stimulation. They're a time of connection with you while your child learns about the food and how to manipulate it. They imitate and learn by watching you.

To create healthy attitudes about food, and reduce the likelihood of food pickiness, it's important to create a positive atmosphere around eating and to have mealtimes be a time of relaxation and enjoyment. If your child is healthy and growing well, you usually don't need to worry. Most children's appetites are right for their age and growth rate. And around the age of two, toddlers go through a phase where they start eating less, often because their growth starts to slow down around this age. Toddlers also often go through phases where they refuse to eat certain foods (even if they loved them the previous week), only want to eat a small number of specific foods, and/or are easily distracted at mealtimes. These are all typical toddler behaviors. They're learning to become an independent person, and one way that they can exert said independence is by self-feeding and choosing what foods they eat. Just as you can't force someone to sleep, you can't force them to eat.

When you offer foods, I highly recommend sitting down to eat with your little one and having some of whatever they're eating on your plate too. Family meals are so important, even if they happen just once a day and with just one parent. If they see you eating something, they'll be more likely to try it. Remember to allow them plenty of time to explore the food and decide what they want to do with it (even if they don't chew and swallow it, they're still interacting with it and learning about it). Talk to your baby or toddler about the food they're exploring and allow them full control over it so that they can develop all those fine motor skills in their hands and mouths.

It's common for young children to react negatively to certain foods. Some are slow to accept new tastes and textures. Keep offering them to your child, and they'll usually start to accept and enjoy them over time. Forcing your child to eat can lead them to resist eating and potentially lead to picky eating.

# PICKY-EATING CAUSES

There are many factors that can lead to picky eating, and how we handle the picky phase can make a difference when it comes to the future of our child's eating habits and health.

## TEMPERAMENT
Some children are more sensitive to change. They tend to be "pickier" and more neophobic (frightened of new things) than other children.

## LACK OF EXPERIENCE
In the first twelve months, a lack of experience with a variety of tastes and textures can also cause picky eating. This can be a result of parents who are anxious and picky eaters themselves. Children often model the eating habits of their primary caregivers. Low resting tongue posture, lack of tongue mobility, and lack of exposure to lumpy foods can cause delayed oral motor

skills, such as the ability to move food around in the mouth and chew. This leads to more gagging and fear of foods. So children who have been eating purees from six months to nine or ten months and then at twelve months are being labeled as "picky eaters" likely haven't had enough practice.

## SENSORY PROCESSING ISSUES

As adults, we're desensitized to the textures, flavors, and smells of most food, but many children aren't. In the first few years of life, mealtimes are all about processing the sensory input received from various foods. To eat textured solid foods, the toddler needs to be able to integrate information from all eight sensory systems simultaneously with every single chewing motion: how the food looks, how it feels, what it sounds like in the mouth, how it tastes and smells, and what adjustments need to be made in terms of balance, location, and pressure being exerted.

Often when kids display picky eating, especially those with food aversions/extreme problem feeding, it's because the touch, taste, sound, or smell of a food is being processed in their brain as unpleasurable or uncomfortable in some way. Think of something that makes you shudder—maybe it's nails on a chalkboard or the idea of eating a sardine. Are you cringing yet? A child who's oversensitive to sensations in the mouth (also called oral defensiveness) may gag on solid or lumpy food and avoid strongly flavored food. Some kids are oversensitive to smells and seek out bland food as a result. Conversely, a child seeking more sensory input may dislike bland or soft food and only eat food that's crunchy, textured, or highly flavored. A child who has sensory-based motor disorder may struggle with the coordination skills needed to use a spoon or knife and fork and may avoid food that takes too much effort to eat. Some children with low muscle tone or poor oral motor coordination may struggle to chew and swallow and may therefore prefer food that doesn't need to be chewed.

## ORAL MOTOR CONCERNS

Picky eating can also result from specific motor challenges in the mouth with respect to muscle tone, strength, chewing patterns, lip closure, tongue mobility and lateralization, and ability of the tongue to manipulate food to make a bolus (ball) and move it from the front to the back of the mouth.

## GI ISSUES/FOOD SENSITIVITIES

Gut issues can affect appetite. As well, a child who has had previous experience with issues such as reflux that led to pain might have learned to be afraid of eating, associating it with vomiting or severe gagging. Children are also very intuitive and often avoid foods that they feel their body cannot handle (e.g., due to a food allergy or intolerance).

## THEY JUST AREN'T HUNGRY

Every child's caloric needs vary, depending on their activity level, growth rate, and metabolism, the latter of which can change throughout the day. Hunger can also be affected by how frequently they eat (does your child graze all day?) and how many liquids they're consuming (are you filling up their belly with water?).

## PROBLEM FEEDING

Now let's take a look at picky eating that seems more extreme. Maybe your child gags when tasting, touching, or even looking at most new foods. Or they melt down at the suggestion of eating something new. Or they have only a handful of foods in their diet.

Think of picky eating as a spectrum. On one end of this spectrum is the average picky eater who eats a decent variety of food but can be particular. Most families don't notice much of a disruption to their lives with this mild version of picky eating, even though it can be annoying. On the other end of the spectrum are extreme picky eaters.

Researchers and practitioners use a variety of terms to describe this end of the spectrum: *problem feeders, extreme picky eaters, picky-eating disorder, food aversion disorder, food phobia, selective eating disorder,* and, well, the list goes on. Unfortunately, there isn't a consistent term among professionals, even though *avoidant/restrictive food intake disorder* has been added to the DSM-V (the diagnostic and statistics manual used by doctors).

The following chart explains some of the signs that might indicate a real concern. Write down all the foods that your child eats—you may even notice that they aren't actually as picky as they seem!

## PICKY EATING VS. PROBLEM FEEDING

- Eats fewer than 30 foods (but usually 20–25 on a regular basis)
- Eats at least one food from almost all textures and food groups
- Has typical food jags
- Tolerates new foods on their plate
- Eats new foods after repeated 15–21 exposures
- Typically eats with family

- Eats fewer than 20 different foods (< 15 consistently)
- Refuses to eat entire food groups
- Refuses to eat one or more textures
- Foods lost to food jags are NOT reacquired
- Very distressed when presented with new foods (even if similar to preferred foods)
- May gag, vomit, shudder at sight or taste of food
- May or may not add new foods in more than 21 exposures
- Rarely eats with family; prefers to eat alone

If your child has fewer than twenty foods in their food repertoire, this may indicate a more serious issue that could require different mealtime strategies and perhaps even specialized feeding therapy.

## MEALTIME STRATEGIES FOR PICKY EATERS

1. **Include them in meal preparation**
   Instead of sneaking veggies into meals, show your child what's going into it so they can learn. Better yet, ask them to help.
2. **Trust your child and their body**
   Children's bodies are incredible regulators of appetite and hunger, if we let them be. They start to lose this at the age of 2-3 years (but it can be reversed).
3. **"You don't have to eat this"**
   When you say this, it removes the pressure to eat and is a powerful way to give them the control they want at meals.
4. **Start small**
   Offer mini bites that won't overwhelm them and just one piece at a time.
5. **Use a "safety" napkin, cup, or plate**
   Let your child spit out food they don't want to chew or swallow.
6. **Offer food multiple times**
   Don't stop at 1, 2, or 3 times (they need at least 15-21 exposures to one food before they try it and like it).
7. **Pair favorite foods with new foods**
   Let them dip it in their favorite condiment or add favorite spices. (Dipping fruit or green vegetables in ketchup is totally fine.)
8. **You have to eat it too!**
   If you happily eat the food and make it accessible, your kids are more likely to try it.
9. **Be mindful of your words and reactions around food**
   No "yucks" or "you won't like that" or "you didn't even try it, how can you say you don't like it?" This only discourages them more.

---

MEALTIME STRATEGIES FOR PICKY EATERS, CONT'D

**10. Do not force feed**
This will just not end well, and children usually resist.

**11. Introduce change gradually**
For really picky eaters or those more sensitive to change, introduce change gradually, systematically, and consistently around meal time. Use the same location, utensils/plates, serving sizes. Attempt to follow the same time schedule for meals.

**12. Provide options but at least one preferred food at every meal**
Trust me, this will make your life so much easier, and it will also help your child feel safe and calm. While it is a good idea to have several foods available on the table, the expectation should not be to eat all of them.

**13. Invite an adventurous friend**
While parents can influence what their child tries, no one can make a bigger difference than a child's friends (this is often why your child will eat things at daycare and not at home).

---

When it comes to picky eaters and problem feeders, don't make every mealtime about trying new foods. Some mealtimes should be stress free, where the child can eat their preferred foods and there are no other expectations. Some mealtimes (snack times are a good place to start) can incorporate some of the food-play strategies below into a game that's more about exploration than biting, chewing, and swallowing. Remember, eating is a sensorial experience, so interacting with new foods at any level is a wonderful way for a child to become more adventurous and accepting of them. Sometimes it also helps to do various whole-body sensory activities throughout the day, to assist with overall sensory processing, paying particular attention to tactile and proprioceptive input—think heavy-work activities such as pushing, pulling, carrying, or even yoga poses. Getting the face, tongue, and cheeks ready too can be fun and stimulating as well.

Here are some food-play ideas to make mealtimes a bit more fun!

- **Blow the food** across the table (e.g., popcorn, cracker pieces, smaller spinach/lettuce leaves, etc.).

- **Make things out of the food**, such as shapes, faces, boats/cars from pepper halves, or pictures (brownies or chocolate pudding for dirt and broccoli for trees, etc.).

- **Match foods that are the same color** (goldfish, gummy bears, M&M's, cucumber pieces, carrot pieces, etc.).

- **Decorate the food** (use small pieces of food to decorate a cake, muffins, or rice cakes using peanut butter or something similar for glue).

- Use toys (e.g., diggers/cars) to **transport the food** to dolls, toy animals, dinosaurs, etc.

- **Use cookie cutters** to make the food into different shapes.

- **Play with the food**. Sing songs (e.g., "Head, Shoulders, Knees, and Toes") while tapping with foods, pretend to put on "makeup" or "face paint" with food items if you don't mind getting a little dirty, have a tea party, build something, or become a detective (have your child find similarities between food items: "Which one is wet like this?" "Which one is the same color?" "Which one is the same shape?").

- **Make paint** (e.g., add food coloring to yogurt or pudding) and finger-paint pictures (or use painting tools if your child refuses to touch it with their hands).

# Chapter Fourteen

# WEANING

Weaning is a big decision for you and your little one and shouldn't be made lightly. A lot of the mamas I work with ask about weaning, and I find that parents often feel the need to night-wean before tackling day-weaning. They think (and are likely told by various people) that if they stop nursing overnight, their baby will sleep longer. And who wouldn't want their baby to sleep longer at night? The hard truth is that weaning at night may or may not help your baby sleep longer because sleep depends on so many other things. And your baby may continue to wake up, and you will have eliminated the one thing that gets them back to sleep fast!

You may have also heard that letting your baby fall asleep while breast-feeding is creating a bad habit and that they'll never learn to self-soothe. This is unrealistic and impractical. And then there's the myth that by nursing at night, your baby will get cavities (yes, this is true for some babies who have softer teeth and a predisposition to cavities, but most babies don't).

Your weaning journey, just like your motherhood journey, is deeply personal. What works for one family won't necessarily work for another, and this is completely okay. If you're breast-feeding and want to keep breast-feeding, nursing day *and* night is a way to protect this breast-feeding relationship. A lot of babies, even those who are older than a year, wake up at night to feed. Whether a baby can go twelve hours without food (or hydration) is unique to each baby. Most babies need at least one to three night-feeds until they're seven to nine months old, and many will continue this until they're well beyond a year old. If your older baby (nine months or older) is waking up every couple of hours at night, there's likely something more going on—a habit, a feeding issue, food sensitivities, sensory challenges, medical reasons, heightened stress reactivity, an emotion/connection/attachment issue, or perhaps something more serious, such as a sleep disorder. And weaning won't fix these.

We decided to night-wean my daughter when she was sixteen months old from three feeds to one and then gradually to none, and we fully weaned her (day and night) when she was three and a half. As I write this chapter, we're nine months from that milestone and my daughter still points to my boobs and talks about "her milk." And every night since she's been weaned, she's found her way into our bed (thank goodness for king-sized beds!). And I'm okay with that. Why? Because when we weaned, she wasn't the one who was ready—I was (also one-hundred-percent okay). I ended that special connection time, that snuggle time, a time that offered her comfort. So she had to find another way to get all that!

When something isn't working for you or your baby, it's okay to make parent-led changes. But know that parent-led changes will often be met with tears of frustration. Remember, tears aren't bad in and of themselves.

It's okay for our children to cry. It's how they communicate and express emotion. It's important to allow them to express their sadness, anger, or frustration. When we support them through the tears, they can get to the other side of the emotion while feeling loved. This is different from letting them cry alone.

# BEFORE YOU START

Again, since weaning is a big decision for both you and your child, consider whether you're making it for the right reasons.

Think about the factors involved in the following reasons to wean:

## YOU FEEL PRESSURED BY FAMILY, FRIENDS, OR YOUR DOCTOR

Peer or social pressure isn't a great reason to night-wean. It can lead to less sleep and perhaps resentment. Think carefully about whether night-weaning is something you actually want or if you're feeling pressured to do it.

## YOU'RE RETURNING TO WORK

Your return to work may cause your baby's sleep to regress a little initially because of reverse cycling. Reverse cycling describes your baby's need to reconnect with you, largely by feeding, after a period of separation (once you return from being at work). If you're looking to wean during the day, you'll need a plan in place for how your baby will get their needed nutrition.

## YOUR BABY IS FEEDING BETTER AT NIGHT THAN DURING THE DAY

Many babies can shift to getting more nutrition at night than in the daytime. You make more breast milk overnight due to hormonal changes associated with your circadian rhythm, so the milk might flow more easily at night, making it easier to extract. But nighttime is also distraction free, calm, and quiet, which makes focusing on feeding a little easier. Nighttime is also the time of biggest separation in a twenty-four-hour period, and it's dark and scary at times, so feeding during the night promotes time for connection and safety.

## YOU WANT ANOTHER BABY

Breast-feeding is commonly seen as a barrier to conceiving. There's a misconception that breast-feeding acts as a sort of contraceptive. This is so far from the truth. Thousands of mamas get pregnant each year while breast-feeding their babies or toddlers. I continued to nurse my first until I was about six months pregnant with my second (at which point I decided I wanted a few months without anyone attached to my boob). Remember that every woman is unique, and while one woman's fertility might be impacted by breast-feeding, another's may not. Some women regain fertility and get pregnant again while exclusively breast-feeding day and night, while others don't regain that fertility until they're totally done breast-feeding. You just never know.

# WEANING METHODS

As with most other things in "baby world," there are many ways to wean. It looks different for each family and even each baby within each family. I highly encourage you to start with a period of observation, where you track your child's normal patterns and behaviors. Some toddlers will self-wean and experience a smooth transition to sleeping through the night. Others may need a gradual approach, in which case you'll benefit from support and a plan. Remember, night-weaning doesn't guarantee that a baby of any age will stop waking at night. But in infants between eighteen and thirty-six months, it can reduce or stop night-waking.

## GRADUAL

This method takes weeks or months. One feeding at a time is dropped (day or night), and nighttime feedings can be spaced out until baby is no longer looking to breast-feed during the night. The common strategy here is "if they don't ask, don't offer." Move along in your routine, and if they ask to breast-feed you can either oblige or offer an alternative, such as milk in a cup, a snack, or even an activity, such as a favorite game. If you're taking a more parent-led approach, you may decide to cut a specific nursing or feeding session in a day and then reduce that even further every week.

You choose how fast or slow you go with this approach. Depending on the age of your baby, you may need to replace the nursing session with a bottle-feed, especially if they're under a year, as breast milk or formula will still be their primary source of nutrition. Usually it's best to cut the feeding session that your baby or toddler is least attached to. The easiest feed to cut is often one during the day, or maybe the one at the first wake in the evening, if it's shortly after bedtime. The harder ones tend to be the ones before naps or bedtime.

## SCHEDULED

Parents use this method when they have a timeline in mind, such as a developmental milestone, an age, a return to work, etc. If you're hoping to wean by a specific date, I encourage you to start the weaning process much earlier, so that you can take a gradual approach if you or your baby need it.

## ABRUPT

This method may occur as a result of sickness, hospital stays, or a medication that is incompatible with breast-feeding (when no alternative medications are possible). This can be painful physically but also emotionally, and it can be even harder if the decision is out of your hands. This approach will require you to really lean on your village for help and perhaps get specialized support from appropriate professionals.

Even though we might expect weaning to be a gradual and linear process, with nursing or feeding sessions gradually decreasing in frequency, length, and volume, it will likely be more of an up-and-down journey with some good days and weeks and others where you feel as if you're going backward. This is normal, and you'll both get through it!

# WHEN TO WEAN

It's generally not recommended to wean fully from the breast or bottle until your baby is twelve months or older. For the first year of life, breast milk or formula should be their main source of nutrition and caloric intake. At around six months you can start introducing solids, but remember that eating solids is a skill that requires time and practice. Solids will still be complementary. By about twelve months of age, your toddler should be pretty proficient at eating solids. They may be eating three meals and possibly two snacks during the day, which should be sufficient for their nutritional needs, making the breast milk or formula a bonus.

Note that your breast milk never loses its nutritional value (but your baby's nutritional requirements increase), so you can keep nursing for as long as you want if it's working for you and your baby.

# NIGHT-WEANING

## NIGHT-WEANING AND SLEEP

As mentioned, many people believe that night-weaning improves baby's sleep. Sleep trainers who use behavioral-based strategies often suggest that parents shouldn't "reward" the baby by feeding them milk at night because that's why they're waking at night—it's a manipulative behavior that must, at all costs, be extinguished. Oh my goodness! Talk about stressing out mamas and causing even more feelings of guilt and shame! This thinking isn't simply narrow-minded—it's just plain wrong.

We've discussed that it's normal for children to wake up at night well into toddlerhood. In fact, everyone wakes up slightly after each sleep cycle (this is called a partial arousal). We readjust, take a sip of water, go to the bathroom, or pull up the blanket. Babies are no different. They just can't take care of those needs on their own yet, so they call out for help. The real issue is whether your baby can begin a new sleep cycle without parental support. This isn't developmentally appropriate until much later than we're led to believe in our Western culture. Children attach through physical contact for the first year and beyond.

Research shows that "20% of babies can sleep 'through the night' (meaning 6 hours) at 6 months of age without intervention. Half of them signal for parental help during an 8-hour period, 5 (out of 6) nights." As well, "70% of all babies 6–18 months wake at least once in the night and nearly 20% of them wake more than three times in the night."[30]

As you can see, night-wakings are completely natural at this age and beyond. Remember that babies wake up for all kinds of reasons. They could be hungry, thirsty, hot/cold, wet/dirty, uncomfortable, in pain, frightened, or in need of love, comfort, and connection to feel safe. Although night-weaning might eventually help your baby sleep for longer chunks at night, it might also mean that you're still supporting your baby back to sleep but have now taken away the easiest (and fastest) method of doing so: nursing or bottle-feeding.

## COMFORT NURSING

If your older baby or toddler is still waking multiple times a night, you may have the sense that they don't need the nutrition, even though they'll gladly suck on a nipple. So what gives?

Sucking is a calming and organizing action that can be used to regulate the nervous system. This regulating mechanism might be why your child seems to be nursing *all the time*, or why they might be attached to their pacifier. There are a few reasons why sucking has this effect.

1.  Everything in the midline of your body is primitively soothing, organizing, and regulating. Which means that anything that happens in the middle of your body (e.g., sucking on a breast, bottle, pacifier, or thumb; chewing on a shirt or gum; rubbing your belly; and even masturbation) is primitively soothing, organizing, and regulating.

2.  Sucking provides a lot of input through the many muscles in our mouth, jaw, and tongue, and these muscles have proprioceptors in them. The proprioceptive sensory system allows us to know where our body is in space, which can help us feel grounded and secure in our environment. You're using all these little muscles when you're chewing, sucking, and blowing, which then stimulates the proprioceptors and releases neurotransmitters (serotonin and dopamine) that have a soothing and calming effect on your body.

3.  Sucking also releases oxytocin and CCK, hormones that are calming and can even help with sleep (bonus!).[31]

Benefits of sucking aside, nursing and bottle-feeding provide your child a chance to be near you, in your arms. Connection with Mama or with their primary caregiver is what it's all about for babies and toddlers (and for us adults, too). When our children are close to us, they feel safe, secure, and calm. Remember, they co-regulate with you. You're their safe haven.

## HOW TO NIGHT-WEAN

Here are a few tips to consider if you're looking to make a small change to your overnight feeding situation.

- If you're breast-feeding, think about your baby's current night-feeds. How many times is your baby actually eating? Try offering both breasts (and even back again) during each night-feed to see if that decreases the number of feedings.
- If your baby is comfort-sucking (which, again, is completely normal), try removing them from the breast when you no longer feel the suck, suck, suck, swallow, and pause.
- Is your baby really full at bedtime? Could you do a nice, long cluster feed before your bedtime routine, maybe again after the bath, and then again as a top-up before bed? If you know that your baby has consumed a lot of milk, could your partner go in and support the baby back to sleep if it's been less than three or four hours? You could then get a good stretch of sleep at the beginning of the night.
- Try a dream-feed before going to bed, to see if that leads to a longer stretch of sleep. (Dream-feeds tend to stop working when your baby is about nine to eleven months, if not earlier, so really tune in and see if this is working or if you're waking your baby up more by doing this.)
- Make a list of all the ways that you could soothe your baby other than feeding. Could you rock them, rub their back, sing to them, or snuggle

them? You could then work toward a feed every three or four hours, for example, and you/your partner could use other soothing methods to get the baby back to sleep in between—this is so important. Often, when you take something away, you need to put something else in its place. I highly recommend adding additional sleep associations *before* you start the weaning process, if time allows for this.

I always recommend talking to your child about the process, no matter how old they are, but especially if they're older than eighteen months. Reading books about weaning to them during the day and before bed is also a great way to start introducing and reinforcing the concept (my favorites can be found at www.kailiets.com/favorites). You can also bring the concept of weaning into your play with your child during the day. And always validate their feelings about how hard or sad this process might be. Let them know that you still love them and are there for mama cuddles whenever they need but there's no more milk.

Please remember that there's no right or wrong way to wean your older baby or toddler. A combination of weaning methods can be used to meet your needs as a family. Sit down and make a plan, set realistic expectations, and consider your needs and your child's.

The most important thing is that you, as the parent, feel supported in your goals and have a clear plan of action. You're in control of how fast or slow you go with your baby. You can keep some feeds or get rid of them all at once. Find a pace that's comfortable for you and your baby and trust yourself and your instincts. You *do* know best!

# SLEEP

Sleepless parents, this section is for you. You were prepared for life to change with your new baby, but of all the changes, sleep loss has you the most frustrated, and you're constantly searching for solutions.

You've read all the books, scrolled the posts on social media, and even Googled "How do I get my baby to sleep at night" on more than one occasion. Maybe you've tried sleep training, or sleep schedules. You're watching wake windows, trying various approaches, or attempting to get your baby into a "drowsy but awake" state—whatever that means! Maybe you've tried all these things and still don't know what to do. Bottom line, you're struggling in the sleep department. And when your pediatrician asks you how baby is sleeping at every visit, you start to feel like a failure. Maybe there's something wrong with your approach, or even your baby. You can't fathom the idea of leaving your precious baby to cry alone in a dark room until they (hopefully) fall asleep. You can't imagine not attending to their needs. But you're wondering how you can function through one more day with heavy eyelids and a cloudy brain.

The good news is that you're in the right place. There's another way to get more sleep without sleep training!

Trust me, Mama, I was there. Kristjan would wake up the second the stroller stopped or his head hit the bassinet mattress. I was stressed out and so confused by all the schedules that were printed and posted around our NYC apartment. I tried the E.A.S.Y. method and couldn't figure out how to stop my baby from falling asleep at the breast in order to play and then sleep. And "you time" (the *Y* in E.A.S.Y.)? What a joke! My son could sleep for three hours on or next to me but rarely alone in his own sleep space. I sometimes spent two hours bouncing on a ball with him in my arms until he finally settled and went to sleep (I now wonder if perhaps he was over-stimulated by all that bouncing).

Regardless of *how* he fell asleep, he never slept for more than two or three hours in a row, and I was exhausted. I started dreading the nights and therefore started going to bed later, essentially self-sabotaging. There came a time when I begrudgingly responded to my son at night when he woke, and sometimes even felt as if I hated him. It was awful! When he was eight and a half months old, I finally caved (well, actually, my husband said "enough is enough") and we got help. Help that felt supportive and in line with our values. That didn't make us leave our baby to cry and "figure it out" alone. That helped me tune back in to and trust my mama instincts and validated the things I was already trying and noticing worked (like nursing to sleep). It changed my life and the trajectory of my career, and it was essentially the catalyst for this book. This is why I'm on a mission to help. I want to help parents find their own path—a path that works for them. I want parents to follow their hearts and instincts.

My aim with this section (and really this whole book) is to help you change patterns while supporting attachment and encouraging responsive parenting. Just know this: you cannot force sleep, and your baby will eventually sleep independently throughout the whole night with or without your help.

I know that sleep is a huge stressor, and it's easy to become totally consumed with trying to get your baby to sleep. The best advice I can give you is to do what you can to encourage good sleep habits, to optimize sleep for your baby, but also focus on optimizing sleep for yourself so that you can get through the sleep-deprived zombie stage, however long it lasts for you.

I approach sleep holistically to make sure that all your baby's needs have been met. I help parents keep the parts of the nighttime parenting that they love and change the pieces that are no longer working for them. My approach is evidence informed, developmentally driven, and attachment focused and will always support responding to your baby in a way that feels good in your heart.

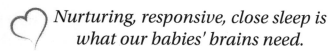

*Nurturing, responsive, close sleep is*
*what our babies' brains need.*

*–Kaili Ets*

I do not believe

- That you must put your baby in a separate room or on a separate sleep surface
- That you must teach your baby to self-soothe
- That leaving your baby to cry unsupported for any length of time is a good thing
- In timed checks (because really, what good are those anyway?)
- That you have to stop doing things that work for you and baby (nursing to sleep, rocking, bouncing, shushing, etc.)

Instead, I will

- Help you feel more connected to your baby and have a happier baby as a result of harnessing your intuition

- Give you some knowledge, tools, and strategies to establish healthy sleep for your family

- Encourage you to respond to, support, and soothe your baby in a way that feels good to you!

- Encourage you to tune in and lean in to your mama instincts rather than urging or forcing you to go against them

- Help you maintain a secure attachment with your baby, which research has shown is hugely significant in increasing emotional regulation in later years[1-4]

As a certified pediatric sleep specialist, I can tell you that sleep is often a bit of a puzzle, and each baby's (and family's) sleep needs are different, just as you and I don't have the same sleep schedule or strategies that help us sleep. There are often many layers that need to be worked through, so put your detective hat on and get curious about your baby and their sleep.

A reminder: My approach is not one-size-fits-all. Every human is unique. What works for one baby may not work for another. I recommend reading, learning, and trying. When you find a strategy that resonates with you, give it a good go. Be consistent with the approach for at least three to five days, assuming it still feels good instinctively, before deciding that it doesn't work.

# FUNDAMENTAL TENETS FOR SLEEP

The reality of infant sleep in our Western world is that the information is often confusing and full of contradictory advice, making it seem enormously complicated. But it doesn't have to be. Here are some of the intentions that I recommend you keep in your back pocket.

- Ensure safe sleep
- Provide loads of soothing for your younger baby
- Sleep at the right time—not by the clock, but by your unique baby's signs
- Establish sleep routines and plenty of sleep associations
- Keep the things you love, and change the things you don't (you don't have to be a martyr)
- Be consistent
- Give yourself and your baby grace
- Know that your child will sleep independently eventually, even without any assistance from you, because that is what biology dictates when we are developmentally ready. I can't tell you when that will be, and in the meantime, there are plenty of things you can do to support sleep. But do remember that you cannot force sleep.

*Chapter Fifteen*

# IT'S TIME TO CHANGE THE NARRATIVE

As a society, we've done a terrible job of supporting parents in the first few years of life with a baby—of normalizing motherhood, the postpartum period, and infant sleep, development, feeding, and more.

We've become obsessed with infant sleep, and the sleep-training market has skyrocketed in the last few decades. "Are they sleeping through the night?" is one of the most common questions, even from well-meaning family and friends, the implication being that your baby should be sleeping through the night from a very early age. But as you'll learn in this chapter, babies don't and shouldn't sleep through the night for a big portion of the first year (and beyond). They wake up. A lot. And guess what? That's biologically normal! Hard, but normal.

Babies are meant to eat at night just as frequently as they eat during the day. They need our support at night just as much as during the day. As discussed earlier in the book, human babies are born about nine months before other mammal babies. A human baby's nervous system is immature, and they require adult support to regulate their heart rate and temperature and meet their needs. We are all they know! We help them figure out this new "outside" world. Independence comes later—much much later!

Think about how teeny-tiny babies are (yes, even that ten-pound baby). Their bellies are about the size of a pea! They can only fill that tiny belly so much at each feed and therefore need to eat frequently. Plus, breast milk gets digested easily and efficiently, so if you're breast-feeding, to grow and thrive your baby will need to fill their belly more frequently than if they're being formula-fed.

Instead of asking new parents "How is your baby sleeping?" we should be asking "How are you coping with the nights?" or "How are you doing with the sleep exhaustion?" Meaning that we normalize the fact that babies wake up (sometimes a lot) and that this is hard and exhausting.

*How can we, as a society, support mamas to optimize sleep for both themselves and their babies?* This is the question we should focus on.

As a result of this obsession with sleep and the boom in the sleep-training market, our expectations around sleep in the first year of life (and beyond) have become unrealistic. We've come so far from remembering and understanding what normal sleep actually is for babies, and we've become more controlling, anxious, overwhelmed, stressed out, confused, frustrated, and busy as a culture.

Most sleep trainers sell you a dream. They tell you that you can "live the dream" and have it all: a happy baby as well as time to cook and clean, socialize with friends, take up new hobbies, and catch up on a long to-do list. They tell you all of this is possible when you have a baby who sleeps "through the night." The sleep-training world wants you to think that sleep, or lack thereof, is a problem that must be solved. This just isn't true. Sleep (or lack thereof) is NOT a behavioral problem.

Sleep isn't an issue in many other cultures as it is in the West. It's time to normalize infant sleep and stop talking about it as though it's a problem that needs to be fixed. And sorry to be the bearer of bad news, but there is no magic sleep solution, or perfect routine or schedule to help your baby fall asleep. I wish there were!

Your baby might be having trouble sleeping for a variety of reasons. Here are just a few to get you thinking.

## WHY YOUR BABY MIGHT BE WAKING FREQUENTLY AT NIGHT

- Developmental changes and new skills being learned
- Feeding difficulties—poor latch, weak suck, tethered oral ties, oral motor dysfunction
- Pain or discomfort due to body tightness, reflux, colic, food allergies/intolerances, or tummy troubles
- Overtired or under-tired
- Nutritional imbalances
- Sensory processing differences and/or temperament
- Separation anxiety
- Changes to their daily routine (starting daycare, parents back to work, etc.)
- And so much more

Or, your baby could be waking a few times a night and that might be totally NORMAL for their age!

Again, we're all unique. There's no way that all babies will sleep the same way or require the same solution to their "sleep difficulties." This is why it's so important to consider your unique baby, family, values, environment, and daily routine—your unique life.

## SLEEP TRAINING (AND WHY I DON'T EVER RECOMMEND IT)

When I hear and read about sleep training, the information usually refers to controlled crying, pick up put down, disappearing chair, rapid return, cry-it-out, timed checks (Ferber), overnight sleep schools (yup, those still exist), or hiring overnight sleep experts to sleep train in your home.

Lots of sleep consultants, programs, plans, and approaches—and even doctors and other health-care professionals—recommend traditional sleep-training approaches. These often involve separation and/or behavioral-based techniques such as not touching your baby, using only your voice to soothe them, only patting their back or bottom, leaving the room—essentially, responding to your baby based not on what you're hearing (or what you instinctively want to do) but on the timing. These various approaches also want you to believe that you must teach a baby to sleep alone and learn to self-soothe, and that the only way to do that is to not respond to their "manipulative cries" at night. Sound familiar?

This is complete nonsense! To go back to an earlier example, you'd never be okay with your partner not responding to you or giving you a hug if you were upset. If they just stood there, not looking at you, and told you to calm down and figure it out, you wouldn't calm down—it would enrage you further, and you have a fully functioning frontal lobe! You've had many years to learn self-regulation skills (which don't fully mature until we're in our twenties). Or what if they put you in a room and closed the door so that you could figure it out and calm down? How would that make you feel?

Let me shout this from the rooftops: a baby cannot be trained to sleep! Sleep is a biological function, just like eating and eliminating. It is NOT within our conscious control.

> *A baby cannot be trained to sleep.*
> *Sleep is a biological function just like*
> *eating and eliminating.*
> *It is NOT within our conscious control.*
>
> *—Kaili Ets*

Here are three truths, and the main reasons I don't believe in or recommend traditional sleep training.

## TRUTH #1: BABIES WAKE BECAUSE IT'S NATURAL AND NORMAL TO DO SO

Babies wake to eat, to hydrate (haven't you ever needed a sip of water in the middle of the night?), because they feel safest when they're close to their parent (isn't that why you love sleeping next to your partner?), and because everyone, including adults, wakes at some point throughout the night.

## TRUTH #2: SLEEP TRAINING DOESN'T TEACH A BABY SLEEP SKILLS; IT DOESN'T TEACH THEM TO SLEEP LONGER OR BETTER

Sleep training teaches babies that their caregiver won't respond to their needs and any effort to signal for comfort will be futile. They'll stop calling out, crying, and/or trying to get your attention. This might suggest that they've "figured out" how to sleep through the night. Nope, they still wake up, but they know they won't get support so what's the point in signaling the need for help? And when they do cry for long periods and eventually fall asleep (from exhaustion), their system will likely be stressed out.

## TRUTH #3: SLEEP TRAINING GOES AGAINST YOUR MAMA INSTINCTS

Your instinct is to rush to your baby when they cry. To soothe them when they're scared, hurt, uncomfortable, or not feeling well. To keep them alive and well by feeding them, caring for their physical needs, and, most of all, loving them. You're likely nodding in agreement, right?

Letting your baby cry for any amount of time without supporting them (as happens with timed checks, the full-extinction method, and even some "gentle sleep training" methods, such as the Sleep Lady Shuffle) goes against these instincts! Why wouldn't you respond to your crying baby? And why is it bad to do this? (It's not.)

You are not creating bad habits by responding to your baby and supporting them back to sleep each time they wake during the night. What you're doing is loving them, nurturing them, supporting their development, and teaching them that you'll always be there when they need you, day and night. You're following what is natural and innate—your mama instincts! They're strong, and if you pause long enough to listen to them, they'll never steer you wrong.

This is why I don't support sleep training and never recommend it to any of the families I work with. Instead, I encourage them, as I'm now encouraging you, to become a sleep detective. View your baby and situation from a place of curiosity rather than feel as though you need to "fix" something. Figure out if your baby is a) sleeping as a baby at their age should be, or b) if there is truly an issue affecting their sleep (whether it's related to development, feeding, reflux, overtiredness, or something else). Look at what's working for you and your baby and what's not.

My aim is to provide parents with tips, tricks, and tools to help them make changes that are developmentally appropriate, that focus on maintaining the trust and attachment between caregiver and baby, and that encourage mamas to follow their instincts during the process.

# DEBUNKING "BAD HABITS"

How many times have you heard that to get your baby to sleep longer, you need to:

- Stop nursing them to sleep
- Stop bed-sharing
- Stop soothing them back to sleep
- Stop using sleep "crutches," such as rocking, walking, bouncing, swaying, etc.

Well, guess what, Mama—all of these things are biologically normal. We, as humans, were designed to do them. Not only that, but they're all amazing when it comes to building a secure attachment with your baby (the kind of attachment we should all strive for!). Being responsive, supportive, and loving HELPS your baby with their development.

## "BAD HABIT" #1: NURSING TO SLEEP

Nursing to sleep is biologically normal for many reasons.

1.  Breast milk produced in the evenings contains more sleep-inducing hormones (e.g., tryptophan, serotonin, and melatonin) than daytime breast milk.[1,2] Tryptophan is a precursor of serotonin, which is vital for brain development. Serotonin has a regulatory effect on our circadian rhythms and is involved in melatonin production. Melatonin plays a big part in regulating our sleep-wake

cycles, and our babies don't start producing this on their own until about twelve to sixteen weeks after birth, when their circadian rhythm matures. Melatonin also relaxes the smooth muscle of the gastrointestinal tract, which might play a role in reducing the symptoms of colic. So nursing to sleep and during the night might make your baby more comfortable.

> *Young infants should not be forced to fall asleep without comfort; they may need to nurse to feel relaxed and safe enough to enter sleep.*
>
> *—Dr. Darcia Narvaez, Psychology Today*

2.  The sucking action of breast-feeding offers proprioceptive stimulation through the muscles of the tongue, cheeks, lips, and jaw, which activates the vagus nerve and has a calming effect. The sucking action also releases sleep-inducing hormones, such as cholecystokinin (CCK), which is thought to contribute to relaxation and sleepiness.[3] CCK is also released in the mother at the same time, which is why you'll often feel relaxed and somewhat sleepy after breast-feeding too—yet another reason to sleep when the baby sleeps.

3.  You make more breast milk in the middle of the night, so why not take advantage of nature? Prolactin, a hormone that helps establish, build, and maintain milk supply, also follows the circadian rhythm. Prolactin levels are higher in nighttime breast milk, particularly in the early hours of the morning, which is often why babies will nurse more then (milk is plentiful and flowing freely).[4] Sigh, I know those are the hardest hours for you, Mama, but take

some comfort in knowing that this is biologically normal (doesn't make it easier but perhaps less heavy on your heart).

> *Most babies nurse several times at night during the first six months.*
>
> —*Sweet Sleep by La Leche League International*

4. Breast-feeding at night might protect against SIDS. The hypothesis is that breast-fed infants wake up more frequently than formula-fed infants because they digest the breast milk more quickly than formula and spend more time in lighter stages of sleep, which could protect against SIDS.[5-7]

At this point, you might be thinking that nursing throughout the night means you'll get less sleep. I get it. It sort of makes logical sense, and sleep trainers use this as one of their selling points. But research shows that women who exclusively breast-feed report significantly more hours of sleep, better physical health, more energy, and lower rates of depression than those who are formula-feeding or doing mixed feedings. Yes, breast-feeding mothers woke more frequently to nurse their babies, but they were more likely to bed-share and woke up lightly rather than fully and fell back asleep faster.[8]

## "BAD HABIT" #2: BED-SHARING

As just mentioned, bed-sharing may actually help you to get more sleep if you're a breast-feeding mama, or at least help you feel better because you're not having to wake up fully, climb out of bed, walk to another room, feed or support your baby back to sleep, and then walk back to bed. You've likely heard that bed-sharing is unsafe and that your baby must sleep in a crib, with nothing in the crib—no blankets, stuffed toys, crib bumpers, nothing—until they're two years old. Just a baby and their crib mattress: the cold, lonely reality of many babies these days.

**Bed-sharing can be quite safe, when done right.** If your baby sleeps well in a crib and that's working for you and your family, no need to change anything. And if having your baby in bed with you allows you both to get more sleep, then that's okay too! See how you get to make the choices for your baby and your family?

Anthropologist James McKenna coined the term *breastsleeping*. He's dedicated his life to researching the relationship between bed-sharing and breast-feeding and has found that in the absence of any known risk factors, breastsleeping is the most advantageous way to parent at night, for both baby and mother.[8] McKenna also talks about how the term *co-sleeping* is commonly misunderstood as *bed-sharing*, and they aren't the same. Co-sleeping is when mom (or primary caregiver) and baby sleep in sensory proximity to one another. This could mean the baby is sleeping in the same bed as you, or in a sidecar, bassinet, pack and play, or even a crib in your room. Bed-sharing means that your baby is sleeping in the same bed as you.[9]

As mammals, we're meant to sleep near our infants. Other mammals do this so they can protect their young from predators. While we don't have to worry about predators, this biological norm (and need) is still ingrained in us. Babies all over the world co-sleep and breast-feed. Many cultures understand that there's no such thing as *just a baby*. There's always a baby and someone. It's much easier for a mother to manage frequent feeds if they're close by. They can also support the baby through separation anxiety, and, most importantly, it's a great way to be close enough to respond in an emergency. Our Western industrialized culture favors separation, individuality, and independence from an early age, but this isn't the case in every culture.

Bed-sharing isn't something to be afraid of. We're fearmongered into thinking it's not safe, under any circumstance, and that our babies must sleep alone. Why? Because society has told us that this is the safest option. But our babies and toddlers want closeness and connection. They want a warm body to snuggle with. They want to hear someone breathing next to them. This helps them feel safe and calm. This is what you prefer, right?

Even if you never planned to bed-share, you've likely found yourself in a bed-sharing or pseudo-bed-sharing situation at one point or another in your life with baby.

Unfortunately, the spur-of-the-moment, middle-of-the-night bed-sharing scenario where you either fell asleep nursing in the armchair or brought your baby into bed "just this once" because you were so utterly and totally exhausted usually isn't that safe (because you likely haven't set up your sleep space safely—see below). Shhh, I won't tell. Heck, I've been there before and I'm willing to bet most, if not all of us, have. The guilt must stop!

Bed-sharing can be extremely hazardous if done unsafely (e.g., you've been drinking or using drugs, the bedding is too soft, there are cords or gaps, the baby is premature, etc.), but research has shown no increased risks with bed-sharing when compared to co-sleeping or crib-sleeping.[9-11] Meaning that bed-sharing is just as safe as crib-sleeping, if done right. So what exactly is safe bed-sharing?

## SAFE BED-SHARING

Can be done safely with proper planning and setup.

- No smoking
- Healthy baby (full term)
- No sweat (no swaddles or blankets; dressed appropriately)
- Baby on back

---

SAFE BED-SHARING, CONT'D

- Sober adults (no alcohol, drugs, or drowsy medication)
- Safe sleep surface (firm mattress, no pillows or loose blankets, no cords)

---

Where your baby sleeps is a personal choice. There are so many options, and all these options can be safe as long as you're following Safe Sleep guidelines. Do what works for you, but also plan for the unexpected (i.e., even if you're set on having your baby sleep in a separate room in their crib, consider setting up your bed to safely bed-share, just in case).

## "BAD HABIT" #3: SOOTHING AND SUPPORTING BACK TO SLEEP

You've likely heard the saying "the way your baby falls asleep is how they'll expect to get back to sleep each and every time." The argument here is that if you always put your child to sleep by holding them, nursing them, or allowing them to use a pacifier, you create a sleep "crutch." Then, when your child wakes up in the middle of the night, they can't go back to sleep on their own because they're unable to recreate their sleeping environment without you—you've created a baby who needs you to feed or rock them in order to sleep.

If this were true, your baby would only ever be able to fall asleep in the exact same way: in the same room, with the same clothes, with the same sheets, and only with you. Sounds a bit ridiculous, right? Your baby can and will fall asleep in different ways and, yes, with different people, if certain conditions are met (more on that later). This is a good thing. It means that different caregivers (your partner, a grandparent, or a daycare provider) can each have specific ways or routines to help your child fall asleep. Phew, that makes life a little easier, doesn't it?

This also means that you can vary the way you put your baby to sleep and back to sleep. You can nurse to sleep at bedtime but not necessarily nurse to sleep at each wake. For naps, you can rock them, wear them, or have them sleep in a crib. This is the beauty of having a variety of sleep associations that are familiar and soothing to your child. They'll find comfort in these associations and be able to relax and sleep. The more sleep associations the better, in my view. Which leads us to the final "bad habit."

## "BAD HABIT" #4: SLEEP CRUTCHES

Piggybacking on the previous "bad habit," as far as I'm concerned, there's no such thing as a "sleep crutch." Everyone, babies in particular, develops sleep associations in their lifetime. These are the things that you associate with bedtime, that allow you to create an environment that's calm, quiet, relaxing, and conducive to sleep. Sleep associations can include singing, touching, hugging, feeding/nursing, bathing, reading, specific relaxation rituals, rocking, bouncing, putting a sleep sack on, a special "good night" phrase, white noise, calming scents, pacifiers, loveys, special sheets, and more.

I love sleep associations and usually recommend incorporating multiple associations into your routine to help your baby fall asleep. The more sleep associations you have, the easier it will be to let go of the ones that are no longer working for you or your baby. They'll also help other people put your baby to sleep. I encourage you to invite your partner to help with naptimes and bedtimes and eventually take over some of these. This will also allow you to have some ME time—fill your cup so that you have enough in there to give to others. And stop worrying that your contact-napping toddler won't be able to sleep at daycare without you. Every caregiver will naturally develop their own strategies and sleep associations.

If you have only one way to get your baby to sleep (e.g., bouncing on a ball—hey, I was there with my first baby!), don't worry, I've got you. Start pairing that one way with another association. Maybe you're feeding AND singing a specific song, or feeding AND rocking in a rocking chair. You can also baby-wear or walk them in a stroller to help baby fall asleep in different ways. Start introducing items into the sleep routine that will become associations, such as a particular blanket or a stuffed animal (for older babies and toddlers).

I absolutely love loveys and recommend them to all the families I work with because they can help with so much more than just sleep. A lovey is a comfort or transition toy. It can be anything—a small stuffed animal, one of those little blankets with an animal head, or a small security blanket. I've even had mamas tell me that their child attached to an old T-shirt and wanted to have that all the time. A lovey is anything snuggly and comforting to hold. Find one that's soft because your child will likely play with it, chew on it, and snuggle with it. The idea is for it to become like a friend, a comfort tool that they can use to help them self-regulate and feel safe and supported. Have the lovey with you at all times—while baby-wearing, during feeds, during car rides, when your baby is upset, and eventually during naps and overnight sleeps (you don't want the security blanket or shirt to be too big to cover the face or cause strangulation). If you build this association ahead of time, you can even send this lovey along if/when your child starts daycare. Learning to love a lovey and associate it with sleep takes time—sometimes weeks or months, depending on the age you start.

Technically, these shouldn't be in your baby's sleep space until baby is at least a year old, due to safety and reducing the risk of SIDS. But again, this is one of those things that you need to make an informed choice about. I introduced a lovey to both my children when they were five months old. I'd have it while we were nursing, when I was baby-wearing, when they were in the car seat, and when they were upset. Around seven months, I put the lovey in their sleep space for naps (a crib or a pack and play). And around nine months, I put the loveys into their crib at night as well.

This isn't what all the pediatric associations recommend for safe sleep, but my children's loveys were those small blankets with the little animal heads on them, and I was confident that my children were strong enough to move them away from their heads and airways. This was an informed choice that I made after looking at the risks and my children's development. Ultimately, you need to make your own decisions. The idea with these items is to have your baby associate them with sleep and calm so that when they wake in the middle of the night, they'll be able to recreate a sleeping environment without your assistance by grabbing the lovey (or the pacifier, etc.).

Can you see now why all these so-called bad habits aren't bad at all? The guilt, stress, and worry that can come from thinking our babies aren't sleeping through the night because we're doing something wrong is so unnecessary. What you're doing is right! You're listening to your baby and tuning in to your mama instincts (even if you don't realize that just yet). Above all else, remember that there's no one right solution or way for each family—because we're all different.

The sleep-training industry wants you to think there's only one way, and that it must be followed to the letter. They need you to believe that, so that they can sell you the dream. But sleep training places the burden of change upon babies. In reality, sleep depends on development, age, what's going on with feeding, what your day looks like, what's happening internally with hormones and sleep cycles, and more.

That said, there are things we can look at and improve to help you and your baby get more sleep. Things that are developmentally appropriate, supportive, and respect both your baby and your instincts!

*Your baby can still get longer stretches of sleep even if you: nurse to sleep, respond to every cry, bed-share, and trust your instincts.*

*—Kaili Ets*

# Chapter Sixteen

# "NORMAL" INFANT SLEEP

What is normal, or typical, sleep for babies anyway? There's so much conflicting advice, and everyone's experience is different. Some babies seem to sleep through the night right away. Others love to play, cry, and eat at night—anything but sleep.

If I could have just one superpower, it would be to wave my magic wand and give mamas and babies everywhere long, restful sleeps every night. Though we cannot force a baby (or anyone, for that matter) to sleep, we can tune in to their cues and create the ideal environment to support their sleep.

My aim with this chapter is to help you set healthy and realistic expectations about your baby's sleep, and also to set you up with healthy habits regarding the things that you can control around promoting sleep.

# SLEEP FOR THE ZERO- TO THREE-MONTH-OLD

In the first three months, anything goes. At this age, babies are unpredictable in terms of their sleep. The worst thing you can do is compare your baby to someone else's and worry that there's a problem to be solved if your baby isn't sleeping through the night (or only wants to sleep on you).

Though it can be normal for some babies to sleep longer stretches at night at this age, don't expect this, as this isn't typical for the average baby! Here are some typical sleep skills in babies three months old and younger.

---

### SLEEP FOR THE 0- TO 3-MONTH-OLD

**IN THE FIRST 3 MONTHS, OR THAT FOURTH TRIMESTER, IT IS NORMAL TO HAVE A BABY WHO:**

- Is unaware of night vs. day
- Sleeps most of the time except to feed
- Doesn't want to sleep in a bassinet or crib
- Only wants to sleep on you, in your arms, or next to you
- Feeds all day and all night
- Passes stool during the night, requiring diaper changes
- Sleeps all day and is up every hour at night

- Is wide awake and alert in the middle of the night
- Is startled awake by their hands
- Doesn't go down while awake and needs to nurse, rock, bounce, etc. to sleep
- Can usually only tolerate being awake for 45-90 mins at a time
- Stops crying when picked up (no, this does not mean they have manipulated you)

---

This is also a time when babies go through a "fussy" period. Babies are born with a stimulus barrier to protect them from getting overwhelmed by the outer world and all the sensory information that bombards their system daily. This stimulus barrier usually starts to disappear around the six-week mark, so your baby may become a little fussier at this point, especially in the evening. There's also usually a growth spurt around three or four months, which means baby is going to want to eat and eat (or cluster feed), and they're working on a lot of developmental skills. These growth spurts happen a few times during the first two years and are often known as sleep regressions. In the short term, baby's sleep will seem more fragmented, but that's because they're growing, and changing, and developing, and that's a lot of work! I much prefer to look at these phases as sleep PROgressions. Changing your mindset around this can make a world of difference. More on that in a bit.

What can you do to get through this stage?

In the first month, just let baby do what they do—let them eat and sleep when they want—and focus on bonding and resting. Around the two- or three-month mark, you may notice that your baby is spending more time awake. This is when you want to start taking note of how long they're awake and creating environments conducive to sleep.

Babies in the first three months of life (that fourth trimester) can sustain being awake for only about forty-five to sixty minutes, which includes feeding and changing, so it will literally feel as if all they do is eat, poop, and sleep—and that's totally fine. You don't need to focus on having baby play at this early age, though you can put them down on the floor for some tummy time if you want (see the tips on this in Chapter Five).

# SLEEP STRATEGIES FOR THE FOURTH TRIMESTER

- Use movement for naps—whether a carrier, stroller, a rocker bassinet, or car rides.

- Consider bed-sharing (following safe bed-sharing guidelines).

- Try the bassinet or crib for the first part of the night and then bed-share (safely) to get more sleep.

- Feed on demand (for breast-fed and bottle-fed babies).

- Set realistic expectations and know what is actually normal for babies at this age.

- Get bodywork done for your baby (and you): I highly recommend 1-3 visits with a craniosacral therapist or an osteopath/chiropractor. Often babies will sleep better after these treatments.

- Look for lactation support to make sure that latch and sucking are efficient. Poor latch can affect further air intake and also cause less milk intake, which can both affect sleep and overall well-being.

- Say no to houseguests. Yes, you're allowed to say no, and I recommend this for at least the first 6 weeks while your body heals and you bond with your baby!

- Keep an eye on the "baby blues" and be sure to speak to your doctor if you just don't feel right.

- Ask for help. Make a specific list of the ways family and friends can best support you (if they don't already know). Post it on your fridge for when someone comes over.

- Hire support, either a postpartum doula, night nurse, or someone like me to help you feel more confident in your baby's development and sleep.

- Communicate with your partner about how you are feeling!

- Don't forget about self-care and filling your own energy or love cup!

# SLEEP FOR THE FOUR- TO SEVEN-MONTH-OLD

You may have this idea that your baby should start sleeping through the night around this time. Some babies do—most do not! Try not to set this unrealistic expectation. You'll save yourself a lot of stress (I promise!). Canadian researchers found that 38 percent of six-month-olds aren't yet sleeping six consecutive hours at night and that 57 percent aren't sleeping eight hours at night.[12] It's normal for your baby to still be waking up at this age (sometimes a lot).

The four-month mark is often when babies come out of that sleepy fourth trimester and wake up to the world, and it's also when the first real sleep *progression* happens. Rolling may start anywhere between four and six months, and you might even see some of those crawling mini-milestones closer to seven months. This can mean more wakefulness at night, as their brain is on overdrive processing all the new growth and skills, and they may also practice their new skills at night. Babies also start to experience the first part of separation anxiety around six months.

---

### SLEEP STRATEGIES FOR THE 4- TO 7-MONTH-OLD

- Acknowledge that this does not last forever and just prep yourself to be gentle with yourself and your baby during this time.

- Feed your baby on demand during the day and offer more frequent feeds if they are distracted.

- Offer breastmilk or formula in an open cup if your 6- or 7-month-old is a distracted feeder during the day.

- Continue to feed them at night (they are often distracted during day feeds and are growing).

---

## SLEEP STRATEGIES FOR THE 4- TO 7-MONTH-OLD, CONT'D

- Get out of the house. Put them in the carrier or stroller and get out of the house. The movement might even sway them to sleep, so bonus!

- Don't expect a schedule, just take each day as it comes and focus on trying to read your baby's cues so they don't get overtired!

- Babies will still likely be taking 3-4 naps, though they may start to fight that last nap. Use motion to get a quick catnap in at the end of the day to make it to bedtime. Even 15 minutes is great!

- Watch for overstimulation and overtiredness: Because baby is more alert, it is easy to get plenty of interaction and stimulation during the day. This is important for development, but overtiredness can become a problem at this age, so you really want to watch your baby and their tired cues.

- Keep wake windows short (about 90 minutes at 4 months to about 2.5 hours at 7 months). Your baby is still small and can become easily overstimulated!

- Begin a bedtime routine, if you don't already have one, so that your child begins to learn and know what is coming next.

- Create a "menu" of sleep associations or ways to fall asleep. If something is no longer working, feel free to stop.

- You can start introducing a lovey as a "friend" and soothing item to help with transitions and be a comfort at night.

- Solids should be saved until the 6-month mark, as they can affect your baby's digestion, which temporarily affects sleep.

## RETHINK SLEEP REGRESSIONS

Let's reframe these.

Sleep is affected by physical, cognitive, emotional, social, and even language development. Just as our personal sleep preferences are different, because we're all different, babies also have different preferences based on their temperaments (personalities). Some are quiet and "easy," others are active, sensitive, loud/vocal, or fussy. This will affect their sleep and what they need to be able to sleep as well.

As mentioned, I prefer to think of sleep regressions as progressions. "Regression" suggests a loss in skill, and babies don't lose the skill of sleeping during this time (even though it may seem like it). As humans, we all know how to sleep, and our bodies will sleep without any effort when the right conditions are met (more on that shortly). What's actually happening is that due to a combination of developmental changes, growth, increased brain development, and changes in sleep-cycle architecture and even length, babies' brains are in overdrive, which often leads to more frequent wakings, some sleep "challenges," and more fussiness—temporarily. But baby is growing and progressing in their skills (yay)! This is what we want.

During these periods of massive growth, your baby's belly is also growing and their nutritional requirements increase. They're expending more energy, which means they need to take in more of it (from food). Add to this the fact that around this age, babies start to become more distracted during feeds. So you'll likely have a baby who is making up for those missed calories at night, when it's calm, dark, quiet, and distraction free.

So yes, your baby will likely wake more frequently during these periods of massive growth, but I promise that it's temporary and that there are always things we can do to help! Doesn't that help reduce the overwhelm a little bit?

It's so important to set age-appropriate expectations!

# SLEEP FOR THE EIGHT- TO TWELVE-MONTH OLD

Even though your baby is getting bigger and older, and likely doubled their birth weight long ago, it's still normal for them to wake up at night in this period. Research shows that at twelve months, 28 percent of infants aren't sleeping six hours straight and 43 percent aren't staying asleep for eight hours.[13] And it's also normal for them to still need one or two feeds at night (because remember, they're constantly growing and developing).

## SLEEP FOR THE 8- TO 12-MONTH-OLD
### DURING THE 8- TO 12-MONTH RANGE, IT IS NORMAL FOR BABIES TO . . .

- Have bedtime battles (even for previously good sleepers)
- Drop the catnap at the end of the day (usually around 9–10 months)
- Need Mom more—there is another bout of separation anxiety that happens around 9–11 months
- Need more snuggles at bedtime
- Have 1–2 longer wakes in the middle of the night
- Reach developmental milestones: independent sitting, pulling to stand, and maybe even learning to walk
- Refuse the afternoon nap (around 11–12 months)—push through . . . it will pass and they still need the afternoon nap!

## SLEEP STRATEGIES FOR THE 8- TO 12-MONTH-OLD

- Remember, this is all just a phase and will pass
- Keep an eye on wake windows, but really watch your baby's cues to prevent overtiredness
- Support them through this leap and show/teach them you are there for them
- Continue to build bond with lovey
- Give lots of space and opportunity to practice new skills
- Practice safe separation (see the Separation Anxiety section in the Development chapter)

### KEEP THE NAP

When babies transition from three naps to two (around eight or nine months), they often drop the midafternoon nap, which can mean some cranky afternoons. To compensate, try to schedule a slightly later lunchtime nap (a longer wake window between nap one and nap two) and an earlier bedtime.

Around eleven or twelve months, you may find that your baby is fighting that afternoon nap, and it can be tempting to think they're ready to drop it. I'm here to encourage you to persevere—your baby likely won't be quite ready for such long wake windows at this point. Instead, try capping the morning nap to get the afternoon nap. You could also incorporate a quiet time or a rest period, where you read or play quietly in their room with the lights dimmed, to reduce the sensory stimulation and help them reset. Or you could even plan for a stroller walk during normal naptime (even fifteen minutes asleep could be enough to get them through to bedtime without too much crankiness).

## SLEEP FOR TODDLERS, PRESCHOOLERS, AND BEYOND

You were likely ready for sleepless nights in the beginning, but you may have expected that your baby would be sleeping through the night by their first birthday. Or maybe you have a toddler who's still waking up at night, perhaps a couple of times, and you're wondering what gives. Yet again, you find yourself scrolling Dr. Google at 3:00 a.m. and going down a rabbit hole of conflicting information. The reality is that some toddlers will sleep the whole night through, but some may not. Both are "normal." Research shows that about 70 percent of toddlers up to eighteen months still wake at night one to three times.[13,14]

It's also typical for toddlers to wake up early in the morning (yes, usually an ungodly time when you just want to roll over and pull the blanket over your head). Then of course comes the time when they really start fighting and eventually drop their midday nap (around two and a half to three and a half years old). Oh the joy of an overtired preschooler at bedtime.

I've talked a lot about how development can impact sleep. The transition out of babyhood into toddlerhood brings about a lot of change. Speech is developing daily; they start walking, running, and jumping; they're eating varied and increasing amounts of foods; more teeth are erupting (sometimes many all at once); and there's another bout with separation anxiety—all of which can mean that sleep is once again disrupted.

In older babies and toddlers, deep sleep predominates the early part of the nighttime sleep and is caused by a buildup of homeostatic sleep pressure due to wakefulness before falling asleep (I'll chat more about this soon). Simply put, there's a fine balance between your child being awake long enough to achieve a consolidated amount of sleep in the early part of the evening and being awake so long that they become overtired. Another common sleep difficulty with toddlers over twelve months is that late-in-the-day naps can mean a very late bedtime. And then of course comes the transition from two naps to one, which can happen anywhere between fourteen and seventeen months and can ensure your toddler is tired and cranky by the end of the day.

At this point, children are also becoming more independent beings and often facing more separation from their parents (i.e., time with a nanny or at daycare, preschool, and eventually kindergarten). They're also learning a lot more about object permanence (the knowledge that something still exists even when it's out of sight), so the separation anxiety is in full force, especially at twelve, eighteen, and twenty-four months.

## CONNECTION AND BEHAVIOR

Although many sleep trainers believe that bedtime-battle behaviors need to be extinguished, you'll likely know what I'm about to say: This is nonsense. These "behaviors" are your child's way of communicating something. They don't yet have the language to put their thoughts and feelings into words, so they do their best to *show you*. As babies this happens through tears. This might still happen in the toddler stage, but toddlers will also start communicating with you in other ways, and often when they're feeling disconnected.

Bedtime is a perfect opportunity for a child who hasn't had enough quality time with their parent during the day to fill their cup with lots of Mommy and Daddy time before they fall asleep. Without that full cup, they won't want to sleep. Almost all bedtime battles at this age are a sign of something going on with attachment, relationship, or needing more connection.

Make sure there's time for connection after a period of separation—but please don't feel guilty if you have only a little time with your child after work. That won't serve you or your family. It's not about the quantity of time but the quality. Carve out time at the end of the day where you can focus on the connection (and not be busy/distracted trying to cook, clean, etc.). Prioritize the connection when you first get home, even for just ten to fifteen minutes. Fill your toddler's love cup first, and then get dinner going. Maybe you go to the park on the way home from daycare, or you read a special book or play a special game when you get home.

If your day runs late, maybe you adjust your little one's bedtime so that they have enough time to connect with you (if possible). If this is always the case, I also recommend accommodating this later bedtime with a later naptime (or plan for a fifteen- to twenty-minute nap in the car on the way home from daycare, if you have a child who falls asleep in the car).

We live in a digital age, and constant attachment to our devices is leading to more disconnect in general, but this especially affects our connection with our littles (and also leads to way more stress and overwhelm in our motherhood journey as we compare, track, and Google everything). Be mindful of how much and when you're using your devices around your children. I'm so very guilty of being on my phone a lot during the day, whether it's for work or just to zone out (yes, as adults we need this occasionally too). But I do make an effort to connect with my children in the morning over breakfast, a few times during the day, and in the evening before dinner. And then of course we get to the bedtime routine—no phones there.

If we don't consciously make these points of connection with our children, to them it may seem that we are constantly busy and that they aren't a priority. So if you're feeling disconnected from your child and you're struggling with bedtime battles, it's often a good idea to put away the technology before dinner and bedtime in favor of prioritizing connection.

You can even make your bedtime routine a special time for connection. Fill a box with special items that only come out at bedtime. They don't need to be expensive, just things that your child likes. Before bedtime, set aside fifteen minutes where your child can choose whom they'd like to spend the time with (if both parents are home) and the activity. This time should happen every night and should never be taken away as a punishment.

# BRIDGING THE SEPARATION OF NIGHTTIME

Nighttime is the biggest separation experience, and your child may battle bedtime because they fear this separation. Drs. Gordon Neufeld and Deborah MacNamara talk a lot about "bridging the nighttime separation."[15-17] As discussed, we can do this by focusing on the next connection, rather than the separation (see Chapter Three). There are many fun ways to bridge this nighttime separation, so let your imagination take over. When we focus on the next connection, we preserve the relationship and make the separation a little easier.

Toddlers are smart, as I'm sure you know if you have one. They'll do their very best to prolong bedtime to get just a little extra connection time with you and hold off that separation just a little longer. They may do this by asking for a cup of water every five minutes, one more book, or another trip to the potty. Perhaps they just want one more hug, or they get out of bed and ask you to tuck them back in (multiple times).

Knowing that this is a result of their innate drive for connection and of that fear of separation (and that they're not manipulating you) should make things a little easier, but you can start to anticipate any and all bedtime needs *before* they happen. A visual bedtime routine schedule to follow (including the water, bathroom trips, and books) can also be a great idea. Essentially, ensure you've taken care of all the things that your child could ask for before you say good night and leave the room, so that there's nothing left to ask for. You can also try the "ticket" strategy—they get five (or any number you choose) tickets to call you back in or ask for something after bedtime, and once those are used up, that's it until the next night.

# Chapter Seventeen

# SLEEP SCIENCE

It's time to dive into the science (or biology) of sleep. This chapter is a bit more science-y, and you might be tempted to skip it, but I highly recommend you give it a go! Understanding infant sleep science is half of the equation when it comes to understanding infant sleep.

We'll look at sleep cycles and how they differ between babies and adults, the hormones involved in sleep, and the two essential factors that lead to sleep: circadian rhythm and homeostatic sleep pressure.

## STATES OF SLEEP

Sleep is vital for our well-being and is the foundation of our arousal and regulation. We often think of sleep as restful. While it's true that sleep is restful for some functions, such as conserving and regenerating our energy and metabolic functions, it's highly active for others. Essentially, sleep is what helps us learn and grow. While we sleep, our brain cells "clean" the brain by getting rid of what's no longer needed and helping to grow and strengthen what is. The process is complex, involving specific cells, neurons, and systems. All we really need to know is that this happens during sleep, especially deep sleep.

There are essentially three states of sleep that make up a sleep cycle:

- Wakeful sleep
- Rapid eye movement (REM) sleep
- Non-rapid eye movement (NREM) sleep

NREM sleep has three stages within it—N1, N2, N3. N1 is a light sleep as we transition between being awake and asleep, and N3 is a deep sleep, also called slow-wave sleep. N3 sleep is the most restorative sleep, and difficult to rouse people from. During deep NREM sleep, your baby may occasionally startle or make sucking motions, but they'll generally be very still and have quiet regular breathing. This N3 stage of sleep is often when it's easiest to transfer a baby or leave them alone to sleep.

REM sleep is considered light and active sleep and is often easier to wake up from. During this state, even small changes in sleep surface and temperature (e.g., from the warm embrace of parental arms to the cold bassinet/crib mattress) can cause a baby to wake. During the dreaming portion of the REM stage, the mind and eyes are active but the body is still (almost paralyzed), a phenomenon known as paradoxical sleep. The reason for this is that our minds don't want us to act out our dreams. You may notice your baby's eyes move from side to side under their eyelids, or maybe they frown or wriggle their limbs. Perhaps their breathing is irregular and they even cry out or whimper—all without waking. This is part of REM sleep.[18,19]

The N3 stage is when our brain categorizes, organizes, and integrates what we learned and thought about during the day, and is also when the greatest amount of growth hormones are released. It's believed that the brain uses the REM phase to process this information. Babies spend more time in REM (active/light) sleep than adults. There also seems to be a relationship between motor skills and REM sleep. As babies develop greater motor skills, you'll see a broadening of the sleep cycles, with more time spent in the REM phase. As well, initially babies don't have muscle paralysis during REM, so they still move and twitch. This may explain why it's common for babies who've been sleeping well for weeks or months to become wakeful as they enter new developmental stages and practice their new skills.

By the time a baby is six to nine months old, they've found their midline, developed more core stability, and have slightly greater control over their motor skills from all the practice, but it isn't until they start walking that the muscle paralysis during the REM phase is fully developed. The theory is that babies don't have enough independent movement skills before this time to fight, flight, hit, run, etc. during their dream state.[20]

The architecture of a sleep cycle also differs between babies and adults. A typical adult sleep cycle looks like this: Awake-N1-N2-N3-N2-REM. Babies, especially those under six months, don't have a distinction between the different NREM stages and their sleep cycles look more like this: Awake-REM-NREM(N3)-REM. Around three to six months, babies start to develop the different NREM stages of sleep, with more of an adultlike sleep structure developing between six and nine months.

The length of our sleep cycles is also different. Adults have a 90- to 120-minute sleep cycle and spend about 75 percent of their sleep time in NREM sleep and about 25 percent in REM sleep. Babies, on the other hand, have a much shorter cycle (45 to 60 minutes) and spend about 50 percent of their sleep in REM sleep and 50 percent in NREM (N3 specifically) sleep. More time in REM sleep, which is a lighter sleep, means that babies spend more time in a sleep state that is easier to be woken up from.[21,22]

As our babies age, their sleep-cycle architecture also changes (phases of sleep but also time spent in REM vs. NREM), which is part of the reason why those pesky sleep PROgressions are so hard. Gradually over the first year, babies spend less time in the REM state and more time in the NREM state. When they reach toddlerhood, their percentages are similar to adults. In general, NREM phases are more prominent in the beginning of the night, which is why this is often referred to as the more restorative sleep period, while the REM phases occur more in the early-morning hours. All of this affects our ability (and our baby's) to fall asleep, transition between sleep cycles, and stay asleep.

Everything you just read might have gone over your head, and that's okay. It went over mine at first too! I've read countless books and articles on the science, and it's so complex that I still don't understand all the intricacies, so take a deep breath and realize it's okay to be confused by all this. One step at a time!

## WHY DON'T THEY WANT TO SLEEP?

It makes sense that babies need sleep to support brain growth and maturation, as well as memory and mood. And babies who get more sleep are more adaptable, approachable, and better able to explore and understand their environment and regulate their emotions. So why in the world does it seem like all they want to do is anything but sleep?

Short sleep cycles, minimal deep sleep, and frequent night-wakings protect young infants from SIDS—sort of like a built-in survival mechanism.[23] We want our babies to be sleeping in this lighter state so that they wake up if they can't breathe properly or are hungry, cold, or wet. Plus, as mentioned, babies spend more time in REM, or the light/active sleep state, than adults, so they wake up much more easily.

## PARTIAL AROUSALS

News flash—nobody sleeps through the night. Wait, what? Yup. So if adults don't, why are we expecting our babies and young children to? I've explained that each of us moves through several sleep cycles each night, and that babies move through these cycles more frequently than adults. As we switch from one sleep cycle to the other, we rouse slightly, and as long as we're not hungry, cold, or have to go to the bathroom, we'll go right back to sleep. Maybe you head to the bathroom or take a sip of water, or perhaps your arm fell asleep and you switch positions. Then you fall back asleep. This is a partial arousal.

Babies don't have the experience or the physical or cognitive ability to shift their position, roll over, take a sip of water, and fall back asleep, so when they experience partial arousals, they may cry out, thrash around, or become startled. If we don't respond, this partial arousal may turn into a full arousal (cue more tears and even screams—unless of course they've learned that they won't get the support). And yes, if they associate your calming and comforting presence with going back to sleep, they may wake more fully and start looking for that support. This isn't a bad thing. We're teaching them, through experience and co-regulation, how to transition from partial arousal back to sleep.

This is part of the reason I love sleep associations (remember when I mentioned that these aren't crutches or bad habits?). If your baby is able to fall back asleep with many different cues (such as rocking, patting, nursing, shushing, or having a lovey or pacifier), it will be easier for them to move through sleep cycles and partial arousals with less support as time goes on, and when they're developmentally ready. Having more sleep associations also allows you to have something to fall back on when one stops working (because it usually does eventually).

Now that you know a little more about sleep-cycle architecture, let's explore the specific hormones involved in sleep.

## SLEEP HORMONES

We are hormonal beings. Hormones aren't just about periods and hot flashes. They're chemical messengers that influence nearly all functions—everything from temperature to heart rate, blood sugar, fertility, mood, and, you guessed it, sleep. They're coursing through and fluctuating in our bodies all day long, helping to keep our systems in balance. Often, as the amount of one hormone increases, another decreases in an effort to achieve homeostasis, or equilibrium.

The two main hormones involved in sleep are melatonin and cortisol, but others play a supportive role, including serotonin (helps with melatonin production), tryptophan (precursor of serotonin), adrenaline (connected to cortisol production), and oxytocin (helps reduce stress and promote calm and relaxation[24]). I won't bore you with all the technical bits of each of the hormones, but I want to give you a general sense of how some of them work in relation to our sleep.

### MELATONIN

In the morning, your body makes cortisol to wake you up, and in the evening, it makes melatonin to make you sleepy. At bedtime, we want melatonin to be high and cortisol to be low. During the night, melatonin will decrease and cortisol will increase, and at a certain point they cross (usually in the early hours of the morning), in preparation for waking up. This applies to adults as much as it does to babies and children.

Melatonin is linked to the circadian rhythm and is made in response to dim light. It doesn't necessarily make you fall asleep, but it makes you sleepy and improves quality of sleep. Daylight (also white/blue light—yes, like the light emitted from regular/LED lights and most electronic devices) inhibits melatonin, which is one of the reasons why naps can take longer to optimize than nighttime sleep—there's no chemical push to sleep during the day. You may hear that blackout curtains are a must, both day *and* night, to counteract exposure to daylight. The reality is that while they may be helpful at night, they can wreak havoc on baby's natural circadian rhythms when used during the day. You may hear someone recommend getting your newborn to nap in the daylight, to help them establish their circadian rhythm. I recommend doing some mini-experiments to figure out what works best for your baby. Trial naps both in the dark and with some light and see how your baby responds. If there's no difference, I'd suggest not using blackout curtains.

Also consider what evening looks like in your house. Are all the lights on? Is your baby's sleep space bright when you enter it? Do you use your phone or a night-light for those middle-of-the-night feedings? These are all things to think about and experiment with. (I'm not expecting you to fumble around in the dark for each wake—trust me, it might seem like a good idea at the time, but it can make things take way longer.) Different light colors affect our circadian rhythm differently. Red/orange light doesn't seem to have as much of a negative effect as blue/white light. I love using salt lamps at night, but my kids now have an essential oil diffuser in their room that has different colors, so we choose the red one (it does feel "softer" on my eyes than the white). You could also try using red lightbulbs in an existing night-light.

Babies don't begin to produce melatonin until about twelve to sixteen weeks, but tryptophan (chemical precursor of serotonin, which then converts to melatonin) is found in nighttime breast milk, which is one of the rea-sons why breast-fed babies fall asleep so easily after a night-feed.[25] This is important to know if you're giving your baby pumped breast milk. Make sure you're labeling the time of day you pumped so that you can give your baby breast milk pumped in the evening for any bottles at night.[26] Unfortunately, formula doesn't contain tryptophan or melatonin and thus does not have the same effect.

Another benefit of melatonin is that it relaxes smooth muscles, including the gastrointestinal lining. It's perhaps partly because of this that breast-fed infants are less fussy and experience less infantile colic than formula-fed infants,[27] which may further improve their sleep.

## CORTISOL

Cortisol significantly impacts sleep as well as emotional regulation and stress. When our stress levels increase, so do our cortisol levels. Cortisol gets a bad rap, but it's important for metabolism, blood sugar, and the immune system.[28] Cortisol also has anti-inflammatory properties. Because cortisol levels are low at night, children (and adults) with itchy-skin conditions often report a worsening of their symptoms at night,[29] which can lead to more frequent wakes due to discomfort.

Cortisol plays a role in the circadian rhythm, and levels are lowest in the evening after we fall asleep. They gradually rise through the night, peaking in the morning to wake us up.

When babies are born, their cortisol rhythms are flipped and they don't know what time of day it is—remember, their circadian rhythm and melato-nin production don't really kick in until twelve to sixteen weeks after birth. Their internal rhythms are also disorganized initially. It's our job as parents to help them organize their bodies in a way that makes life easier for them, not necessarily for us. How? We help them synchronize their circadian rhythm and help them anticipate what's going to happen next. We do this by having consistent rhythms and routines to our day, including light exposure (ideally natural light) and sleep and feeds at somewhat consistent intervals. I'm not suggesting you keep a rigid schedule. I highly recommend following your baby's lead in terms of sleeping and feeding, especially for the first six to nine months. Keep an eye on your baby and watch their cues, and tune in to the natural rhythm that starts to unfold as well.

While cortisol naturally peaks in the morning to wake us up, it can also be increased by other things in our lives, namely stress. For babies and children, cortisol levels increase if they're overtired, perhaps from lengthy wakes at night or poor naps during the day. They also experience stress when left to cry unattended or unsupported for prolonged periods. As well, overstimulation and sensory processing challenges can increase stress in our babies. If babies' cortisol levels increase too much during the day, they may go to sleep with higher-than-normal cortisol levels and end up waking more frequently at night and too early in the morning.

When adults are tired, we "crash." Unfortunately, the opposite is often true for children. They get "wired" and seem to fight sleep even more. This is part of the reason why older babies and toddlers who miss their optimal bedtime window get more active and rambunctious. What they need is to move their bodies to get rid of this excess cortisol. So instead of battling bedtime, try your best to go with the flow—let them climb, move, and play and then try to slowly reduce stimulation and find quieter activities.

Phew, that talk about cortisol was intense, right? I don't want you to get all stressed out (thereby increasing your cortisol levels) about whether you're creating more stress in your baby's life. Most likely you're not. Stress is a part of life, but now you have some biological reasons to back up why responsive and supportive parenting, day *and* night, is key! It helps to balance our hormones too.

## OXYTOCIN

Finally, a quick note about the "love" hormone. Oxytocin increases with eye gazing, physical affection, and during breast-feeding, and it's also indirectly associated with sleep. It can aid in counteracting stress (and the resulting increase in cortisol) by helping us feel calm, relaxed, and happy. And when we're calm, relaxed, and happy, we're more likely to fall asleep and stay asleep more easily.

# TWO BASIC FACTORS THAT IMPACT SLEEP

Sleep cycles and sleep hormones are important to consider and be aware of, but when it comes down to it, sleep is dependent on two biological factors: 1) circadian rhythm and 2) homeostatic sleep pressure.

## CIRCADIAN RHYTHM

Our circadian rhythm is sort of like our internal clock. It's involved in many of our internal functions, such as our sleep-wake cycle, hunger/thirst and the optimal times for absorbing and digesting foods, and when we need to use the bathroom. It regulates our body temperature, immune system, mood, alertness, and the production of various hormones, some of which we just discussed.

Another cool thing about the circadian rhythm is that it's strongly connected to the eyes and affected by exposure to light and dark. Our bodies change in response to light and darkness in conjunction with this biological clock. When the sun rises, our blood pressure and body temperature rise. As the sun goes down, our metabolism slows and we get sleepy. While we're sleeping, our bodies repair themselves, and when we enter a deep sleep, our body temperature drops. Though our circadian rhythm is largely affected by daylight, noise, activity, social cues, and habits all have an effect on it too. Circadian rhythmicity is usually established anywhere from one to six months after birth,[30] but around twelve to sixteen weeks is when babies start to release melatonin.

## HOMEOSTATIC SLEEP PRESSURE

Circadian rhythm is half the battle when preparing for sleep. The other half is homeostatic sleep pressure (HSP), which is essentially a biological sensor that indicates how strongly we need sleep at a given time. HSP is present at birth and is controlled by how long you've been awake—meaning the longer we're awake, the more sleep pressure we have, which then triggers hormones that make us feel sleepy. Sleep pressure builds throughout the day and is affected by age and maturity and, to some extent, cultural factors (in some cultures it is the norm to take multiple naps during the day and have a shorter nighttime sleep duration). Normally our sleep pressure is highest at night, coinciding with our circadian rhythm. As you can imagine, it's quite difficult to fall asleep with low sleep pressure, but for babies and children, it's also hard to sleep with high sleep pressure (as is the case for an overtired or overstimulated baby).

The sleep gate zone is the sweet spot—the time when it's easy to fall asleep due to HSP and the circadian rhythm being aligned. Sleep pressure is high and the circadian rhythm is signaling sleep (with high levels of melatonin and low levels of cortisol). Right before the sleep gate zone comes the wake maintenance zone, which counteracts sleep pressure and makes you feel temporarily more awake, making it harder to fall asleep. This is why you sometimes see little ones getting a second wind during your naptime or bedtime routine. Attempting sleep too early is likely to backfire (and lead to those "battles"), or you may find yourself spending all day in a dark room rocking and bouncing your baby, at which point you run the risk of having an overtired baby (I've been there, and it's NOT fun!). But again, remember it varies between individuals. It's so important for us to be in tune with our babies, to have a rhythm or flow in our day that offers a balance of physical activity along with time for rest, but also to know that we cannot force our babies to sleep.

Another fun fact is that we only need a certain amount of sleep in a twenty-four-hour period, and this changes with age, getting shorter and shorter. And the more sleep you get during the day, the lower your sleep pressure will be at night. This is part of the reason why newborns seem to sleep all the time but also wake every hour at night. They can't handle being awake for too long because their sleep pressure rises much faster than that of older babies or adults, and they get overstimulated and overtired more quickly. They sleep a lot during the day because they're not yet able to consolidate longer chunks of sleep at night—their sleep-pressure drive hasn't had a chance to ramp up. As babies get older, their sleep pressure accumulates more slowly, meaning they'll be awake longer, the intervals between naps will grow, and they'll gradually start to have longer chunks of sleep at night.

It's helpful to keep in mind that a baby has a sleep need distributed across a twenty-four-hour period and divided into daytime naps and nighttime sleep. This is why I recommend examining your nap timings and lengths during the day, as a starting point, when starting to work toward more consolidated chunks of sleep at night.

## SLEEP PRESSURE ANALOGY

Picture an empty cup, and a bunch of pompoms. The empty cup represents your baby and their body, and the pompoms are the sleep pressure. Sleep pressure is created as we spend time awake, but it is also created through daily activities and sensory stimulation. So things like going for a walk in the stroller, playing at the playground, rolling and moving around on the floor and exploring our bodies, as well as splashing in the bath and eating solids fill the cup. Sleep pressure decreases with naps and overnight sleep. Ultimately, our night sleep will empty our entire cup by the morning and we start by filling it back up with sleep pressure (or pompoms) throughout the day. The goal is that we want our body (cup) to be full of sleep pressure (pompoms) at bedtime, but not so much that it is overflowing.

By now you might be thinking "How in the world do I know how long my baby should be awake, how long they should sleep, and how much is too much or not enough?" It can be confusing, which is why the prescriptive schedules and plans don't work and why they create even more stress for you (and your baby). Again, the key is to tune in to your baby and what they're showing you through their mood and behavior, and to also tune in to your heart and what it's telling you.

# WAKE WINDOWS

Before I talk more about naps (because you probably have baby-nap questions), I want to chat about wake windows, which help build sleep pressure until babies need a reprieve (aka a nap). I had no clue about wake windows until my eldest was about eight and a half months old. I just assumed he would fall asleep when he was tired (which seemed to be never). Once I learned about wake windows, my life changed because I finally understood that he was overtired.

That said, wake windows are only a small piece of the larger sleep puzzle. The sleep-training world would have you think otherwise with all the sleep schedules and plans based on age.

Wake windows are also called awake times or wake intervals. They're the optimal amount of time a baby is awake before needing a nap or sleeping at night. Remember, we need to find a balance between daytime and nighttime sleep to optimize nighttime sleep. Having an idea of what typical wake windows and sleep totals are for different ages can be useful. Finding the "right" window of time for *your* baby is also useful to help prevent overstimulation and overtiredness, which can lead to fussiness and more difficulty falling and staying asleep. What I DON'T want you to do is start obsessing about rigidly following any specific timing (I see this a lot with the mamas I work with).

There's a huge range when it comes to normal and healthy wake windows. Every baby is different and has different sleep needs, so looking at charts and requirements isn't the best (or only) way to figure out what works for *your* baby. But it can be a useful starting point, especially if you're unsure how much sleep your child should be getting or what your baby's tired cues are. I recommend spending some time watching your baby to learn what their specific tired or sleepy cues are and logging their sleep times to figure out the perfect window for your unique baby. And not forever—for three days or so. I'll chat about tired/sleepy cues soon.

I've created a guide, based on a few different sources, and included it here to help you see the average sleep totals in a twenty-four-hour period for babies of varying ages. Again, use it as a starting point. Use it to guide you in terms of making sure your baby isn't getting overtired while also making sure that they have enough sleep-pressure buildup to get longer stretches at night. Use it to help you figure out if your baby is perhaps getting too much daytime sleep, which might be impacting their nighttime sleep. And remember that not all babies are the same—some will need more sleep and some will need less, but this guide will give you an idea so that you can start to play around with naps versus night sleep. It might also be helpful to know that babies and toddlers are generally able to extend their wake windows about fifteen to twenty minutes every three weeks.

## SLEEP TOTALS

This table summarizes the average sleep needs for babies in the first three years. Remember, these are only averages. Every baby is different, and the reality is that we cannot control a baby's wake window or their schedule.

Many sleep consultants and traditional sleep-training approaches will use wake windows and schedules as a very crucial part of getting babies to nap during the day and sleep through the night. However, this is only one piece of the sleep puzzle. Use this guide as a starting point.

Having an idea of what typical wake windows and sleep totals are for different ages can be very useful and easy to keep in mind. It can bring more attention to the idea of building enough sleep pressure before nighttime sleep so that babies can gradually start to sleep longer stretches when they are developmentally ready. This guide is also useful to help prevent overstimulation and overtiredness, which can lead to fussiness and more difficulty falling and staying asleep (naps and bedtime/overnight).

Wake windows are the optimal amount of time a baby is awake before needing to go for another nap or go to sleep for the night. We need to find a balance between daytime and nighttime sleep in order to optimize nighttime sleep.

Please remember that it is more important to become aware of and watch YOUR baby's tired cues and use these sleep totals as guide (rather than needing to adhere to them rigidly). I recommend that you spend some time logging your baby's sleep times to figure out the perfect window for your unique baby.

| Age | 1st Wake Window | Remaining Wake Windows | Number of Naps | Total hrs of Daytime Sleep | Total hrs of Nighttime Sleep | Total hrs of Sleep in 24 hrs |
|---|---|---|---|---|---|---|
| 0–2 mths | 45–60 mins | 45–60 mins | Evenly spread throughout day and night | Varies | Varies | 14–17 |
| 3–4 mths | 90–120 mins | 90–120 mins | 4 | 3.5–5 | 9–10 | 12.5–15 |
| 5–7 mths | 1.5–2.25 hrs | 1.5–2.75 hrs | 3–4 | 2.5–3 | 10–11 | 12–14 |
| 8–9 mths | 2–3 hrs | 2.5–3.5 hrs | 2–3 | 2–3 | 10–11 | 12–14 |
| 10–12 mths | 2.5–3 hrs | 3–4 hrs | 2 | 2–3 | 10–11 | 11–14 |
| 12–16 mths | 3–3.5 hrs | 3–4.5 hrs | 2 | 1.5–3 | 10–11 | 11.5–14 |
| 17–24 mths | 4–6 hrs | 4.5–5 hrs | 1 | 1.5–3 | 10–11 | 11.5–14 |
| 2–2.5 yrs | 5–6 hrs | 5.5–6 hrs | 1 | 1–2 | 10–12 | 10–13 |
| 2.5–3 yrs | 6 hrs | 6 hrs | 1 | 1–2 | 10–12 | 10–13 |

*This table has been adapted from various sources: Baby-Led Sleep & Well-being Certification, Lyndsey Hookway Holistic Sleep Coaching, and other sleep schedules.*

**Note** also that nighttime sleep doesn't necessarily mean continuous, unbroken sleep. Unless your baby is waking up for hour-long middle-of-the-night parties, the partial arousals (where you might do a quick feed, a cuddle, or a diaper change) aren't full wakes.

And please try not to compare your baby to other people's babies, even if they're the same age. I know, easier said than done, but seriously, Mama, the faster you stop comparing and worrying about what everyone else is doing or saying, the faster your overall stress and overwhelm will fade. It took me almost nine months to figure that out!

# Chapter Eighteen

# NAPS

Okay, the time has come to talk about naps! Naptime, or lack thereof, is among the top struggles I see mamas facing in those first two to three years of motherhood. I get it. My firstborn wasn't a good napper, at least not in the way I defined it at the time. He'd nap for twenty to thirty minutes in his own sleep space but could nap for two or three hours when on or next to me. He'd fall asleep in the carrier or stroller only if we were moving, but as soon as we stopped, his eyes would pop open. Oh, and he hated the car! Sound familiar?

My daughter, on the other hand, was a great napper. She'd fuss a little, I'd feed her and put her down in her own sleep space, and she'd sleep for three hours at a time. It was so different and unexpected that the first several times I went in to check if she was okay! The difference with her was that

I was more confident in myself, in the sleep process, in noticing her cues, and also in optimizing the environment.

At first, your newborn will pretty much sleep wherever they are. They're able to stay awake for only short windows of time. Follow your baby's lead and put them down when you see signs that they're tired, knowing that initially their naps will be inconsistent.

At around five or six months, a daytime sleep pattern will emerge and the intricate balance between circadian rhythm and HSP will become more important. At this point, your baby will likely be taking about three or four naps per day (depending on the length of the naps). The transition will often happen naturally. As babies get closer to nine months, it's likely that they'll transition from three naps to two, and from two to one around fourteen to sixteen months.

## NAP LENGTHS

It's not just the number of naps but also their length that can determine how many naps your baby needs. Some babies have a couple of two-hour naps every day, while others have four or five twenty- to thirty-minute naps. Your baby's temperament is also a factor. They may be happy to go with the flow or they might thrive on consistency. Babies who are easily over-stimulated tend to have shorter naps as the day progresses, likely because their nervous systems are becoming more and more overloaded (sensory input is cumulative) and their cortisol levels are increasing. These babies may do well with at least one long nap during the day, and often this can be achieved by wearing them in a wrap or carrier and going for a long walk or bed-sharing with them for one of the naps.

I often see mamas striving to get those one- or two-hour naps (and then feeling like a failure when they don't). I've also heard that naps under thirty-five minutes aren't restorative because babies haven't completed a full sleep cycle, and that naps need to be on a flat, nonmoving surface to be restorative. Oh my goodness, talk about stressful for you and your baby! Constantly feeling as if your baby isn't napping enough, fighting them to nap longer, and struggling to get them sleeping on their own in the crib is enough to make any parent tear their hair out, don't you think?

Know that none of the above is true when you look at biologically normal infant behavior or sleep science. The best way to tell if a baby is getting enough sleep is to take note of their mood and behavior. Does sleep come easily for them? Are they happy, content, and easygoing when they wake up? If yes, then your baby is likely getting what they need. If they're crying, cranky, or upset when they wake up, they're likely still tired. Some babies take long daytime naps (like my daughter), and many are simply catnappers (like my son), especially babies who aren't yet mobile. So stop looking at the clock and start tuning in to your baby.

## TO EXTEND THE NAP OR NOT?

As mentioned, if your baby wakes up fussing, grumpy, or crying, then they're likely still tired and a longer nap would be beneficial. In this case, you can try to extend the nap (if you have the flexibility)—but please don't get tied to the goal of making the longer nap happen. Try feeding them and see if they fall back to sleep, or put them in a carrier or stroller and go for a walk (the motion may lull them back to sleep). Or if they regularly wake up cranky at the thirty-minute mark, try going in around the twenty-five-minute mark, gently rousing them, and then helping them resettle. The idea here is that your baby may have a thirty-minute sleep cycle and might not be able to transition between cycles on their own just yet, so essentially you're offering support. Now, this strategy might backfire, so be ready for that. Give these strategies a try and see what happens. If your baby isn't settling back down relatively easily, then stop and keep going about your day.

If your baby wakes up tired and cranky and you can't resettle them or lengthen the nap, their wake window before the next nap will generally be a bit shorter than usual. So be on the lookout for the tired signs and put them down for their next nap a bit earlier. This will also move up the rest of the day and bedtime as well. The next day is a fresh start.

## WHY NAPS ARE IMPORTANT

Though the length and place of naps aren't too important, whether your baby naps or doesn't is. Because of that HSP, we want babies to nap at least a little bit during the day to relieve some of that sleep pressure and minimize stress (and the crankiness that comes from that stress). Some research has shown that it's the distribution of sleep that's important (rather than the length) in terms of preventing elevated cortisol, so evenly distributing daytime naps makes sense.[31]

All babies are different, but evidence reveals that not enough sleep in the day can do the following:

- Make falling asleep at night difficult
- Shorten the sleep cycle
- Shorten the duration of sleep
- Make sleep more fragmented
- Cause early rising
- Lead to fussy behavior or hyperactivity

Also, baby naps give you a chance to decompress and have some time to yourself, which is very much needed for mental health and well-being.

There are hundreds of blogs, tables, and charts suggesting how many naps your baby needs at different ages. I hope you can see now that it isn't such an easy answer and will depend on your baby.

## NAP TRANSITIONS

As babies grow, their wake windows get longer and their overall sleep needs gradually lessen. They'll shift from needing four naps, to three, to two, to one, and eventually to none. Nap transitions can be another tricky time for a lot of parents—and a time when being flexible will be key (and less stressful). Usually, your baby will start to resist that last nap of the day no matter what you try. Instead of thinking about it as dropping that last nap, think about it as your baby showing they're able to be up for longer periods during the day because their wake windows are lengthening.

Now, if you lengthen baby's wake window and their naps get even shorter, they probably aren't quite ready for this transition. It's also common during nap transitions to have some days where they take three naps, for example, and others where they take only two. This is okay. Try to be flexible and adjust bedtime to be either later (if three naps) or earlier (if two naps) to accommodate. The reason for this is that you want to make sure the wake window before bed isn't too long, which can lead to overtiredness and a buildup of cortisol.

In general I don't love bedtimes before 5:30 p.m., mainly because we cannot expect our babies to sleep for more than eleven or twelve hours in a row. A bedtime that's too early may lead to early rising simply because of the length of time they've been asleep. You may find that your baby needs a catnap (fifteen to thirty minutes) at the end of the day in order to make it to a more acceptable bedtime. It's often easier if this nap is a contact or moving nap. A slight drop in sleep pressure will help your baby make it to bedtime without having an overfull cup.

Be aware that around eleven or twelve months, babies will start to fight that second nap. It might be tempting to think that it's time to transition to one, but I urge you to persevere. Often around this age there's a lot of development happening, which might be leading to sleep disruption in the short term. Your almost-toddler is likely not able to sustain being awake for many hours at a time and still very much needs the two naps to prevent overtiredness (unless one nap is three hours long, in which case that might be enough). Initially, you may need to cap the first nap (to an hour) in order to get the second nap (even if it's only thirty minutes). If the second nap still isn't happening, try capping the first nap even more (to forty or even thirty minutes) to get the second nap. Keep offering the second nap, even if it's just a rest period to reduce the stimulation around them. Think of it as a reset.

## TIRED CUES AND NAPTIME STRATEGIES

Trust that your baby knows when they need to sleep. Your job is to create the optimal timing and environment for that sleep to happen. The first step is to tune in to their cues. There are the obvious ones, such as yawning or rubbing their eyes, but these are usually late tired cues and mean your baby is ready for that nap *now*! There are often more subtle, seemingly random, cues, including red cheeks, rubbing of ears, clumsiness, getting bored with toys, and a blank stare. Maybe they clench and unclench their fists or need to be held a lot more and fuss when you try to put them down. Tune in and observe what they do *before* you see the eye rubbing and yawning.

This will take some trial and error, but spend a few days watching your baby and see what works best for them and what will work for you. Consider what's happening around sleep times. Is your baby waking up hungry (maybe they didn't get a full feed right before sleep)? Are there intake issues due to latch, sucking ability, or TOTs? Are they overstimulated before sleep times? Creating a stimulating learning environment for babies is good, but too much of a good thing can be overwhelming. Does your baby need more help winding down and switching from an active/alert state to a quieter state conducive to sleep? This is why having a naptime routine—which could be a mini-version of your bedtime routine or totally different—is important.

## TIRED CUES

| EARLY CUES | TIRED CUES | LATE CUES | OVERTIRED |
| --- | --- | --- | --- |
| • Red eyebrows, eyes, cheeks | • Yawning | • Intensely crying | • Arching back |
| • Averting eye contact | • Rubbing eye(s) | • Arching back | • Pushing away |
| • Turning head | • Pulling ears/hair | • Hands fisted | • Emotional |
| • Blankly staring / Staring into space | • Fussy; clingy | | • Hyperactive |
| • Quiet and disengaged | • Sucking fingers | | • Not wanting to be fed (even though hungry) |
| | • Frowning | | |
| | • Clumsiness | | |
| | • Bored with toys | | |

You want it to be simple and transportable (e.g., lovey, book, song, nursing, sleep). Or maybe your baby is highly active and they'd benefit from more physical activity shortly before naptime to use up excess energy. These babies will likely still need a bit of a wind-down routine as well, to switch states. And of course, all babies thrive when they get plenty of outdoor time with fresh air, which will also help with regulating their circadian rhythm.

While tuning in to your baby's tired cues is a good first step, there may be other reasons for nap refusals: a huge developmental leap (life is too exciting, frustrating, or scary to sleep); too much excitement during the day; separation anxiety; a major change in your day (e.g., your returning to work or their starting daycare); overtiredness (especially during nap transitions); and fear of missing out (on this fun new world they're living in). Luckily there are plenty of things you can try.

# NAPTIME STRATEGIES

We cannot force a baby to sleep during the day, just as we cannot force a baby to sleep at night. Here is a recap of a few things you do to make naptime a little more enjoyable and to avoid those battles.

- Know your baby's tired cues.

- Make sure that you are quick to move once you see those tired signs in order to avoid the second wind.

- Know (and accept) your baby's temperament—easygoing babies will tend to sleep longer, whereas sensitive and high-needs babies will tend to take shorter naps.

- Make sure the environment is set up for sleep before you enter the room. Having the lights dim and the white noise on when you walk in will help baby to relax.

- Consider motion naps, co-sleeping naps, and baby-wearing naps to avoid naptime battles. These are NOT creating bad habits and are just as restorative as sleeping on a still surface. Sleeping in the crib is not always necessary.

- Build a strong naptime routine as a shortened version of the nighttime routine.

- Use a variety of sleep associations in order to parent your baby to sleep—nursing, rocking, routines, loveys, and white noise are all really great options.

- Tune in to your baby and whether they need more wind-down time or perhaps more physical activity to wear themselves out.

- Don't fight the nap! If things get too frustrating, stop, take a break, and try again later.

- Be flexible. Having a variety of ways to support the baby's nap will help you avoid power struggles.

See? Naps don't have to be rigid or stressful. Treat each day as a new one, do your best, and know that that's good enough! Follow your baby and trust your instincts, and let go of this need to "fight" or obsess about sleep. Try your best to go with the flow. Trust me, life will get easier and much more enjoyable when you stop focusing so much on what you should or shouldn't do.

# Chapter Nineteen

# HOW FEEDING AND TEMPERAMENT CAN AFFECT SLEEP

I discussed feeding in detail in Section Two, but here's a quick recap of why sleep can be impacted by feeding in general.

## FEEDING AND SLEEP

Initially, babies have teeny-tiny bellies and can only hold so much nutrition at any given time. They need to wake and eat frequently to gain weight and grow. If your baby isn't getting a full belly for whatever reason, they'll continue to be hungry, which can result in frequent wakes. If they're taking in a lot of air due to a poor latch while they feed, this can be uncomfortable and can potentially be the underlying cause of colic and reflux, both of which can affect a baby's ability to feel comfortable and calm for sleep. If your baby is allergic, intolerant, or sensitive to something in your breast milk or in the formula, this can affect their digestive system and lead to discomfort, gas, constipation, or reflux.

As their bellies grow and they become more efficient eaters, sometimes distraction can play a role in not getting a full belly and therefore not sleeping well. Once they start to eat more solids, they can gradually go longer and longer stretches without eating. Knowing what is age appropriate will help you to decide what's best for your baby in terms of offering full feeds or frequent shorter feeds (e.g., if baby is distracted), timing of feeds (I recommend feeding on demand as much as possible), and introduction of solids, while also figuring out causes of potential discomfort. All of this will help you put more pieces of the sleep puzzle together.

Once your baby is on the move more, they'll expend more energy and calories, which will lead to needing more energy and calories. The bottom line is that babies need to eat. It takes a baby at least six to nine months to grow a belly big enough to accommodate enough calories to go longer periods without needing to fill up again. Babies will often wake for one or two feeds well into their second year of life. This is normal (and definitely not what you hear in our society today).

Unfortunately, a lot of the baby sleep books and sleep trainers out there are using outdated research based on infants who were formula-fed. And much of the research was from the eighties (or earlier), when it was still recommended that babies be placed on their bellies to sleep, which has been shown to lead to deeper sleep. (That doesn't mean you should put your baby to sleep on their belly now. While belly sleeping isn't dangerous in and of itself, it's one of the risk factors for SIDS, so let's not go there.)

So if your younger baby is waking frequently at night, before assuming that they have a "sleep problem," please promise me that you'll rule out any feeding difficulties before trying more extreme approaches, such as night-weaning or spacing out night feedings. Often once feeding challenges are fixed, sleep will improve on its own. Seek out feeding support first if you think there may be something going on with your baby's feeding abilities (see Chapters Nine and Eleven for signs and symptoms to look out for).

## TEMPERAMENT AND SLEEP

As mentioned frequently throughout this book, we're all unique beings with preferences and moods. Some adults are easygoing while others are more high-strung. Some are passive. Some are always on the move. The same goes for babies. You may have even had an idea of your baby's personality while they were growing in your womb!

While we can't change underlying temperament, we can shape and support our baby's temperament through our parenting style, our environment, and numerous other factors. All children, regardless of temperament style, need reliably responsive care, but some may need more or less support. This is true especially for those babies with more-sensitive temperaments who need considerably more help with regulation. And if you're a caregiver of a more-sensitive baby, you'll also need to lean on outside support so that you don't get burned out.

Since babies can't voice their preferences, we need to get curious and tune in. Knowing your child's strengths, difficulties, character, and behaviors will help you have a more enjoyable parenting experience as well as a better understanding of what they need for sleep. It will help you avoid strategies that are likely to fail because they're a bad fit for your parenting style and/ or will damage your child's confidence and attachment.

Temperament could be a whole book in itself, but because it's an important piece of the sleep puzzle, we'll briefly discuss the main styles.

An individual's temperament consists of nine main personality traits.

These traits can be categorized into temperament styles: easygoing, active, cautious, and a combination of these. Personality traits and temperament styles are what make children (and all of us) unique in how they respond to the world. These are general personality traits, which means that most people don't fit neatly into one specific category 100 percent of the time. But for now, we'll go with this for the sake of simplicity.

## MY CHILD'S TEMPERAMENT STYLE IS . . .

| | | Activity level–level and extent of motor activity | | | | | |
|---|---|---|---|---|---|---|---|
| 1 | calm, content, inactive most of time | 1 | 2 | 3 | 4 | 5 | highly active, always "on the go" |
| | | **Adaptibility–of behavior to changes in the environment** | | | | | |
| 2 | adapts easily to change, highly portable | 1 | 2 | 3 | 4 | 5 | likes familiar environment, does not adapt easily, unsettled by change |
| | | **Regularity–of functions like eating, elimination, and sleep** | | | | | |
| 3 | eating, sleeping, and bathroom habits are regular, like clockwork | 1 | 2 | 3 | 4 | 5 | eating, sleeping, bathroom habits are irregular; resists routine |
| | | **Sensitivity–to sensory stimuli** | | | | | |
| 4 | not overly sensitive to pain, sounds, light, and temperature; oblivious | 1 | 2 | 3 | 4 | 5 | highly sensitive to pain, sounds, light, and temperature |
| | | **Distractibility** | | | | | |
| 5 | highly focused, not easily distracted | 1 | 2 | 3 | 4 | 5 | easily distracted, unable to ignore distractions |

| | | | | | | | |
|---|---|---|---|---|---|---|---|
| | **Mood** | | | | | | |
| 6 | Overall positive mood: cheerful, friendly, pleasant, and happy | 1 | 2 | 3 | 4 | 5 | overall negative mood: often angry and grumpy; doesn't smile |
| | **Persistence–attention span and persistence in an activity** | | | | | | |
| 7 | sticks with projects until they are done, doesn't give up | 1 | 2 | 3 | 4 | 5 | does not stick with projects until they are done; gives up easily or loses interest |
| | **Intensity–energy level or responses** | | | | | | |
| 8 | emotional reactions are mild and low key; "easygoing" | 1 | 2 | 3 | 4 | 5 | emotional reactions are intense and exaggerated; "drama queen" |
| | **Approach/Withdrawal–response to new object or person** | | | | | | |
| 9 | curious, keen, accepting; willing to try new things; comfortable in social situations | 1 | 2 | 3 | 4 | 5 | wary of strangers, apprehensive, withdraws in social situations; doesn't try new things |

It can be easier to manage specific temperament styles if you shift your mindset about them. Often, we view "sensitive," "high needs," "fussy," and "demanding" as more negative personality traits. But what if you reframed this by considering what these traits might mean in the future? Your baby with "high needs" may be a fun, confident, and curious preschooler and a self-assured, independent teenager. Often the same characteristics we find to be challenging in infancy can be traits we want for our children as they grow up. A reframe like this can make things a little less stressful. This is by no means intended to diminish how hard it is in the moment. You need to take care of yourself too—reach out for support, ask for help, and recharge your battery.

# TEMPERAMENT STYLES

I've adapted the temperament styles by paraphrasing the common definitions and adding my experience in sensory processing. In my opinion, sensory responsiveness (how we respond to sensory stimulation in our environment) is a central component of temperament.

## EASYGOING

These babies are generally content and ready to go with the flow. They usually have normal eating and sleeping habits and can easily adapt to changing situations without becoming distressed. These babies usually don't overreact or become upset easily and will adapt to whatever schedule you choose, even day to day. They typically have the most regular sleeping habits. Since these babies are often so laid-back, it's important to build intentional one-to-one time to connect with them. You may want to play or cuddle before bedtime and after your baby wakes up even if they aren't crying or fussing.

## ACTIVE

About 10 percent of babies fit into the "high needs" (previously called "difficult") temperament category. These children are often described as being very active, always on the move. They have intense reactions, a negative mood, and tend to have irregular routines. They often have long and frequent crying episodes. They're also assertive, persistent, and decisive.

I find that this category can be broken down further based on arousal level. Your baby may be active or spirited because they have a low arousal level and are looking for *more* input to help their body feel grounded in space and against gravity. It's possible that their daily life input just isn't enough because they have a high threshold for sensory stimulation and are under-registering it in their brain and nervous system (previously discussed in Chapter Two). They need to be highly active—bouncing off the walls, jumping on the bed, climbing on everything—to feel where their body is in space. These babies often need opportunities to burn off energy, so it's helpful to add some rough-and-tumble play before your bedtime routine. As your baby gets older, it's also helpful to add in as much freedom of choice (and physical activity) as possible.

On the other end of the arousal spectrum are babies who are active because they have a high arousal level and their fight-or-flight stress response is being activated. They're attacking/fighting or withdrawing/fleeing due to a lower sensory threshold, over-registration, or an increased sensitivity to sensory input. These children are often more irritable, angry, or fussy, easily upset by sensory stimulation, and have intense reactions to situations. They're more irregular in their eating habits and are fearful around new people or in new situations. They are often labeled as "high needs" because they demand a lot of attention from you. Because these babies have intense reactions to situations, they may struggle with any changes to their sleep routine and need a much more gradual approach. Talk to your baby and prepare them in advance for any changes.

## CAUTIOUS

About 5 to 15 percent of babies fall into this category. This is the "slow to warm up" temperament. These babies are typically withdrawn, shy, and may react strongly or with no reaction to new situations. They tend to be less active and sometimes fussier. These babies often display a low activity level, but again, their arousal levels can be either high or low.

A baby with high arousal (and low activity) avoids things. They're more sensitive to, and over-register, sensory input and often avoid it. They "shut down" easily. They might avoid different textures or movement. They may appear to always be on high alert or anxious and very observant. These babies can become uncomfortable with and unsure of changes to their routine. For these babies, it's best to try to maintain a consistent routine, keep your promises, and give them time to become comfortable and familiar with any changes to their routine.

In contrast, a baby who has low arousal (and low activity) is usually quiet, perhaps labeled as "easy." They under-register sensory input and don't really notice it coming in, so they don't have the motivation (or want/ need) to act on it. They move more slowly and often stay back and observe rather than be in the action. They tend to miss or take longer to respond to events in their environment, and may meet their milestones later as a result. They're the kids who might have their heads on the table at school or maybe even seem to "have their head in the clouds." They usually tend to blend into the background and often go unnoticed in the classroom (the quiet, well-behaved kid).

## HIGHLY SENSITIVE BABIES

Those in this group often don't fit into the neat little categories above, or perhaps fit into more than one. Highly sensitive people can become over-whelmed by sensory input (and this can be minor or more significant, such as with SPD). Highly sensitive people may fall into the high arousal, low activity category (more avoidant and cautious), or the high arousal, high activity category (spirited, high needs). These children are easily bothered by stimulation, and their bodies create a stress response that kicks their sympathetic nervous system into high gear and signals their body to fight, flee, or freeze. This then increases their adrenaline and cortisol levels, thereby making it harder to sleep.

Often these babies sleep less than others because it's difficult for them to calm down enough to sleep. They also tend to struggle more with sleep when they're teething or if their sleep environment (e.g., sleep sack, fit or feel of pajamas, feel of sheets, etc.) isn't perfect. They often rely on sleep interventions (rocking, swinging, sucking, body contact, etc.). It's important to understand and tune in to your baby's personality and preferences so that you can better navigate exactly what they're sensitive to and what support they need. Depending on how sensitive your child is, it can be helpful to get additional support from an occupational therapist trained in sensory processing.

And then of course there's the combination-temperament type, which makes up about 40 percent of babies—because it's rare for a person to fit into one box or category.

We also need to recognize that we, as parents, often have certain expectations regarding behavior, but these expectations come from our own temperament style and personality traits, as well as how we were raised. If your child is more like one parent than the other, which is often the case, then ask your partner how they would (or think about how you would) react or what they would have done in certain situations—and then try this with your baby. On the flip side, think about whether there are any pieces of your child's behavior that trigger you. Maybe your temperament styles are quite different.

The following strategies are great reminders for everyone, but especially for parents who have highly sensitive or "higher needs" babies.

# SLEEP TIPS FOR TEMPERAMENT

## 1. Start slowly

You may need to only work on getting nap timings optimized, or only work on getting a calming and consistent bedtime routine, or perhaps only focus on layering in sleep association so that when you take one away, you have something else to fall back on to help calm and support your baby to sleep. Maybe you are choosing to work on a sleep location for the first nap and the first wake. Sometimes a little improvement can give you a boost of confidence that you haven't had before.

## 2. Consistency is key

Consistent and repetitive patterns are key. This sounds easy, but trust me, it is often harder than you think. You are exhausted and you want something (anything) to change ASAP. Often we so desperately want results that we forget changing a habit takes time (and doesn't happen overnight). I encourage you to be consistent, especially in the first 4-5 days/nights, and don't give up. I promise you will see some improvement, even if it is small! Once your baby can detect the pattern or routine, and things become familiar and predictable (and seen as "safe" by the brain), they will be able to calm and settle in.

## 3. Parenting a sensitive/high-needs kiddo is hard!

Parenting a sensitive, high-needs, or intense baby is not at all like you expect or like the experience of your friends who are parents. You may feel like it's your fault and doubt your ability to make the right choices, but know that it is not your fault, and you are doing a great job, Mama!

## 4. Two steps forward, one step back

There are many variables that may impact sleep with our babies and children, especially those with higher needs and who are more sensitive. They are more prone to sensory-processing sensitivities

## SLEEP TIPS FOR TEMPERAMENT, CONT'D

and reflux, and they often have lags in development. Sometimes, supporting sleep doesn't work within a usual timeline. It's often impossible to know how it will go until you try. You might see some great changes initially and then a plateau. Or things that worked before stop working. Or maybe change is taking longer than you thought. Babies with higher needs will often take longer with any change than easier and more flexible babies. As long as the changes are feeling good in your heart, I invite you to keep going. Keep trying. And if something no longer seems to be working, or doesn't feel right anymore, then change it.

### 5. Sometimes you need to let go of tired cues

If you wait for the nonstop children to be tired, you may be waiting a long time. While some children start to look drowsy or more droopy when they're running out of steam, often the really active children rev up. They can become more wired and then impossible to put down. Watch the clock and try to get ahead of their second wind.

### 6. Have a calming bedtime routine

Tune in to your child and see what calms them down at bedtime. Sometimes a bath or reading books actually stimulates your baby, which can be especially true for the more sensitive and alert kids. If you find these activities too exciting, think about whether you can move them to a routine earlier in the evening. Instead, try some gently rocking in a rocking chair or just rocking their body as they lie in their sleep space, or give them some firm squeezes (I like to call them Hug Squeezes) along their body from the head down to the feet to help them calm down. Even just holding them in a bear hug can be calming at times. Notice whether patting their bum or perhaps just shushing with your voice helps them feel calm and quiet. You can also try humming. See what works and doesn't work for your unique child.

Hopefully you have a clearer picture of why temperament and sensory processing can impact sleep and why it's so important to tune in to the baby you have in front of you. Our temperament dictates what type of environment, activity level, and conditions we need to feel fully calm and relaxed at night.

Also consider what we discussed about the hormones melatonin and cortisol earlier in this section. Some research published in the occupational therapy field examines the connection between sensory processing differences and sleep.[32-34] One study found that children with increased sensory sensitivities (specifically, children with auditory, olfactory, and visual sensitivities) had higher levels of cortisol and lower levels of melatonin before sleep, and as a result, had more difficulty sleeping.[35]

The relationship between temperament and sleep is also why sleep training has such different effects on different babies. Some babies hardly make a peep, while others cry so much they vomit—yes, horrid, I know.

One thing that we can do for all our babies, regardless of temperament type, is to build a strong attachment with them so that they learn that we, their parents, will always be responsive and supportive. This secure attachment can help them thrive—and sleep!

*Chapter Twenty*

# RHYTHMS, ROUTINES, AND SCHEDULES

Thanks in large part to sleep-training culture, there's a lot of pressure on us parents to make sure our children are on a strict sleep schedule with strict wake windows. Ever heard that 7:00 p.m. to 7:00 a.m. is the ideal time for sleeping? Or perhaps you've been told to follow the 2-3-4 wake window system—meaning that you put your baby down for a nap two hours after they wake up in the morning, then you have them awake for three hours before they nap again, and then awake for four hours before bedtime. I tried both those schedules and failed miserably. I couldn't figure out how to get my son to stay awake for all those hours during the day, and when I tried to get him to sleep for 7:00 p.m., I'd invariably spend two hours bouncing him on a yoga ball while silently cursing him and beating myself up because clearly I was doing something wrong. Phew, talk about stressful.

By now you know that there's no *one* schedule that could be perfect for every baby at the same age—it's just not possible. Instead, I prefer to look at rhythms and routines when I support my clients with sleep. As adults, we thrive on rhythms, routines, and consistency, and these things are especially important for our children. Familiar, predictable, and rhythmic things are all viewed by the brain as "safe," which means that they leave us feeling calmer and more regulated than things that are unfamiliar, unpredictable, and new, which put our nervous system into fight-or-flight, thereby increasing cortisol levels.

## RHYTHMS

We live on earth, so our lives are affected by the natural world, which follows rhythms: night and day, seasons, moon cycles, etc. We also have rhythms inside our bodies—remember those circadian rhythms we talked about earlier in this section? We women also have a menstrual cycle (or rhythm).

Most parents provide their children with weekly and daily rhythms unconsciously. You might have daily activities such as mealtimes, dog walks, or reading a book before bed. Maybe you always go outside after breakfast, have a cup of coffee or tea as your baby naps, and sit on the couch watching Netflix after they go to bed. Perhaps you have a mom-and-baby class on a certain day of the week, or your toddler goes to daycare two days a week. These common activities allow our children (and us) to identify where we are in the week, creating patterns and familiarity in day-to-day life. Rhythms may develop unexpectedly, and they may change (as your baby ages, for example), but we naturally move back to a rhythm each time. It's important that the rhythm flows, rather than jolts us from one activity to the next.

So how are rhythms different from routines and schedules?

# ROUTINES AND SCHEDULES

While rhythms are broad and free flowing, routines are more structured—they involve things happening in the same order. And schedules are often more rigid and time dependent, which isn't necessarily a bad thing (many of us have work schedules with specific timings of events).

Children thrive on following the natural rhythms of the day, and with some predictability in various routines, but they don't need to have strict schedules. When I finally stopped trying to schedule our days and leaned in to going with the flow, allowing my baby to nap when and where he wanted and letting go of the need to attend specific classes on time or even at all, our lives became much less overwhelming and stressful. By letting go of a rigid schedule, I also let go of the "shoulds." This made me (and probably my son) feel as if a weight had been lifted off my shoulders and I could just breathe and be. I could follow the natural flow of our day, whatever that might be on any given day.

Do you think you might want to try that? Just for a little while, to see how it goes? Combining some predictability with some flexibility can give you a sense of freedom. Let's be honest—at first, life with a new baby can feel chaotic, but if you relax and observe your baby, you'll find gentle patterns emerging. You can build on these patterns, creating a daily rhythm to suit you both.

Strict schedules don't necessarily make life easier for you as a mama. Being tied to particular naptimes and sleep places can make getting out and about, visiting friends, and taking holidays more complicated. Remember, your needs and those of your baby will change with time and from day to day. Following your baby's rhythms will help you meet those needs when there are growth spurts or illnesses. It will also give you confidence to adapt when necessary (e.g., for a doctor's appointment or holiday travel). When your baby is attached to you, rather than a schedule, problems are less likely and you might feel more relaxed about managing the day.

I like to think of routines as a set of activities that happen in the same order before the same event each day. We all have morning and evening routines, even if we're not conscious of them. Here's my morning routine: I roll to my right side and hang my legs over the bed, go to the bathroom, wash my hands, wash my face, put cream on, brush my teeth, brush my hair, and then go downstairs to grab a cup of hot water with lemon, followed by coffee. I do this every morning, in pretty much the same order. I also have a specific bedtime routine. Do you see how a routine is a bit different from a rhythm? Following routines within the rhythm of your day and week can offer natural order to your life—predictability with room for flexibility and fun. The key is consistency. The activities don't need to happen at the exact same time each day, but they should happen every day in the same order (or as close to as possible).

It's never too early to start building a bedtime routine into your child's day. Maybe it involves singing certain songs, dimming the lights, and maintaining a quieter environment. Bedtime routines can become longer, with more steps involved, as your child grows and matures. A consistent bedtime routine allows your baby to associate certain activities with sleepy time. This concept may seem simple enough, but sometimes it takes some trial and error to find what activities work well for your family and your baby. Finding activities that help your baby relax sounds simple enough, right? Remember that we all have different preferences, and what one baby finds relaxing, another baby might find stimulating. And if your baby doesn't enjoy something, it's likely to set off their stress response. You really have to tune in to your baby during each part of the routine to see how they respond.

Make sure the activities in the routine are also enjoyable for you (if bouncing on a ball for two hours before bed isn't sustainable, then don't do that). Routines are also a great time to involve your partner, which can be important for everyone. Maybe your partner does bathtime, and then you do pajamas, song, and feed. Gradually you can have your partner take over more and more pieces of the routine.

---

## BEDTIME ROUTINE IDEAS

- Take an evening walk in stroller when it is dark out
- Play make-believe in the bedroom with laughing and/or dancing
- Give a massage (gentle but firm pressure is usually best vs. a light touch) leading up to (or after) bathtime with Mom or Dad
- Bathtime can be relaxing for some kids and set tone for winding down, but it can be alerting for others
- Use a white noise machine in the room (consistent is often better received than intermittent)
- Close the blinds and use only a dim bedside lamp (red/orange light if possible) while getting ready for bed
- Change into clean, soft pajamas ideally made from natural fibers to allow for breathability
- Read a bedtime story from a picture book
- Nurse and snuggle
- Sing a lullaby or other song(s)
- Speak in a soothing, calm voice and say good night and I love you (or whatever your words are)

---

#### BEDTIME ROUTINE IDEAS, CONT'D

- Create a bedtime book that is personalized for your child. In the OT world, we call this a social story. It can be as simple as taking pictures of your child at each stage of their bedtime routine (i.e., bath, lotion massage, diaper change, pjs, brushing teeth, reading books, rocking in the rocking chair, nursing, singing, etc.). Then add some simple text to each page (or make it up on the fly). Read this book as part of your bedtime routine. Bonus tip: have pictures with each of the parents doing parts of the bedtime routine, so that your child becomes used to both of you doing parts of it.

---

Your naptime routine might be a shortened version of your bedtime routine, or it could be a different (but consistent) routine.

Along with bedtime and naptime routines, have a middle-of-the-night routine. I'm not suggesting you do a whole bunch of activities—rather, keep your activities simple but consistent. For example, try to keep everything as dark and cool as possible and in night mode at night, even when you're changing their diaper or feeding them. Whisper and limit your talking. You want your baby to understand that it's nighttime and that nighttime is for sleeping. Another thing to think about is diaper changes. When that cold air hits their bums, most babies will scream or open their eyes, and then we'll be stuck with going through our soothing options to get them back to sleep (sigh). Most disposable diapers can hold a lot of pee. Some babies might not even feel wet, so maybe part of your routine is that you only change your baby if there's poo or leakage. That said, some babies are very sensitive to wetness and may need a dry diaper to sleep better. These are all things to think about and trial, to see what works for your baby.

We've talked about presleep routines, but did you know that our whole day affects our ability to sleep at night?

Waking up at the same time every morning helps our circadian rhythm function optimally. This is the case for both children and adults. It isn't as important in the newborn phase, but by about six months, your baby's circadian rhythm is more mature and thrives on consistency and routine. Yes, getting up at the same time as our babies often means rising early, with the sun, because children have much more sensitive circadian rhythms. Much of my sleep education and research indicates that between 6:00 a.m. and 7:00 a.m. is a very normal time to get up with our babies, especially after about six months.

If your family rhythm is to have later bedtimes and later wake times, that's fine, though this will require you to make sure you keep the bedroom very dark until your desired wake-up time (which might be difficult depending on where you live and the changing seasons). When it's time to get up, I recommend opening the blinds and filling the room with sunshine—essentially, creating a dramatic wake-up experience, which will not only let your baby know it's morning time but will also help their circadian rhythm.

By now you might be nodding about this concept of rhythms and routines but wondering what happens when life happens? Babies get sick, they go through periods of massive development in the first two years, and then of course there's the seemingly never-ending teething. What if you get off track? I get this question a lot because each of the above scenarios often means that your little one needs extra cuddles and/or round-the-clock nursing sessions, i.e., your routines go out the window. Try not to get stressed out and discouraged. Just remember what worked last time in terms of your sleep routines and try again once your baby is feeling better. They may need extra doses of comfort for a while, but you'll get through it together and your baby will learn that they can always count on you.

Thinking of your day in terms of rhythms and routines versus schedules can be freeing. It can help ease the stress and overwhelm a little bit, allowing you to go with the flow and trust your mama instincts! That said, if you're someone who loves schedules and they're working for you and your baby, then keep doing that. Same goes for pretty much everything in your parenting journey.

> *If it is working for you (and your baby/family), keep it. If it is no longer working for you or your baby, that is when you change it.*
>
> *–Kaili Ets*

# Chapter Twenty-One

# MAKING SLEEP CHANGES

As mamas, we want the best for our babies and we often give selflessly. But remember, we're not meant to be martyrs! If something is no longer working for you, it's one-hundred-percent okay to make a change. That means that even if bouncing or rocking your baby for hours at bedtime gets them to sleep but you hate it, it's time to make a change. If your baby stops falling asleep while nursing, it's time to make a change. And yes, you can change it in a way that's responsive and supportive rather than just taking it away and leaving your baby to "figure it out."

Sometimes making a change means accepting that, in the short term, things may seem as if they're getting worse. This is totally normal. Change is hard for all of us, and it takes time to form new habits that stick. Change is scary and sends our stress system into high gear. Your baby may wake more often after you make a change, but if you stick with it, things will progress and your baby will start sleeping for longer stretches. **Consistency is key** with this—and, of course, following your heart!

When you make a change, I highly recommend considering your parenting values. If you're against traditional sleep-training methods, then don't resort to them. If you don't like the idea of bed-sharing or it's not comfortable for you, then don't do that either. Also consider whether the strategies you've chosen for the changes feel light or heavy. Do they feel right or wrong? Do they make your heart happy or make it hurt? These questions might sound a little silly, but trust me, you'll know in your heart and your body whether the changes you want to make are the right ones for your baby and your family. Trust those feelings!

Once you make changes, you'll need to tune in to your baby to see how they're responding to them. Are the changes happening too fast for them? Are they getting upset every time you try the new way? Do you feel as if they're okay with the changes and how you're supporting them through them? You'll also need to listen to yourself and how you feel regarding your baby's emotions around the changes—because there will be emotions. Remember, change is hard and scary for all of us. Your baby will have feelings about the changes, and they may communicate them through tears and perhaps even aggression (e.g., hitting, grabbing, biting, kicking, squirming, etc.). This is okay, as long as we're there to support them! As discussed, our job as parents isn't to stop the emotion, even though that tends to be our first instinct (to make it better). Our job is to support and guide our children through the emotion. To allow them to express and release their emotions.

# SLEEP-SURFACE TRANSITIONS

Changing sleep locations works best when it's done gradually and you're tuning in to your baby to see how they're reacting. I highly recommend making this change during a time when your baby isn't having a developmental leap, sick, or experiencing a big change in your life (e.g., a new baby arrives). I also recommend doing it when their separation anxiety is relatively low, so generally before six to eight months or after about eighteen months. Separation anxiety usually peaks between nine and eighteen months, so this wouldn't be an ideal time (though it's not impossible). Also, remember these are guidelines and your baby will be unique, so no comparing, okay?

A few things to consider:

- What will make your child feel safe and comfortable in the new space? Temperament comes into play here.
- If your child is old enough, maybe you could let them pick the bed, sheets, or decorations for their new room.
- Play and have a good time in the new sleep space during the day. This will help your child become familiar with it, which in turn will help them feel calm and safe in it.
- Start with naps in the new space. I often recommend the first nap of the day, if you have the flexibility to choose. It's usually the easiest nap so will make the transition a little easier on everyone. (If this first nap happens during the school drop-off for your older child, then it's not the ideal time for your family.)
- Begin the night in the new sleep location. When your child wakes, you can choose to keep them in the new sleep location if they're comfortable or take them into your room or another sleep space after the first wake or subsequent wakes. You choose what works best for you!

Elaborating on the last point, if, for example, you want to transition your child from your bed to a solitary sleep surface, you'll need to decide if you want to have them in a crib (recommended for younger babies) or a mattress on the floor (something to consider for toddlers). Put your baby on that separate sleep surface at the beginning of the night and then support them back to sleep on that separate surface for each wake. How many times you support them back to sleep in that new sleep space is totally up to you. It's also okay to take them back to your bed at some point, for however long this works for both of you. Just remember that nighttime is the biggest separation, and if they're in a new environment (new bed and/or new room) and they have a new routine (sleeping alone vs. with you) it will initially be a bit scary.

## TRANSFERS

Transferring a sleeping child is tricky and can take time to master. The timing of transfers will depend on how old your child is. In the fourth trimester, babies spend about 50 percent of their time in REM sleep and 50 percent in NREM (N3) sleep. They're in REM for about the first twenty to twenty-five minutes of their sleep cycle. You'll likely have a more successful transfer if you wait out this stretch and then transfer them once they're in the NREM (N3) stage of sleep. You'll know your infant has reached this stage when their eyes stop fluttering under their eyelids and their breathing is more regular.

Around three to six months, there's a shift and babies start to go through more NREM stages (1 and 2) instead of going right into deep sleep, and the REM phase happens toward the end of the sleep cycle instead of at the beginning. What this means is that it may be easier to transfer your little one soon after they fall asleep rather than waiting the twenty to twenty-five minutes.

As much as this all sounds good on paper, transferring a sleeping baby is still a work of art and often much more difficult than I just made it seem. When you transfer your baby into a crib, for example, think about the way you physically do the transfer. Often we instinctively put our baby down gently with the head and shoulders making contact with the surface first. This can be scary for babies, as it can make them feel as if they're falling. Instead, focus on putting your baby down by their legs, bottom, trunk, shoulders, and then their head. Hold them as close to your body as possible while you *slowly* move through the transfer.

Your baby might startle, as being on their back can feel vulnerable. (You might be thinking, "What about the Back to Sleep campaign?" That was put in place to reduce the risk of SIDS, and it has, but back sleeping is only ONE factor in SIDS reduction.) Sometimes it's helpful to turn them over to their side once their body is on the mattress, just for a moment, while they settle, and then slowly roll them over to their back. If you're transferring for a nap and you'll be awake and around to supervise, you can leave your baby in the side-lying position, which might be more comfortable for them. This is especially important if your baby was born with or is developing a flat spot anywhere on their head—this isn't what's recommended in the Safe Sleep guidelines, but it's my professional opinion based on my training and education in infant/child development, sleep, and craniosacral therapy and my many years of working with babies. For added comfort, you could heat the crib sheets with a warmed-up towel or perhaps a heating blanket until it's time for the transfer. Remove the heat source and gently and slowly place your baby onto the warm sheets, so that the temperature transition, from the warmth of your body to the sleep surface, isn't as drastic.

Sometimes it takes a more-gradual approach, especially if you've been doing contact naps for many months. Start with the goal of transferring your baby from sleeping on you to sleeping next to you on the bed. After a few days, you can gradually move away from your baby (perhaps to the other side of the bed initially and then eventually off the bed and out of the room). Once your baby is used to staying asleep without being on you or next to you, you can work toward practicing jostling them slightly. After you've transferred them to the bed, place your hands underneath them and move them just a little—don't pick them up. When your baby continues to stay asleep with this jostling, you can practice lifting them and putting them back down in the same spot. When they're used to this, you can pick them up, walk around, and then put them back in the same spot. Finally, you can try to transfer them directly into the crib. Yes, this approach is a lot more time-consuming, but it can be very helpful for more-sensitive babies who get alarmed or startle easily. Essentially, you're helping them safely get used to the feeling of being moved and put down while they're asleep.

Another great strategy for transfers—and transitions in general—is to introduce a comfort object (e.g., a lovey) that smells like you to help your child retain that sense of security, sameness, and comfort. This will also take time because you're building an attachment between your baby and this comfort object. I introduced a lovey to each of my kids around the five-month mark, but it wasn't until about nine or ten months that they started to look for and take comfort in the lovey. This might seem like a long time, but to this day (at the time of writing they're four and seven years old) those same loveys bring them comfort when they're sad and also at night. They help my kids feel safe and calm.

Remember, you're building new habits and change takes time! Don't give up after the first or the fifth attempt. Humans thrive on consistency and routine—our children are no different. So keep at it!

# HOW TO SUPPORT YOUR BABY TO SLEEP AND BACK TO SLEEP

Parents often come to me for help when they're making changes to how they support their baby to sleep. Either they've heard that their baby must be falling asleep independently and therefore think they're creating bad habits by nursing, rocking, walking, or holding their baby so they fall asleep (they're not), or they're so tired, both physically and emotionally, that they can't keep doing what they've been doing and feel stuck.

Before you take a sleep association away, you'll want to layer in additional sleep associations. Your baby will start to associate the new ones with the old, calming ones, and over time these new ones will feel safe to them. This is called habit stacking.

Gradually, you'll reduce how long you do the sleep association you want to get rid of and the newer one will take over. This might look like adding a bum pat and a song while nursing or bouncing your little one. You'll start nursing or bouncing for less and less time but still keep the bum pat and the song. Finally, you'll stop the nursing or bouncing and just sit or stand while doing the bum pat and song. If you're standing while bouncing, the next step might be to sit and do the bum pat and song instead of standing. And then when your baby is sleeping, you can transfer them. It will take some time—usually four to five days but sometimes more, depending on your baby's temperament—to add the new sleep associations before you start making the changes. And remember, change will be easier with consistency.

Tune in to your baby every step of the way. Are they even tired? How long is it taking them to fall asleep? Maybe you need to start bedtime a little later so that you're only rocking or bouncing for five minutes instead of forty-five. This all takes a little trial and error. Tune in to your heart as well. What feels right to you?

Another change you can make is to have your partner take some of the wakes. And again, it will often be easier if you spend some time building your partner in as a sleep association before you make the switch completely.

# IT MIGHT BE EASIER FOR YOU TO MAKE THE CHANGES

We often put a lot of pressure on our little ones to make sleep changes and get used to new things when perhaps we should put the onus on us, parents with mature adult brains, to make changes when it comes to *our* sleep.

Dealing with frequent night-wakings is exhausting. Yes, you get used to the sleep deprivation to a certain extent, but nights are still hard, and perhaps you're starting to resent them or your baby. Hey, no judgment here. This was totally me with my first. By eight and a half months I was done! I hated the nights. As mentioned, I'd sabotage myself by staying up late, convincing myself it was easier to respond to my baby this way. Then I'd be frustrated and even angry when responding to him. It was horrible. This wasn't the way I wanted to feel or to parent. This is when I reached out for help—thank goodness! It changed my life.

We cannot force anyone to sleep, but we can make changes to our sleep habits and hygiene to help us deal with the exhaustion. Often the easiest change to make is to your bedtime. This is something you can control to a certain extent. While you cannot force yourself to sleep, you can choose to go to bed earlier (that might mean when your baby goes to bed), so that you're at least getting more rest. Instead of getting extra sleep by sleeping in in the morning, you get the extra hours in the evening. This is called the reverse sleep-in.

You can also nap, or at least rest your body, when your baby naps. Perhaps this means embracing the contact naps and lying back to listen to a podcast or audiobook, or maybe taking a longer nap next to your baby in bed (make sure to set up your bed for safe bed-sharing).

You could also ask your partner to alternate wakes with you, split the nights (with one taking the first half and the other taking the second half), or even have them take the whole night once in a while. Trust me, a whole night of sleep (even just six hours in a row) can make a world of difference. You may need to move yourself to another bedroom and put earplugs in, and of course make sure you've practiced bottle-feeding and have pumped some milk for your partner if you're breast-feeding, so they can take over the night-feeds as well. You can also ask your partner to take the baby in the mornings so that you can have a few extra hours of sleep (bonus if they take the baby out of the house so it's quiet).

# Chapter Twenty-Two

# SLEEP CHALLENGES AND SOLUTIONS

Let's discuss the most common challenges that parents face when it comes to their children's sleep and ways to alleviate them.

## FALSE STARTS

We've all had the experience of our baby waking up shortly after we put them to sleep. Maybe it takes you a while to get them to sleep and you can't understand why they won't sleep for more than forty-five to sixty minutes in a row. My first was like this. I'd spend one or two hours bouncing on the ball with him until he was asleep only to have him wake up forty-five minutes later. I didn't know it at the time, but this is often called a false start.

It's usually a false start if a baby wakes within the first forty-five minutes to an hour after falling asleep at bedtime or has many wakings in the first few hours of the night, before midnight. The first stretch of sleep, in the early part of the night, is thought to be the most restorative for a baby because they typically spend more time in the NREM (N3) phase. After about four to six months, once sleep becomes more about the balance of HSP and circadian rhythm, we want to see babies sleeping longer chunks between their bedtime (which could be as early as 6:00 p.m.) and midnight.

False starts are often a sign that a baby's sleep rhythms are imbalanced. It could mean that their total daytime sleep hours are low, that they've had a too-long wake window before bed and are overtired, or perhaps that they're napping too frequently, leading to not enough sleep-pressure buildup. False starts could also mean that your baby is uncomfortable due to a gassy tummy, constipation, or food sensitivities. Tune in to your baby, especially their tired cues, and put on your detective hat to figure out what's disrupting their sleep.

A good place to start is to look at nap timings and consider whether your baby is getting adequate awake times for their body. Tune in to their tired cues and start experimenting with timings. This is one of the reasons I really hate the 2-3-4 schedule. For most babies, if their longest wake window is before bed, it leads to overtiredness and these false starts. What generally works best for the many families I've worked with over the past few years is to have the first wake window, before nap one, the shortest of the day and the last wake window, before bed, the second shortest. All other wake windows in the day can be slightly longer. And by "slightly" I mean fifteen to thirty minutes at first. We want to make sure that baby isn't overtired before bed but tired enough. It's a fine balance and will take some experimenting to see what works best for your unique baby, which is why relying on a rigid schedule is usually not the best idea.

If your baby is waking up every forty-five to sixty minutes all night, it's likely more to do with an inability to fall back asleep after the partial arousal. Perhaps they've gotten used to and need the type of sleep support that you offer when putting them to sleep at the start of the night. Again, this isn't necessarily a bad thing, but if your baby is waking after each sleep cycle needing the same input to fall back asleep, you're going to be exhausted and probably done with it. Then it's time to make a change.

# SPLIT NIGHTS (MIDDLE-OF-THE-NIGHT PARTIES)

When we brought our son home after he was born, one of our first visitors gave us this little block decoration that said something along the lines of "It's 3:00 a.m. and time to party." At the time I thought it was so funny and cute and it went right up onto the bookshelf. Ha! Little did I know what that 3:00 a.m. party time felt like, especially when it happened multiple nights in a row. Not fun at all! This party is called a split night. It's when your baby wakes up in the middle of the night and seems to be fully awake, ready to play, and no attempt at putting them back to sleep works. There are a few reasons why this might be happening.

First, from an evolutionary perspective, before artificial light existed, humans would go to sleep around sundown and would wake up for a few hours in the middle of the night, which is often when their creativity would flow or lovemaking would happen (yes, this is really what some of the literature says).[36,37] Then they'd go back to sleep until the sun came up. This is called bimodal sleep, and it's ingrained in our circadian rhythm initially.

Another reason split nights can happen, especially between eight and ten months, is because your baby is learning a ton of new skills. There's so much development happening physically (motor skills), cognitively (babbling and separation anxiety), and emotionally (hello, stranger danger).

Because we consolidate our memories and learning while we sleep, and also relive our daily experiences as we learn new skills, our babies' brains are on overdrive during these periods of development. Which means that yes, they might be awake and ready to play and practice those new skills at 3:00 a.m. This happens to so many families I support, and it happened to me, with both my kids.

One of the best things I can recommend is to not fight the wake. This will ultimately reduce your stress, anxiety, and overwhelm, I promise. Let your baby get their movement needs out. I took my son into the living room (mainly because I wanted to solidify the idea that his bedroom and crib were for sleeping) but would keep everything in night mode (dark, quiet, calm). I'd set him up with some quiet toys and make sure the area was safe and somewhat babyproofed and then grab a pillow and blanket off the couch and curl around him. And then I'd close my eyes and pretend to sleep. No talking, no playing. After about twenty minutes or so, my son would usually get bored, stop babbling, and often come and curl up next to me, which was the cue to take him back to bed. Instead of fighting this wake-up, I embraced it while also finding a way to get some rest so that I wasn't as exhausted the next day. This lasted for about three weeks and then one day just stopped. Other mamas have told me that they lie down on the floor (or a mattress) next to the crib and let their babies just crawl and move around the room until they're tired. The choice is yours, but trust me, by embracing the wake rather than fighting it, you'll feel so much less stressed out.

The third reason split nights can happen is due to imbalanced daytime and nighttime sleep. The total amount of daytime sleep is too high and/or the bedtime is too early and you're expecting your baby to sleep too much overnight. This leads to sleep pressure not being in line with your baby's circadian rhythm. These factors work separately, but together they push your baby's sleep through the whole night, ideally between ten and twelve hours (that doesn't mean in a row). Remember that around six months, HSP becomes an important factor in longer stretches of night sleep. If enough sleep pressure hasn't accumulated before bedtime, babies can wake after eight or nine hours of sleep feeling well rested and not able to resettle.

Be careful, though, as there's a fine line between not enough sleep pressure and too much sleep pressure, which can lead to overtiredness and false starts. I recommend considering how many hours of sleep they're getting during the day first. Is it on the higher end for their age? If so, try capping some of the naps, especially the last one of the day. I usually recommend that the last nap doesn't go any later than about 4:00 or 5:00 p.m. (sometimes 5:30 p.m. for babies under nine months). You'll then need a long-enough wake window before bed to raise that sleep pressure again, making sure to tune in to your baby. Sometimes early bedtimes are great, especially if your baby is in an overtired cycle, but these are meant to be a short-term solution. We cannot expect our babies or toddlers to sleep more than ten to twelve hours overnight, so their split night may be a result of their getting nine to ten hours of sleep (especially if you have a low-sleep-total baby) and waking up after they get that.

Another strategy, after you've looked at daytime sleep, is the faded bedtime. Essentially, you move bedtime later, and thereby shorten the night, until the split night disappears, and then you gradually extend the night again. Start by shifting bedtime later each night by fifteen minutes. To get the bedtime later, you may need to experiment with daytime naps—perhaps add a catnap (even if that means it's a fifteen-minute stroller nap) at the end of the day; extend the wake windows slightly, especially if you're moving that last nap of the day later; or try to extend the nap lengths by doing motion naps, contact naps, or nursing back to sleep.

These are short-term solutions while you're working on condensing the nighttime sleep to eliminate the split night. While moving the bedtime later, you'll also need to start waking your baby fifteen minutes earlier each day, which will help to condense that night even more. This strategy will usually take between five and seven days to start working. Try to follow your baby's natural rhythms and guide them through the changes.

## EARLY RISING

Having a baby who wakes up early is exhausting and one of the most common reasons that families look for sleep support. Early waking is usually considered any time before 6:00 a.m. Some people are naturally early risers and are okay with starting the day that early, while for others this is way too early and they don't function well.

You may have heard of the concept of chronotypes, but in case you haven't, here are the basics. Your chronotype is closely related to your circadian rhythm and is the natural inclination of your body to sleep at a certain time—in other words, whether you're an early bird or a night owl. Your chronotype is relatively permanent, though it may change slightly throughout your lifespan as your circadian rhythm and hormones change. Toddlers tend to prefer earlier mornings while teenagers lean more toward the late evenings. As we enter older adulthood, this again shifts to an early-morning preference.

In the early hours of the morning, usually between two and six, our cortisol levels start to increase (and our melatonin levels decrease) as our bodies get us ready to wake up. Sleep pressure is much lower at this time because of the many hours of sleep that have happened. And then of course the sun starts to rise, which triggers the circadian rhythm. All these things are at play with early rising, and though we can try to nudge later waking, sometimes it's not possible. Along with these biological processes, overtiredness can play a role in early rising. Overtiredness can cause false starts, frequent wakes overnight, and early rising due to increased cortisol levels. As well, if the first nap of the day is too early (e.g., before 8:30 a.m.), this can reinforce early rising. Developmental progressions or leaps are also a time when early rising can happen, though these are generally phases that last only two or three weeks. The changing of seasons and daylight savings time can also impact early rising because of the changes in the environment (e.g., the room isn't dark enough, or there's a drastic temperature change and your baby isn't dressed appropriately). Put on your detective hat!

"Okay, Kaili, I get it, but what can I *do* about early rising?"

Unfortunately there's no magic solution, but there are various parent-led strategies you can try, to encourage sleeping past 6:00 a.m.

## STRATEGY: REVERSE SLEEP-IN

The easiest way to cope with early wakings is to adjust your own life (much easier than forcing your child to sleep later). Consider going to bed an hour or two earlier at night so that you don't feel so exhausted because of your early starts.

## STRATEGY: CONSIDER THE ENVIRONMENT

I highly recommend considering the sleep environment around the time (or just before) your baby is waking up. Is there a loud vehicle that drives by in the morning? Can you hear the traffic of the day starting? Does the heat kick in, making the room warmer? Perhaps a sliver of light is poking through the curtains. (Blackout blinds can help, but they aren't a magic solution for everybody.) Also think about your child's diet and rule out any tummy issues, as well as skin rashes and eczema, which can act up at night and be especially noticeable in the early-morning hours when we spend more time in light sleep.

## STRATEGY: SPECIAL MORNING TOYS

One of the first things I recommend to parents, especially those with toddlers who are early risers, is to create a special box of quiet toys that your child can play with either in their room or in yours until your preferred wake-up time. This strategy will take some time to implement, but with consistency it will become part of your child's routine. You may have to set boundaries around this morning playtime. For example, they have to play quietly by themselves on the floor of your room and not jump on Mommy and Daddy and ask them to play. Pretend to be asleep and keep things in night mode as much as possible.

You can also start to teach toddlers (usually eighteen months and older) the concept of a wake-up time with a Gro Clock, or something of the sort. Teach them to stay in bed (or in their room) until the sun comes out on the clock. Initially, you may have to set the clock to only about fifteen minutes after their normal wake-up time. Then you can slowly move it later and later every few days until you get to a wake-up time you're comfortable with.

## STRATEGY: WORK WITH THE CIRCADIAN RHYTHM

In the morning, have a *very* dramatic wake-up. Fling open the curtains, say a cheery "good morning" (I know it will be hard, but take a deep breath and put on your best smile), and start your day. Initially, you'll do this when your child wakes up (assuming you can't get them back to sleep). Then you can move it by fifteen minutes or so every few days. So if your child is waking at 5:00 a.m., you may have to start the dramatic wake-up at 5:00 a.m., then 5:15 a.m., then 5:30 a.m., until you get to your ideal wake-up time. (Truthfully, this will likely still not be as late as you want. It takes about seven to ten days to shift the circadian rhythm.) At first, your child may not actually be asleep this whole time, but you'll want to keep everything in night mode (dark, calm, quiet) until the dramatic wake-up time. This works well with the faded bedtime strategy.

## STRATEGY: FADED BEDTIME

I discussed this strategy in detail earlier in the chapter. The idea is to use your child's total sleep hours overnight to move the wake time in the morning. Only use this strategy if your child is having early wakes because of too much sleep versus too little in a twenty-four-hour period because if they're already overtired, this strategy will most likely backfire. You may have to add a catnap in the late afternoon or early evening, otherwise you run the risk of a wake window that's too long before bed, which can lead to overtiredness and make the nights and mornings even harder. As you gradually move the bedtime back to a more reasonable time, you can also drop the catnap.

## STRATEGY: EARLY BEDTIME

If your child is overtired and waking because there's too much cortisol running through their bloodstream at the end of the day, an early bedtime might be the key to creating a later wake-up time. I know this might seem odd, but children are affected by overtiredness more than adults and, as mentioned, get into a wired state that makes it difficult to go to sleep and stay asleep. So an earlier bedtime may help reset their system. How early will depend on your child's age and when their last nap of the day was. The gap between the last nap and bedtime should be no longer than their maximum wake interval. If they can go only three hours without getting overtired during the day, make sure that they're in bed and asleep by the three-hour mark at bedtime as well. If you're running into the issue of your child becoming overtired before 5:30 or 6:00 p.m. (I don't recommend a bedtime earlier than this), the solution might be a catnap and then a slightly later bedtime. The key is to try to prevent the overtiredness that can happen with a long wake window before bed.

## STRATEGY: WAKE TO SLEEP

This involves setting an alarm for yourself and gently rousing your baby *before* they usually wake up for the day. If your baby is waking up at 5:30 a.m., you'd go in at 5:15 or even 5:00. After rousing them (just slightly) out of sleep, you then resettle them. The idea is to get them to enter a new sleep cycle and sleep a bit longer. Every three or four days, go in about fifteen minutes later. Once you reach the ideal wake-up time (remember, we can't expect more than ten to twelve hours of overnight sleep for our little ones), do a dramatic wake-up. It's very possible that your child will fully wake up when you rouse them. If this happens, do your best to settle them back to sleep, or have a special box of toys that they can play with in the dark until your ideal wake-up. You may want to play around with the timing of when you wake them and how gently you rouse them. Follow your instincts. Don't be afraid to experiment.

Making any adjustments to your baby's sleep, especially when dealing with early rising, will require a series of parent-led changes. You'll also need to tune in to your baby's natural rhythm and give them the chance to adjust to the changes before assessing whether they've worked. It can take up to three weeks, or sometimes even more, to change a person's circadian rhythm, and your child's temperament and reaction to change will also be factors.

# NAPTIME AND BEDTIME BATTLES

Children often fight naptime or bedtime because they aren't tired enough or they're overtired. Both are somewhat-easy fixes that simply require some experimentation with wake windows. Generally, a baby's or toddler's wake window will extend about fifteen minutes every three or so weeks, as their sleep-pressure needs change. Watching their tired cues while also trying to lengthen their awake time can really help reduce these sleep-time battles.

Consider your own energy and ability to co-regulate. If you hate naptime or bedtime because you're exhausted trying to get your baby to sleep, you might be feeling frustrated, exasperated, and angry. Your baby will pick up on this energy and learn that bedtime is stressful—and stress is viewed by our primitive brain as not safe. Think about what makes you feel calm, relaxed, and ready for sleep and then think about what energy you're bringing to naptime and bedtime with your baby. With my first, I'm sure that my anxiety contributed to my struggles!

Sometimes children, especially highly sensitive ones, may just need more time in the dark to wind down and be quiet and calm. Consider whether your sleep associations are overstimulating. I'd bounce my son for hours each night to get him to fall asleep in my arms. It wasn't working for either of us and, in hindsight, was likely overstimulating him. After I reached out for support, I made a change. I would nurse, bounce for five minutes, and then stop and just hold him while still sitting on the ball for a few minutes. Then I'd put him to bed. There were tears initially because of the change, but in a few days my back was much happier, as was my baby. We eventually removed the ball completely, replacing it with a rocking chair (more comfortable). We also built in other sleep associations—reading in the rocking chair then nursing in the chair as I sang and rocked. When he was done nursing, I stopped singing and just rocked for another few minutes and then he went into bed. After we did this for about three weeks consistently, bedtime started to become more manageable, and dare I say enjoyable. This is possible for you too, I promise!

A few other things might lead to bedtime battles: nutritional imbalances (low iron or magnesium), which can cause restlessness and difficulty falling asleep; breathing-related issues or reflux, especially while they're lying flat on their back; and physical discomfort. I talk more about specific strategies for bedtime battles with toddlers in Chapters Three and Sixteen. Bedtime battles tend to happen more frequently with toddlers due to nighttime separation and the connection piece, so if you have a toddler, revisit those chapters.

# Chapter Twenty-Three

# SLEEP INTERRUPTERS

Children evolve and grow. That means there will be bumps in the road along the way. Teething, digestive issues, illness, travel, daylight savings time, family changes, and your returning to work, among many other interrupters, can all affect your baby's sleep. Know that it's okay to respond to and support your baby through these interrupters and then get back on track with your normal rhythms, routines, and boundaries.

## TEETHING

Teething can be so challenging, and it's frequently the scapegoat for everything in the first two years—frequent wakes, fussiness, clinginess, drooling, changes in sleep patterns, and so much more. And while teething can be a factor in these things, it's often not always the cause, or the primary cause.

Your baby was born with all twenty primary teeth below their gumline. The teeth don't cut through the gums, as you might assume. It's actually the gums that break apart to allow the teeth to erupt and move through. Baby teeth can come through as early as a few months after birth (my son had his first two teeth by four and a half months), but many babies don't have teeth until they are six to twelve months old (my daughter didn't get any teeth until she was one and then got a whole bunch at once). Teething continues well into toddlerhood. Usually by age three your child will have their full set of baby (milk) teeth.

Teething happens in stages, and each stage is usually about eight days. There's controversy around what symptoms are related to teething and whether those symptoms have any effect on sleep. In my experience with my kids and working with many mamas, I can confidently say that teething presents a variety of symptoms that can negatively impact sleep. My kids experienced diarrhea, gum irritation and swelling, and low-grade fevers. A friend of mine knew when her son was teething because he'd always get a runny nose and a rash on his cheeks and mouth. Some children gnaw and chew on everything, nurse nonstop, or go on a nursing strike. There's also the possibility of tummy discomfort from the changes in the body's pH levels due to the increased salivation that can happen during teething. Let's also remember that nighttime is mostly distraction free, so it's easier to pay attention to the discomfort of teething—and if you've ever had a toothache, you know that it gets worse when you're lying down because the pressure in your head increases (at least it does for me!). These symptoms have shown up in various studies as well. Is teething miserable for all babies? Definitely not. Does it cause every problem with sleep? Also no.

The other thing to remember is that if your baby is more sensitive, has sensory processing differences, or is just more high needs in general, they may be more affected by the discomfort of teething and may actually experience it as excruciating pain because their nervous system is just that much more sensitive.

## TEETHING TIPS

### 1.  Cold

Teething toys, cold washcloth, or cold food (i.e., cucumber, frozen banana, etc.), breast-milk ice cubes in a mesh feeder, or even frozen breast-milk Q-tips. Put teething toys or a wet washcloth into the freezer to make them cold and then let baby chew on them to relieve the discomfort. Freeze some Q-tips soaked in breast milk and then rub directly on gums, or put your breast milk into the ice cube tray and let baby suck on the cubes for some relief (and the bonus of nutrition).

### 2.  Homeopathic remedies

Things like Camilia drops can work wonders for your baby. Make sure to read and follow the instructions on the package (I learned that the hard way and assumed it was just one vial per time when in fact it was three vials each time). Be careful of the ones with benzocaine in them, as it is not great for babies.

### 3.  Essential oils

We swear by Copaiba in my house (it is seriously amazing and so gentle for babies) and is great with helping to relieve pain and inflammation. Lavender can also be soothing on the jawline. Clove oil can also help, but it is a stronger oil and therefore would need to be much more heavily diluted than Copaiba or Lavender. Valerian is another great option to ease irritability and may also afford temporary pain relief (please see the Gentle, Natural Tools in Your Mama Toolbox chapter for more specifics on essential oil use with babies and kids). You need to use essential oils and homeopathic remedies in general more frequently than you would regular medicine, as they get absorbed and processed in the body faster (or you can use the actual herb if they are plants, though they won't be as potent).

**4.  Amber necklaces/anklets**

This is a controversial one, but hey, so are many other things in the sleep and baby world. The theory is that when amber is worn against the skin, the warmth of the skin allows the amber to release trace amounts of the succinic acid, providing the analgesic and anti-inflammatory properties to the wearer. These necklaces (or anklets) are NOT meant to be chewed on and should be appropriately sized for your baby so that they cannot get it into their mouths. Amber is used and has been used for thousands of years in European countries with good success. For me personally, these worked wonderfully for both my babies, and I noticed a significant reduction in drooling and fussiness when they wore them regularly. But this choice is one you need to make on your own.

**5.  Medication**

For me, this is a choice that I use as a last resort, and please be careful if you label all fussiness, crying, night wakings and such as teething, because overdoing medications like Tylenol or Advil can really wreak havoc on our bodies, and our babies are even smaller with less mature detoxifying systems. So I highly recommend you only use this option when you have tried everything else and your baby is still in pain. And of course, make sure to talk to your doctor about dosing and frequency of use.

# DIGESTIVE ISSUES

A newborn's digestive system is immature, not fully functional, and quite vulnerable to infection. In the first six months, your baby has what's often referred to as an "open gut," which means that the small intestine allows larger molecules to pass directly into the bloodstream. As the digestive system matures, it gradually develops the ability to produce enzymes to digest food and antibodies to protect itself.

Sometimes babies take in too much air while feeding (poor latch, weak suck, or bobbing on/off the breast or bottle). If you're breast-feeding, I highly recommend seeing an IBCLC to check your baby's tongue and tongue function, latch, and feeding position. If you're bottle-feeding, make sure you're using the correct-sized bottle and nipple and are doing paced bottle-feeding.

Certain foods traveling through breast milk can lead to gassiness or constipation. Dairy can cause inflammation and congestion as well as issues with gas and constipation. In fact, a UK study revealed that in a group of thirteen-month-olds who were waking often at night for no apparent reason, most slept significantly better when they were taken off cow's milk and milk products.[39] Eggs, gluten, soy, and corn are other big culprits. I always recommend getting assistance from a naturopath, dietician, or nutritionist to help you sort out any food allergies or sensitivities.

Gassy babies often want to suck because it helps to soothe them in the short term. This can be misinterpreted as rooting and still being hungry. And if you feed them more and they don't need it, this can lead to more pressure in the belly, leading to gas, constipation, reflux, and bloating, all of which are very uncomfortable for baby and can lead to more crying, which then leads to more air being taken in. It's a negative cycle.

If your baby is very gassy, it's a good idea to get into the habit of burping them a few times during the feed, whether they're breast-fed or bottle-fed, especially in the first four to six months. If your baby falls asleep during a feed, don't worry too much about burping them, as you don't want to wake them up just to burp. What you can do instead is put your baby's chin over your right shoulder and position their body diagonally across your chest, so their bum and legs are toward your left side. Then gently lean back. There's no need to pat your baby on their back or bum in this position if you don't want to. Just stay leaned back for a few minutes. This will allow any air bubbles that might be stuck to come out.

If baby is crying or uncomfortable, even after you've tried to burp them, gently tilt their chin up, give them a warm bath, lay them on their back and hold up their feet to help air escape, massage their belly, or cycle their feet (hold baby underneath their knees and drive the knees toward the belly button and not out to the side, which is a great hip stretch but does nothing for the stomach).

The introduction of solids can also increase gas and constipation, especially if the introduction happens before your baby's digestive system is ready to handle them. As I discussed in the feeding section, babies don't have all the digestive enzymes that adults do. If they're eating too many foods their body cannot handle or too close to bedtime, they might experience poor digestion. Undigested food can cause unpleasant reactions, such as stomach upset, gas, and constipation, all of which can lead to discomfort, hormonal changes (more on this shortly), and ultimately poor sleep. Think about it—if you eat a large meal immediately before going to bed, digestion continues while you're asleep. As a result, you may wake up with heartburn, indigestion, acid reflux, constipation, or other unpleasant, sleep-disrupting symptoms. This can happen to babies and toddlers too, especially those who have reflux and/or are eating solids that might not be agreeing with their bodies. If your baby has food intolerances or allergies, these will further aggravate things.

Digestive issues can lead to hormonal changes, which can then affect sleep. Remember that the body maintains a delicate balance of hormones and chemicals that cycle through the body each day. Two of the primary hormones that affect sleep are melatonin and cortisol. Serotonin, a precursor of melatonin, is found mostly in the gut. Digestive issues can harm serotonin, preventing it from being converted to melatonin. When that happens, melatonin production drops and cortisol levels increase.

Luckily, there are things we can do to help. Be conscious of your baby's diet and your own (if you're breast-feeding) or of what's in the formula. Chocolate, dairy, caffeine, and foods that contain phytic acid (found on the surface of most grains, nuts, seeds, and beans) can cause tummy troubles for infants. For older babies on solids, think back to see if their sleep problems worsened after a new food was introduced. By process of elimination, experiment to see if removing a particular food helps their digestion and sleep.

## FOOD ALLERGIES

Food allergies are on the rise among children. It's estimated that 6 million children under eighteen suffer from food allergies, which is double what it was in 2007.[40] Sleep challenges can be a side effect of food allergies and sensitivities, especially daytime drowsiness, sluggishness, or "brain fog" or inability to focus, as well as difficulty falling asleep and staying asleep at naptime and bedtime. It's hard to relax and fall asleep when you have a bloated belly, gas, indigestion, or reflux/heartburn. Food allergies and sensitivities can also cause other problems, such as ear infections, that lead to sleeplessness. Food sensitivities sometimes have delayed reactions, so your child may not necessarily show any symptoms for hours or even a day or two after eating a particular food.

## ILLNESS

If your baby is sick, they might need more comforting, attention, and nursing. This is totally normal, so please do whatever you need to take care of your little one and help them feel better. Knowing that they are safe, secure, and can count on you is so important for building secure attachment and for your child's development. You might be worried that the increased attention will get you off track or reverse some of the work you've already done around your baby's sleep, but try not to stress out about this. Think about yourself when you're sick—all you want to do is curl up somewhere nice and warm, maybe have your partner bring you some tea. This helps you feel calm, comforted, and held. It's the same for our babies.

Yes, sleep will be different during this time (you'll likely get less of it as you comfort your sick child at night more frequently). It's common for babies to need *more* sleep (both day and night) when they're fighting an infection. Allow them to nap longer, go to bed earlier, and sleep in longer—in other words, put your normal rhythms, routines, and loving boundaries on hold. Do whatever you need to get through until your baby feels better. It's only temporary! After a few days, when your baby is back to their healthy, energetic self, you can get back on track. The return to pre-illness rhythms, routines, and loving boundaries often happens faster than you might think.

## TRAVEL

Travel can be challenging, especially for more-sensitive babies, but it's likely a bigger deal for us adults than for most babies. On average, it takes your body one day to adjust for every hour of time difference you experience, but it's believed that babies adjust faster than that. It's also believed that acclimating to a new time zone is harder when traveling east because going east requires falling asleep earlier than you normally would, which is usually difficult from a biological standpoint (our circadian rhythm is strong and loves consistency). On the other hand, flying west requires you to stay up later, which is usually easier for adults but may not be as easy for our babies and could lead to overtiredness. Follow your baby's cues and try your best to go with the flow.

Before making any adjustments, consider how long you'll be traveling for. If you're only going to be away for one week and you're crossing three time zones or fewer, keep your baby on the same schedule if possible. If you'll be in a time zone that's significantly different, or you're going for a longer time, you can shift bedtime and naps by fifteen minutes a day for one to two weeks before traveling. You can also use daylight and darkness to your advantage. Rather than shifting your baby's schedule gradually, simply adjust your baby on the first full day in the new location by getting them up at their normal wake-up time in the morning and exposing them to bright sunlight. Do your best to keep your baby up and exposed to light until the appropriate naptimes and bedtime in the new time zone.

For example, if you arrive in the day and your baby thinks it's night, keep doing naps until it's nighttime in the place you're visiting rather than letting your baby sleep for hours and hours. If you want to plan your travel around the direction you're flying, the suggestion is to travel later in the day when flying east, so your baby will be ready for bed as soon as you get there. When traveling west, the suggestion is to fly in the morning and allow only one or two naps, depending on the age of your baby, in the afternoon when you arrive. Put your child to bed at the usual time. Although it will feel early, your baby likely missed a nap, so this should work.

Bring as much of the child's sleep environment as you can—crib sheets, white noise machine, lovey, sleep sack, etc.—to make it as similar to home as possible. Familiar and predictable will help your baby feel safer amid all the other changes. If you're not sleeping in a hotel, I recommend packing travel blackout blinds, a dark sheet you can hang on the window, or even black garbage bags, which you can tape to the window. Darkness makes the body shift into sleep faster. And don't forget that exposure to lots of sunlight while away is key. Use the carrier and stroller to get in your baby's naps. Busy days and lots of fresh air will help. It adjusts the circadian rhythm and allows the body to control the wake-sleep cycles.

Remember that no matter how well prepared you are and how much planning you've done, traveling and experiencing a new environment can be very overwhelming for a baby. The more stress and tension that you create around travel, the worse it will be for your baby—and you! If you're traveling for a vacation, you'll want to rest, relax, and enjoy.

# DAYLIGHT SAVINGS

Once you have children, you inevitably start to curse daylight savings time. It throws yet another curveball in the joy of parenting. And if your child already doesn't sleep that well, this is an especially hard time of year. While most of us don't love to "spring forward," as it means losing an hour of sleep, pre-kids, we loved to "fall back."

Unfortunately, this is usually no longer the case post-kids. Children are much more in tune with their internal rhythms, and their circadian rhythm doesn't change just because we change the time on our clocks. Often, "falling back" means extra-early rising for children. A quick strategy is to assume your baby or toddler will get up at their usual time (which will look early on the clock) and go to bed earlier yourself the night before. If you find that easier said than done, here are my top-five tips for making this transition a bit easier for everyone.

1.  **Use light and darkness to your advantage**. Our circadian rhythm is largely regulated by light and darkness, which help our body to produce the necessary hormones to help us stay awake (cortisol) and go to sleep (melatonin). Keep the lights off for an extra fifteen minutes each morning and the lights on for an extra fifteen minutes at bedtime.

2.   **Adjust your schedule**. If you have a baby under six months and/or an easygoing baby, you may not have to do anything—lucky you! Some children don't seem to be affected by it at all, and for babies under six months, I usually don't recommend schedules. Instead, focus on following baby's tired cues (using wake windows as a guide) to make sure they don't get overtired. Usually you can go with the flow and let their bodies (and routines) adjust naturally. Most babies will adapt to a one-hour time change on their own within a couple of weeks. The "go with the flow" method is what still works for our family. The idea of scheduling and planning for the time change is much too stressful for me, so I don't. This is the beauty of doing motherhood your way!

If scheduling and planning helps you feel more prepared, then adjusting your schedule in preparation for the time change can do wonders, especially for babies over six months. You can do this in one of two ways.

A) About four to six days before the time change, start moving bedtime forward by ten to fifteen minutes each night (if your baby is very sensitive or has other sensory processing differences, you may need to go with every two to three nights) until you reach that hour. Daily routines and activities will also need to be adjusted by ten to fifteen minutes.

B) If the idea of working on this for a whole week is overwhelming, do this the weekend of the time change. Adjust each wake window by fifteen minutes throughout the day, which will also push bedtime (and ideally wake-up time the next morning).

3.  **Continue (or create) a consistent, relaxing pre-bed routine**. Keeping your regular bedtime routine as consistent as possible is so important, as it helps to cue your baby that sleep is coming. For babies over six months, it's best to have them wake up at the same time every day (which will eventually lead to a consistent bedtime too), including on weekends. For babies under six months, don't worry too much about the consistent bedtime/wake time and follow their tired cues. As part of the bedtime routine, choose things that you also enjoy and will help to relax you—maybe warm bath, lotion massage, diaper change, PJs, sleep sack, and nursing. This signals that it's time to relax, unwind, and prepare for sleep.

4.  **Be kind to yourself and your baby**. Change is hard, and shifting a child's circadian rhythm takes time. It may be a couple of weeks before everyone is back to normal. Know that during the transition, there may be more fussiness, clinginess, overtiredness, and meltdowns or bedtime battles. Our children co-regulate with us, so if we can stay calm, they have a better chance of staying calm. Self-care will help everyone get through.

5.  **Ask for help**! Navigating sleep during any kind of change can be difficult. I know that the struggle is real! Ask for help from your partner, family, and friends, and reach out for professional support if you need it. The time change in March is often easier than the one in November for kids. You may not need to do anything, and if your child is waking up too early before this time change, it might even help to encourage sleeping longer. If your baby or toddler is on the more-sensitive side and gets overtired easily, gradually shifting their whole day *earlier* by fifteen minutes each

day can help. Many of the strategies I mentioned above will work, and even though your child will likely sleep a little later, you may still want to go to bed at your usual time, otherwise you could end up losing some sleep.

## SIBLINGS SHARING A ROOM

Some families may want or need a baby and a toddler to share a room. This was my situation. We had a two-bedroom apartment, so we transitioned my daughter into sharing a room with my son when she was nine months old (he was three years old). It worked beautifully. Not right away, but still much better than I initially expected, and both children adapted well within about three weeks. They've developed a strong bond and love sharing a room to this day, even though we now have more space and they could have separate rooms if they wanted.

Babies and toddlers will adapt to almost anything with consistency and time. Siblings will get used to each other. Before starting this room-sharing, though, it's important to address each child's sleep challenges in their current location so that they're sleeping for longer stretches. If your six-month-old is struggling to sleep for more than two hours, or the toddler is waking up a lot at night, moving them into the same room is only going to mean less sleep for everyone, unless you decide to bed-share with one of them. When I transitioned my daughter into sharing a room with her brother, she was waking up about three times at night and it worked fine. My son was sleeping through the night, and though he'd wake a little when I came in to feed my daughter, he'd go back to sleep easily with a little hug and a kiss on the cheek.

Though you can choose when you want to transition your baby into sharing a room with a sibling, the Safe Sleep guidelines advise having baby in your room for the first six to twelve months. It's often helpful to wait until your youngest is sleeping for three- to four-hour chunks, if time and space allow for this option. And don't forget, making changes and forming new habits takes time. Your children will need to get used to sharing the space. I also found that a joint bedtime and bedtime routine works best for my children (at least it has for the past four years). But you ultimately decide what works best for your children, which may depend on their ages as well.

## RETURNING TO WORK

Your return to work is often a hard transition for both you and baby. There are many changes to prepare for. Who will be taking care of your baby? Will they be at home with another caregiver (your partner, a grandparent, or a nanny)? Will they be at a daycare in a center or in a home-care situation? Will they be going a few days a week or the whole week? Full days or half days? In an ideal world you'll have a few weeks to practice the transition and get your baby used to (and familiar with) their new caregiver and the setting. Initially, you may want to be in the new setting with the other caregiver while your baby is getting used to the environment, if possible. If this isn't possible, perhaps you can leave your baby for an hour or two the first day then shift to half a day and then the whole day. The more gradual the process, the easier it will be.

That said, emotions will likely arise with this change. Remember that tears in and of themselves aren't bad. What's important is to make sure that your child is being supported and comforted in a loving way when they're expressing their emotions. This is something you may want to talk to your new caregiver about.

You'll also want to be aware of your own energy in the time leading up to your return to work. In general, children are open, energetic beings who are sensitive to the energies around them. This means that they'll feel your energy around this big transition. If you have any doubts, anxieties, sadness, or worries, your baby will pick up on those. They'll also sense how confident you feel with their new caregiver. Do your best to exude confidence that the caregiver you chose will take good care of your child and support them whenever they need. Tell your child that you are going to miss them but that you can't wait to see them at the end of the day. I'm not suggesting you mask your true feelings—just be conscious of what you're projecting to the world and your baby.

One way to make the separation easier is to have a transitional object, such as a lovey, a blanket, or even a laminated picture of your family, that your child can keep with them throughout the day. My children's loveys were their best friends when they went to childcare. During the transition phase and naps, they were allowed to hold their loveys, but for the remainder of the day their loveys stayed in their backpacks as per the daycare rules (but they could go and give them quick hugs as needed). This worked well for us, but remember, I started building that attachment to the loveys when they were around four or five months old—it takes time!

This change in routine will mean that you and your baby have less time together during the day. This can result in clinginess, fussiness, and bed-time battles, and it may mean more frequent wakes overnight initially. This is because they miss you and need that connection to restore order to the relationship. Make sure to carve out some moments for special connection when you get home from work and before bed, so that you can fill your child's "love cup." Be fully engaged and present during this time (it doesn't have to be long—even fifteen minutes is great!): put your phone away and don't be doing chores. You'll want to bridge the separation overnight as well, as I discussed earlier in the sleep section.

If you're breast-feeding, make plans to ensure the new caregiver has your breast milk, and practice bottle-feeding with your baby beforehand. You'll also need to think about where you can pump during the day while you're at work, and get yourself the proper equipment for that.

A lot of mamas who are planning their return to work ask me about naps, sleep location, and support falling asleep. Many are nursing to sleep and either holding their baby for all or some naps and worry that their babies won't sleep without these associations in the new environment. Know that your baby will get used to whatever the new process is for sleeping. Yes, there will be a time of transition, and it may take a few weeks for your baby to get some quality naps in, but it will happen. You can let your childcare provider know how your baby likes to fall asleep at home, but also trust that they do this day in and day out and have their own methods and sleep cues that work too. Trust your caregiver and trust your baby! Sometimes sending in familiar crib sheets or even their white noise machine can help them feel safe, which may make sleep come more easily.

## A NEW BABY

If you have a child who isn't sleeping through the night and you're wanting to have or are already expecting another baby, you likely have questions and worries. You're most likely wondering how in the world you'll ever sleep when you have two or more children who aren't sleeping through the night.

A new baby is a lot to get used to for everyone involved, but especially for the soon-to-be older sibling. Helping your toddler prepare for the change ahead of time and involving them in the transition and with the new baby can often work wonders. Think about whether you want to make any big changes to your toddler's sleep (sleep location, how you support them back to sleep at night, etc.) either a few months before the birth of your new baby or a few months after. It's never a good idea to make lots of changes at the same time, and having a new baby in the house (and sharing the attention) is going to be a big change in and of itself.

If you're currently supporting your toddler to sleep and back to sleep at night, can you start involving your partner? Ideally, work toward someone else supporting your older child back to sleep at night so that you can focus on taking care of your new baby. Many families end up using floor beds for this purpose. One parent sleeps with the older child in one room while the other parent sleeps with the newborn in another room. This often allows everyone to get more sleep initially. Of course, this isn't always feasible. You'll have to determine what works best for your family.

If your older child is used to bed-sharing with you and you aren't able to put another adult-sized mattress in another room, transitioning your older child to a new sleep location before or after baby arrives is often the way to go, remembering that this will take time and consistency. It can be helpful to have a small floor bed in your room for your older child to use when they need it (e.g., if they wake up at night and need to feel safe and comforted but it isn't safe for them to climb into your bed because of the new baby). My son was almost two and a half when my daughter was born, and he was sleeping in his own crib in his own room (just across the hall) at that point. He was still waking up at night on occasion, so my husband would go in to support him. This worked well because we put the new strategy in place before my daughter was born.

Jealousy is another thing to consider when preparing for a new baby. It's totally normal for the older sibling to be jealous, and there are a few things you can do to help. You can read books about becoming a big brother or sister and about bringing home a new baby, and you can talk about what life will look like when the new baby arrives. You can also get your older child involved by getting them to read stories, sing songs, show pictures, or talk about their day to the baby in your belly. Maybe they can help you decide on the outfit the new baby will wear home, or choose a special gift to give the new baby. I knew my son cherished his monkey lovey, so I had him help me pick out a lovey to gift his baby sister. Then he helped me wrap it with a gift bag and tissue paper that he chose. When we brought my daughter home from the hospital, my son gave her the gift and also helped her open it. It was a very special moment, and each time she cried, I'd ask him to find the lovey and bring it to her. Eventually, he started doing this on his own.

To alleviate his jealousy, we'd also have him help with other things. I'd ask him to get me a diaper, choose a book to read all together, help me bathe her, and so on. When my daughter got older, I started asking my son to show her how to do tummy time and how to roll, and he even started helping her roll at times (he pulled on her hips one day while she was in tummy time and flipped her over—super cute, after my initial OMG moment).

Because I knew that jealousy often results from feeling less connected, less special, less important, I also made sure that he got some special one-on-one dates with my husband or me—a ride on the streetcar, a treat at a coffee shop, or even just a trip to the park. It worked well! And then at bed-time, he and I would have one-on-one time while my husband took care of the baby. We'd have tickle fights and play peekaboo in our bed, which was a fun place for him to be. All these strategies worked well to mitigate some of the stress and jealousy that can result from a change in routine. Baby-wearing my daughter for much of the day made my life easier at home with a toddler as well!

Many of these strategies will work for you too. Remember to put yourself in your older child's shoes and think about how they must be feeling now that they're no longer getting all the attention. It's a lot for a child to process. If your older child is acting in ways that suggest they don't like their sibling, know that they aren't intending to be mean or hurtful. They're reacting to all the change, which is scary. Do your best to put some strategies in place and make some special time with your older child to let them know they're still loved (and that they have a lot to teach their younger sibling).

Phew! This was an intense and full section because sleep is one of the biggest "pain points" of motherhood. Try not to get frustrated. Almost all children eventually sleep better. Those who continue to struggle usually have an underlying problem or condition.

Most of all, remember that the support you're offering your child isn't why they're struggling with sleep. In fact, it's likely exactly what your child needs.

*Section Four*

# MAMA TOOLS

Now that you know more about your child's brain, development, feeding, sleep, and more, I want to shift gears and focus on you. You matter too, Mama!

All too often our society is focused solely on the baby. We so rarely ask the parents how they're doing—how they're coping with the nights, or the feeds, or their fears. While my work is primarily focused on helping you feel more confident when it comes to your baby, I also care about you! I want to make motherhood a little less stressful and a little more enjoyable for you.

The next two chapters are meant to help you realize that taking care of yourself isn't selfish but necessary. That asking for help isn't a sign of weakness but a sign of strength. I also want to arm you with additional tools (many of which are free and easy to use) that can help you on your motherhood journey.

# Chapter Twenty-Four

# YOU MATTER TOO, MAMA

We enter motherhood having some idea of the tasks associated with this new season of life. We know we'll be changing diapers, feeding our baby, dressing them, etc. But it's hard to imagine just how much there is to think about in regards to being a parent.

Keeping a mental tally of which breast you last nursed on, what size in each specific brand of clothing fits your baby the best and what size they'll need for the next season, when to buy more diapers and wipes before the next blowout, when your baby is due for their checkups, what are the best first foods for your baby and how to introduce them, what motor milestones your baby should be hitting at each age, how long their wake windows should be . . . it's a lot. Never mind what's for dinner!

There's just so much to keep track of. This is the mental load of motherhood. The invisible workload that we have as mamas (and as women in general) plays a big role in our mental health and well-being.

And then we ping-pong from feelings of euphoria and joy to anxiety and overwhelm and back again, not to mention the feelings of loss regarding the life you previously had, perhaps served with a side of guilt because you wanted this baby so how can you love this baby while also mourning your pre-baby life?

It's totally normal to love motherhood and also to struggle with it. You are not alone.

## MAMA MENTAL HEALTH

Your mental health is an important piece of your motherhood journey. Many new mamas develop something called "the baby blues" following their baby's birth. Baby blues are common and can last for up to two weeks. The symptoms include mood swings, crying spells, irritability, loss of appetite, decreased concentration, and trouble sleeping. These are due to the hormonal changes and the psychological upheaval of becoming a new parent. The baby blues are temporary and treatable. It's important to get support and help getting back to a routine.

When the symptoms last longer than two weeks and are more intense, and eventually interfere with a mother's ability to care for baby and handle other daily tasks, it's usually postpartum depression or postpartum mood and anxiety disorder (PMAD). PMAD affects approximately one in five women and one in ten men—yes, dads can suffer from postpartum mood disorders. PMAD is likely under-reported, and only about 15 percent of mothers seek professional treatment.[1,2]

It's important to realize that PMAD can develop any time during the first year, and often occurs after about three months, so just because you were fine at your six-week postpartum visit doesn't mean you're coping well now. Often we don't even realize we have it, largely due to the stigma and lack of resources.

PMAD can happen due to physical reasons, such as a genetic predisposition or a sensitivity to hormonal changes, or psychosocial factors, such as inadequate support (remember, we were never meant to raise our babies in isolation but to give birth and raise them in a community) or feeling as if you have to be Supermom. It can also be due to concurrent stressors, such as sleep disruption, poor nutrition, health challenges, interpersonal stress, and cultural stress and barriers. Many of these things occur easily in the first year of motherhood. This is why taking care of your mental health is just as important as getting sleep when you need it and eating a diet filled with nutritious food and plenty of water.

Other health issues can have symptoms similar to PMAD symptoms, so it's important to rule these out. Low iron can lead to restless sleep (for your baby too, if you're breast-feeding) and difficulty staying asleep. Thyroid and pituitary imbalances can often mimic depression or anxiety—you might feel hot and sweaty, have difficulty sleeping, and have issues making milk. Often the side effects of medications (e.g., those to increase milk supply) can include anxiety. And then there are the effects of unresolved trauma from a traumatic pregnancy or birth experience or of post-traumatic stress disorder from something entirely different. Alcohol and drug use can also lead to many of the same symptoms as PMAD.

Screening is important, as is tuning in to what your gut is telling you. Don't feel guilty or embarrassed about any negative feelings or thoughts that may arise. Much of the time we don't even recognize that what we're feeling is depression—we just feel as if we're failing. You might be experiencing panic attacks or having trouble sleeping and eating. Or you might be angry a lot of the time for no apparent reason.

# EXPECTED AND UNEXPECTED SYMPTOMS OF PMAD

| EXPECTED | UNEXPECTED |
|---|---|
| • Sadness, crying jags | • Agitation and anxiety |
| • Feeling overwhelmed | • Anger, rage |
| • Irritability, agitation, anger | • Insomnia |
| • Sleep disturbance | • Mania |
| • Appetite changes | • OCD-like behaviors |
| • Mood swings; apathy | • Protectiveness and hypervigilance |
| • Exhaustion | • Non-psychotic intrusive thoughts and images |

I highly recommend completing the Edinburgh Postnatal Depression Scale (it can be found easily in a Google search). Ideally, complete this with your health-care provider or a mental health professional who can interpret the results and have a conversation with you. This tool is not meant to be used in isolation but as a starting point.

Just as you'd go to the doctor if you had a cough that wouldn't go away, or if you felt something else was physically wrong, please don't hesitate to reach out for help if you're having a tough time coping with motherhood. Don't hide the symptoms because they can get much worse—and you want to enjoy motherhood and your baby. You can seek support from your primary care provider, your child's pediatrician, or from a mental health professional such as a social worker or psychotherapist. Don't feel ashamed for reaching out or needing help in the first place. If you can get support in the early stages, it will help you feel much better immediately or even three weeks to three months later. PMAD won't last forever.

## THE IMPORTANCE OF SELF-CARE

Often as we start the journey of motherhood, we feel intense pressure to abandon our needs in order to make sure that our baby feels loved and secure. We want our babies to know that we're there for them, that we love them, and that we never want them to feel abandoned. As a result, we endure months of sleepless nights, keep our baby with us when we go to the bathroom, don't take a shower, don't sit down for a meal, and don't let anyone else care for our babies so we can go for a walk, to the gym, or just to the coffee shop by ourselves. But the truth is, we cannot take care of our child—or anyone we love—if we aren't taking care of ourselves. Overwhelm, exhaustion, frustration, and irritability are all signs that your cup is empty. You have no juice left in you to put in the effort to self-regulate, am I right? An empty cup means you have nothing left to give, which can quickly lead to burnout and a higher chance of developing PMAD.

*You cannot take care of your baby, toddler,*
*or those you love if your "love cup" is empty.*
−Kaili Ets

This is where self-care comes in. Yes, I get it. The term *self-care* is often accompanied by a bunch of nodding and maybe some groans or exaggerated sighs. Somewhere along the way, it became a trendy catchall term—something people feel they "should" do. And it feels next to impossible with a new baby. But true self-care helps you cope better with stress and prioritize what's important to you. You'll be better able to take care of others when you take time to meet your own needs.

Self-care involves nurturing your body, mind, and spirit. It involves building yourself up so that your internal resources don't become depleted. It involves being as good to yourself as you would be to someone you care about. It requires you to show up for yourself and encourages you to ask for help when you need it. Self-care means doing things that bring you joy, that fill your "love cup," that make you feel good! When you feel good, you're calmer, and when you're calmer, you can better regulate yourself. Self-care doesn't mean leaving all your responsibilities and going away for a four-day spa retreat—although it could!

My mission is to reduce the overwhelm of motherhood, one mama and baby at a time. Learning about your baby's development and sleep and getting support around their daily functioning will help, but we need to take care of YOU as well, Mama! I want you to continue to build a strong bond with your baby, but for that to happen, they need a healthy caregiver. Someone who can leave them in the care of another person who loves them so that you, Mama, can eat a meal (so that your body has the energy to make it through the rest of the day), take a shower (so that you can feel like yourself), or go for a walk (so that you have time to breathe). Taking time for you means that your child will have a more patient, relaxed, happy, and healthy caregiver. This is important for your nervous system and also your baby's, for that co-regulation dance you do.

I invite you to find two or three small things that you can do each day that bring you joy, make you feel good, or help you feel taken care of. Maybe you make a cup of tea and sit down for ten minutes to enjoy it while it's hot. Or maybe you take a long bath in the evening while your partner takes care of baby.

Here are a few more ideas.

## MAMA SELF-CARE IDEAS

### Drink lots of water

This one is pretty self-explanatory, but water is really, really important. It will make you feel better, keep you energized, and also help that mama brain fog. And if you are breast-feeding, you need even more water. So get yourself a fun water bottle and get drinking!

### Eat the rainbow and pre-plan meals

Make time for eating and focus on balanced, healthy nutrition (prepare in advance if needed—cut up a bunch of fresh veggies on Sunday and store in the fridge and have nuts on hand; peanut butter or avocado on toast is also great!).

### Smile

Even if you don't feel like it, science has discovered that if you turn up the corners of your mouth into a smile shape, you actually start to feel happier! Smiling releases neurotransmitters called endorphins. Endorphins make you feel happier. And, guess what . . . the brain doesn't know how to differentiate between a fake smile and a real one; it reads the positioning of the facial muscles and acts accordingly.

### Get outside

Sit in the sunlight each morning and soak up the Vitamin D rays. Go for a walk by yourself, or even take your baby to the park and be mindful of the way the environment feels around you (i.e., the wind on your face, the sun warming your hands, the smell of fresh-cut grass).

### Move your body

Go for a walk, dance, do yoga, attend a mommy bootcamp class. Move your body, with or without your baby!

**Build your village**

Ask for help! I know this is so hard for many of us to do, but it really is so important. Have someone come over and cook you a meal, throw in a load of laundry, or take your baby/toddler out for a walk while you nap. Consider hiring a postnatal doula or a mother's helper so that you can get some things done around the house or take some time for yourself. Could you delegate a list of household tasks to your partner?

**Meditate**

Meditation is known to help improve mood, deepen sleep, and develop a sense of inner peace and calm. It can reduce stress levels, decrease cortisol, and contribute to an increase in immunity and relaxation. It can also reduce high blood pressure and even aid in concentration. With so many benefits for just a few minutes a day of your time, this is one self-care ritual you don't want to miss out on. Try just two to three minutes per session at first and build up gradually over time.

**Mindfulness**

Pause for a moment, use mindfulness to listen to the birds, appreciate the blue sky, be in the moment, and breathe.

**Date days/nights**

Set up regular date days or nights, either with your partner or a good friend. Grab coffee, go out for dinner, or have a movie night in. Socializing and feeling a little like your old self can do wonders.

**Be kind to yourself**

Positive self-talk! Tell yourself you are loved and keep a gratitude list. Be kind to yourself and forgive yourself often. You are a wonderful and capable parent!

---

MAMA SELF-CARE IDEAS, CONT'D

**Take time for you—Just be**

Find the old YOU! Get your hair done, dress nicely, be active, do the things you used to do. Nurture yourself with a good book and a hot bubble bath, play relaxing music, and escape for a little while. Making this a part of your daily or weekly routine can help you feel more relaxed and rejuvenated.

---

Most importantly, let go! Let go of the need to do it all. Let go of the need to be in control. Let go of the need to sacrifice "me time" for your baby. Self-care is about prioritizing your needs and teaching your baby by example how to love and respect themselves.

Finally, I'm putting this here to remind you that you're doing your very best, and that's all that your child needs! Make this your new Mama Mantra.

 *You are enough, you have done enough,*
*you are doing enough!*

*—Kaili Ets*

# Chapter Twenty-Five

# GENTLE, NATURAL TOOLS FOR YOUR MAMA TOOLBOX

Finally, I want to share a few of my favorite tools that I've collected for my motherhood toolbox over the past seven years of being a mama. I often recommend these to the mamas that I work with. Use this chapter as a guide when you need a quick strategy for whatever comes your way.

## BREAST MILK

This is an amazing "tool" to have in your back pocket. It can be used for much more than just nutrition and sleep! Breast milk has analgesic and even healing properties, so it can often help to soothe sore gums during teething and can heal most topical things, including the eye gunk in your newborn's eyes or even a diaper rash. When in doubt, use breast milk!

# MASSAGE

If you've ever had a massage, you know how calming it is, and touch is a great way to bond with your baby while also supporting development. Our skin has countless receptors. Deep touch in particular activates the proprioceptors of our muscles and joints, releasing dopamine, which has a very calming effect on the body. Massage has been found to help babies gain weight (so it's a great addition to your routine if you have a preemie or if your baby is on the lower end of the weight curve) and optimize sleep latency and total sleep duration for moms and babies. Lotion seems to improve this effect, so using something as simple as fractionated coconut oil, grapeseed oil, or olive oil is wonderful. Add in some soothing and calming essential oils (such as lavender or frankincense) and you're golden.

# REFLEXOLOGY

Tied in with massage is reflexology, which uses specialized compression techniques on reflex points on the feet, hands, ears, and face. These points relate to certain body parts, organs, and glands that, when stimulated, help restore balance, reduce stress, relieve tension, and promote self-healing. Reflexology can help with sleep, teething, digestion, reflux, and more. You can easily find a foot reflexology chart by searching on Google.

# BABY-WEARING

You've likely heard about the many benefits of baby-wearing. It's a win-win situation. You can do pretty much anything with the carrier—breast-feed on demand, move your body, get some baby naps in, have your hands free to cook dinner (or get some work done), and take care of an older toddler—and you usually you have a calmer, happier baby because they're nice and close to you (their most favorite place to be). I loved wearing both of my children and learned early on to never leave home without my carrier (though I will say it took some practice to get it right and comfortable for both baby and me). It's something I recommend to all the moms I work with.

## HUMMING

The vibrations that humming produces ground us, help slow our breathing, and activate our parasympathetic nervous system (rest/digest system). If you're holding your baby and humming, then they can also feel and benefit from these vibrations as well. It's a great way to soothe and co-regulate with your baby, especially during those 3:00 a.m. wake-ups when you have zero interest in bouncing, rocking, or walking your little one to calm them down. Try humming instead. This is also a great one for partners to have in their toolbox. You can say "hummmmmm," use the "om" mantra, or try something different altogether. It's about the vibration itself and not what it sounds like.

## TIBETAN SINGING BOWLS

This might seem random, but I love to use singing bowls with babies, especially fussy ones, and I bring one to all my Babies @ Play classes. You might have seen or heard singing bowls in a meditation or yoga class, and perhaps you've experienced the magical calming quality they bring but never thought to use them with your child. Sound therapy stimulates the auditory system while also developing the ear muscles and bringing the body into balance (think of it as a recalibration). The vibrations from these bowls engage the parasympathetic nervous system (just as humming does). Trust me on this—it's powerful for calming fussy or crying babies.

# SWADDLING

Swaddling has been done all over the world, in various cultures, for thousands of years, with the aim of calming a baby and reducing night-wakings. In Western culture, it has become controversial. There are a lot of questions about whether swaddling is safe or detrimental to a baby's development. Some health-care professionals and sleep consultants are even saying that swaddling prevents the Moro (startle) reflex from being integrated and is causing SPD. Rest assured, this isn't true.

Swaddling is something I recommend on occasion, particularly if you have a very sensitive baby who has big startle reactions and becomes upset by them, or if your baby is very upset or fussy and is having a hard time calming. Swaddling can also help you get a few solid hours of sleep if you find yourself in a sleep-crisis situation and you're so utterly exhausted that you're not functioning well. That said, swaddling doesn't work for many babies.

From my perspective, based on development and neurobiology, here are four reasons why swaddling may be helpful.

1.  The Moro reflex is hugely active in newborns and isn't integrated until three or four months. For some babies, this can mean big startles that really upset or wake them. The swaddle helps to prevent the reflex from being expressed to the point of waking up the baby. While swaddling may inhibit the Moro while they're sleeping (or needing to be calmed), babies get plenty of time during a twenty-four-hour period to be unswaddled (and integrate the reflex)—during diaper changes, feeding, playtime, and when being held.

2.  Babies are born with a C-shaped spine, so sleeping on their back
    in an extended position (with arms and legs out) is quite unnatural
    for them, especially in those first few weeks of life outside the
    womb. The swaddle, when done correctly, helps mimic the fetal
    position. In some parts of Europe, it's recommended that babies
    be placed on their sides to sleep (and switching sides each night
    is encouraged). This helps the baby maintain the fetal position,
    in which case the swaddle isn't needed or recommended.

3.  Swaddling helps babies feel sensory input similar to what they
    experienced in the womb—warm, tight, and cozy with something
    for them to kick and stretch against. When they have to learn all
    about gravity and this new freedom of movement (along with
    all the other sensory input from lights, sounds, and touch), the
    swaddle can help soothe and calm them by mimicking the womb
    and providing deep pressure (proprioceptive input), which also
    has a regulating, organizing, and calming effect on the body.

4.  When done right, swaddling can help regulate a baby's temper-
    ature. Ideally your baby is wearing only a diaper or a short-sleeved
    onesie when being swaddled. Long-sleeved and/or fleece pajamas
    can easily lead to overheating. Support for temperature regulation
    can be helpful in the first few months of life, as babies aren't able
    to regulate their temperature yet.

So why is swaddling such a controversial topic these days? It's true that
tightly swaddling a baby could lead to them sleeping too deeply too soon,
which is one of the many risk factors for SIDS, but other studies show that
it helps to keep the baby on their back, which is thought to lower the risk of

SIDS. There are many different angles currently being researched when it comes to swaddling, sleep, and SIDS. It's also true that baby's sleeping too deeply can impact your breast-feeding relationship with your baby if your body is still learning the amount of milk your baby needs. But this would also be the case if you had a unicorn baby who slept in eight-hour chunks from four weeks old without a swaddle. It's also true that babies who are swaddled too tightly may develop a problem with their hips (hip dysplasia).

In my opinion—garnered from clinical training and experience as an occupational therapist, various sleep certifications, and all the training, reading, and research I've done on sensory processing, primitive reflexes, and sleep—swaddling can be done safely. The key is moderation. I tried swaddling my son and he absolutely hated it. He'd do Houdini moves to get out of the various swaddles I attempted. My daughter, on the other hand, slept on her side without a swaddle for supervised naps during the day and loved the swaddle at night. We transitioned her out at about three and a half months, when she started to roll to her side. We only got three- to four-hour chunks of sleep with the swaddle on, so I wasn't concerned that she was sleeping too deeply or not getting enough feeds at night, and it helped me feel more rested.

## GENERAL TIPS FOR SWADDLING

Here are some general guidelines that I always discuss with my clients when they have made the informed decision to swaddle.

- Swaddles shouldn't be kept on baby throughout feedings (I definitely NEVER recommend this, as it also affects digestion).
- Swaddles shouldn't be kept on for longer than they need to be (i.e., when baby is not sleeping or needing the swaddle to help them calm).

GENERAL TIPS FOR SWADDLIN, CONT'D

- Some say to not swaddle baby during the day for naps and only swaddle at night to promote longer nighttime sleep stretches—remember that sleeping for too long may impact your breast-feeding relationship, especially in that fourth trimester when swaddling is used.

- There needs to be more education around proper and safe swaddling techniques. The straitjacket swaddle with arms straight down by their sides and wrapped tightly from shoulders to hips is not the best or safest option, though this one does seem to be the one that even the Houdini babies cannot squirm out of. In my opinion, if you have to swaddle your baby that straight and tight, it is no longer mimicking the curled fetal position or the environment of the womb and is likely not even that comfortable for the baby. And ultimately, our goal with the swaddling is to make the baby feel safer and more comfortable rather than make them sleep through the night, right?

- Swaddling should definitely be stopped once the baby starts to roll, which is usually around the 3-4 month mark (or even earlier at around 8-10 weeks when it might happen unexpectedly).

Whether or not you swaddle really depends on your unique baby and family. Read your baby's cues and watch for any signs of distress. Keep in mind the importance of varying a baby's position throughout the day, whether they're swaddled to sleep or not. And if you do decide to swaddle your baby, here are some tips to transition out of the swaddle when that time comes (because it will come, likely sooner than you think).

# HOW TO TRANSITION OUT OF A SWADDLE

### 1. Loosen up

Over the course of the week, you can gradually reduce the tightness of the swaddle. This allows the baby to get used to more wiggle room. Toward the end of the week, you may find that your baby has managed to get their arms out or has broken out of the swaddle. Make sure there are no loose blankets in the crib that could cover the baby's face and nose.

### 2. Use a swaddle transition sleep sack

Removing arms from a swaddle provides a lot of freedom, but it can be too big of a step for some babies, especially more sensitive babies. To help your baby with a more gradual transition, you can try using a swaddle transition sleep sack like the Zipadee-Zip or other brand. It provides a womb-like environment but with the full range of movement to roll over and wiggle around safely and freely.

### 3. One arm at a time

Start with unswaddling one arm at a time. When wrapping the baby up for bed, remove one arm and swaddle the other one in. Keep this up for two to three days, and then unswaddle the other arm too (wrapping only the torso). After five or six days, eliminate the swaddle altogether. A swaddle transition sleep sack would be a great option here as well.

### 4. Cold turkey

Stop swaddling. Period. This is effective but also results in quite a few tears. It might be a few days before you will see any improvement.

In order to make this transition in the most respectful way possible, you want to consider your baby's temperament and how they respond to change. If there are tears, then support them through the tears and consider whether the change was too much, too soon. You may want to consider removing the swaddle during the daytime first before moving on to nights, or perhaps putting them to sleep at night without the swaddle but swaddling them in the early hours of the morning when you desperately need more sleep.

## AROMATHERAPY

I love essential oils (okay, I may be slightly obsessed!). And guess what? You don't have to be an aromatherapist to use essential oils! Essential oils are distilled from plants (flowers, bark or resin from trees, roots, bushes, fruit rinds, and herbs). Because their molecules are similar to human cells, they're easily absorbed by the body. Distillation makes essential oils about one hundred to ten thousand times more concentrated (and more powerful) than the plants they came from. They can support every system in the body and are used extensively for emotional and spiritual support. Although essential oils seem to be the hottest trend in our society, they aren't new—ancient civilizations depended on them and valued them so highly that some people would be buried with their essential oils! Many cultures around the world still use them.

The powerful aromas of oils can help with everything from boosting your mood to giving you energy to tackle all that the day throws your way. You can include essential oils in your daytime routine to reduce stress and promote circadian rhythms and in your nighttime routine to promote relaxation as well as melatonin production. Our sense of smell is directly linked to the limbic system, which is linked to emotions, heart rate, blood pressure, breathing, memory, stress, and hormone balance.

You can also use essential oils for their immune-boosting and therapeutic benefits, for both you and your baby. Yes, you read that right! You can safely use essential oils with your baby if you follow a few simple guidelines.

First, make sure your oils are high grade and authentic, meaning that they aren't adulterated in any way (not diluted with a carrier oil, not mixed with other essential oils, and don't contain synthetic chemicals or alcohol). Unfortunately, we live in a world where the bottom line often outweighs quality. Most essential oils found on store shelves (even stores such as Whole Foods) have been manipulated in some way to increase the quantity. To make a high-quality oil that has therapeutic and healing properties, soil quality, climate, humidity, harvesting, and distilling properties must be considered, to make sure that each plant is being grown and harvested at the right time and distilled at the right temperature. Most essential oil brands found in big box stores aren't going the extra mile to consider all those things. Many plants are sprayed with pesticides, not harvested at the right time of day, or are distilled for a shorter time at higher temperatures. Lower-grade essential oils may smell nice, but they don't contain the therapeutic constituents needed to improve your health. The quality of the oil will impact function and potency.

Based on my own extensive research, I've chosen to use only Young Living essential oils. They're the world leader in essential oils (they've also been around the longest—over twenty-eight years at the time of writing), and they own or co-op farms all over the world, where they grow their plants in soil free of pesticides and herbicides. Their plants are grown in the proper climate, harvested at peak times to maximize the quality, and distilled for the right amount of time at the right temperatures to maintain as much of the healing constituents of that oil as possible. Their oils also undergo extensive testing in-house and through independent third parties for quality. These tests must meet (or exceed) the standards for the Association française de normalisation and the International Organization for Standardization, and in Canada many of their oils are now recognized as natural health products.

Of course the choice is yours, and I highly encourage you to do your own research. This means doing some actual reading—more than just the label. As is the case with most things found on our store shelves these days, there's no regulation for labeling essential oils. The label can say "100 percent pure" even if the bottle contains only a small percentage of that pure essential oil (I've heard that the percentage can be as low as 5 to 10 percent). This means that the rest of the bottle's contents could include synthetic chemicals that mimic the chemical constituents of the oil, a fatty carrier oil, such as fractionated coconut oil (which doesn't have a smell), alcohol, water, or even other essential oils used to make the oil smell sweeter and less earthy.

Second, when using essential oils with babies (because their skin is so delicate and their bodies are smaller), make sure that you're properly diluting the oils, at least until you know how they respond to them. A good rule of thumb is to dilute one drop of essential oil in one tablespoon of a fatty carrier oil (coconut, avocado, jojoba, grapeseed, extra virgin olive oil, etc.). Babies also get the benefits of essential oils through breast milk (about 1 percent of what mom uses). I love to apply the essential oils on the feet, along the spines, and on the backs of the necks of everyone in my house. My daughter was anointed with oils as soon as she was born. It was magical. You can also rub the pure essential oil (right from the bottle with no carrier oil) onto your baby's pajamas or sheets. Young Living has also gone a step further by developing products specifically for children. You can find everything from toxic-free wipes to baby shampoos and lotions and, my personal favorite, the Seedling Tender Tush diaper area balm (great for diaper rashes as well as cuts, scrapes, dry and cracked lips, and even other types of skin rashes). My kids are now long out of diapers and we still use the Tender Tush ointment on a regular basis (and yes, we still call it the "bum cream").

Third, be sure to keep oils out of eyes, ear canals, and other bodily crevices. Keep them in the diffuser, rub them on your baby's pajamas or sheets, or dilute them and apply to the skin. Should you ever get oil in your eye (or your baby's eye), use a fatty carrier oil (olive or coconut), yogurt, or milk to dilute and remove—NOT water (oil and water don't mix).

## DILUTION GUIDE

To reduce the need to measure all the time and always have oils on hand, I love to make roller bottles so that I can just grab and go.

| AGE | ESSENTIAL OILS | CARRIER OIL | 10 ML ROLLER |
|---|---|---|---|
| Newborn to 6 months | 1 drop | 4 teaspoons | 1-3 drops EO; fill rest with carrier oil |
| 6 months-2 years | 1 drop | 2 teaspoons | 3-6 drops |
| 2-5 years | 1 drop | 1 teaspoon | 9-15 drops |
| 5-10 years | 2 drops | 1 teaspoon | 12-30 drops |
| 10-18 years | 5 drops | 1 teaspoon | 1:3 or 1:1 (drop of EO: carrier oil) |

Finally, remember the motto "less is best" when starting with a new oil. You can always add more, but it's pretty much impossible to take it away. Try diffusing it for twenty minutes at first, or on an intermittent setting, and then shift to longer periods (we use our diffusers throughout the day and night).

So what oils are best for babies and young children? Don't worry, I've got you! Please visit pages 355 for some DIY aromatherapy recipes.

# CONCLUSION

Wow, Mama, you made it to the end of this book! Thank you so much for trusting me on your motherhood journey.

My goal with this book was to arm you with clarity around what "biologically normal" looks like for babies and toddlers at various stages—to help you understand how our babies' brains are different from ours and why focusing on connection, comfort, and co-regulation is so important. There's absolutely no reason to feel guilty, ashamed, or as if you're doing something wrong when you respond to and support your child in a way that feels good in your heart, day *and* night.

My hope is that this book has inspired you and empowered you to make some small but significant shifts. Maybe you make some changes around your baby's sleep, or perhaps you stop feeling as though you need to teach your baby all the things.

I hope that you can see this book as a good friend, therapist, and mentor as you navigate the wild ride of motherhood in the first few years. I hope that you realize that your intuition, your mama instincts, have always been there, inside of you. I hope that you tune in to your baby, tune in to what resonates with you and your family, what feels right and light in your heart. I hope that you trust that you know what's best for your baby and your family. And I hope that you feel as if you have the permission, or rather the ability, to let go of the overwhelm, the stress, the comparison that so often creeps in, so that you can celebrate your journey with your baby, watching as it twists and turns with each new phase. No matter what happens, you will get through it, and you will be okay. You deserve to enjoy motherhood.

This book is the culmination of everything I've learned over many years and with which I support mamas worldwide. I'd love to hear from you and how you've used *Mothering from Within* to support you on your motherhood journey. Please send me a message and let me know!

And if you'd like more personalized support on your journey, please reach out to me. I'd be honored to empower and guide you and your little one.

XO,

*Kaili*

# RESOURCES FOR PARENTS

Parents often ask me what my favorite books, sleep sacks, blackout curtains, teething toys, and even social media accounts are. I've compiled them in a list here. I hope you find them useful too!

www.kailiets.com/favorites

# WHAT'S NEXT?

Mama,

I truly hope that this book helped you build the foundation to start trusting yourself (and your baby) in your motherhood journey. You do know what's best for your family! Earmark your favorite pages and go back to any topic that you need assistance or some friendly advice on. If you feel as if you need a little more support, or would like personalized support, here are a few ways we can continue this journey together.

## MY COMMUNITY

If you're an exhausted mama (who isn't?) with a zero- to two-year-old baby, I invite you to join my community of mamas. We all need a village to support us on our motherhood journeys, and sometimes it's helpful to have a virtual village where you can come for trustworthy support. I offer loads of free training in this group and love to go live a few times a week on new topics. It's a great place to get some of your questions answered.

Join us here: www.kailiets.com/community

## BABIES @ PLAY CLASSES

My Babies @ Play classes are supportive parent-baby classes where we talk openly about health, sleep, and development. You'll learn a variety of skills to promote your child's development through songs, activities focused on baby, and, most of all, finding YOUR inner child and having FUN! I run these classes multiple times a year in person (and also offer them online as part of my Holistic Baby Development course), and they're sold out almost every session. Mamas constantly tell me that they wish they'd found these classes sooner, and I have a course that teaches other therapists to run them in their areas.

You can grab all the details here: https://www.kailiets.com/classes

## PERSONALIZED SUPPORT

I help overwhelmed and exhausted moms with zero- to two-year-old babies create clear action plans around their babies' sleep, feeding, development, and overall functioning, so they can tune in to and trust their mama instincts and feel confident in the supermoms they are. I offer virtual support worldwide and in-person support for local moms. If you'd like to explore 1:1 support, coaching, and having a "holistic baby guru" in your back pocket, please reach out to me at kaili@kailiets.com or visit my website www.kailiets.com to book a Right-Fit Call.

# DIY AROMATHERAPY RECIPES

**Chest Rub**

½ cup extra virgin coconut oil (add 1/4 cup of shredded beeswax or cocoa butter to keep it solid)

5 drops R.C (can also use Myrtle/ Ravintsara/Tea Tree)

3 drops Orange (or Lemon)

Melt Coconut oil over medium heat. Cool and stir in essential oils. Transfer to container & refrigerate. Apply to chest, back, and bottom of feet (cover with socks) at each diaper change.

**Skin Rashes or Eczema**

1/3 cup of shea butter

1/4 cup of coconut oil

10-15 drops of essential oil (Melrose, Lavender, or Frankincense)

Melt shea butter and coconut oil using a double broiler method. Allow to cool & add essential oils. Whip with hand mixer. Apply to affected area.

### Tummy Troubles

*1 drop Lavender, Digize, Peppermint, or Dill*
*1 tbsp carrier oil*
Massage onto tummy. You can also place one drop of Roman Chamomile in a bowl of warm water, wet a washcloth, wring, and lay over baby's belly.

### Immune Support

*"I Feel Sick" Roller (10 ml)*
*5 drops each of Copaiba, Frankincense, Myrrh*
*2 drops Lemon*
Fill with carrier oil. Roll onto bottom of feet + spine.

*Immune Boost Roller (10ml)*
*10 drops Thieves*
*5 drops Lemon*
Fill with carrier oil. Roll onto bottom of feet + spine daily

### Calming & Soothing (great for fussy or crying babies)

*Peace & Calming, Lavender, Stress Away, Joy, or Ylang Ylang*
Diffuse, place a drop on baby's clothing or Mom's neck for baby to smell, rub on baby's feet or back of the neck (diluted).

If you want to make a 10 ml roller:
*5 drops each of Rose (or Gentle Baby), Geranium, Ylang Ylang*
Fill with carrier oil. Apply to back of neck, feet, or on Mom's body for baby to smell.

### Bumps & Bruises

*1/2 cup coconut oil (melted). Allow to cool.*

*Add in 20 drops Melrose*

*10 drops Lavender*

*5 drops Helichrysum*

Place in a small glass jar. Apply to desired area.

You can also put this into a 10 ml roller bottle with:

*7 drops Melrose*

*3 drops Lavender*

*1 drop Helichrysum*

Fill with carrier oil of choice. Apply as needed.

### Muscle Aches/Growing Pains

*1–2 drops of Panaway, Lavender, Copaiba, Deep Relief, or Idaho Balsam Fir*

Dilute with carrier oil or Ortho Ease Massage oil. Rub on affected area. This has been a GREAT tool for my growing kids!

### Bum Cream

*1/2 cup coconut oil*

*1/4 cup shea butter*

*1 tsp beeswax*

*Melt all ingredients over low heat. Let cool.*

*Add 20 drops Gentle Baby essential oil.*

Apply as needed. Or use Tender Tush or Seedlings diaper cream + Gentle Baby. Apply directly to area.

### DIY Wipes

*1½ cup water*

*1 tbsp castille soap*

*1 tsp carrier oil*

*10 drops Geranium, Lavender, or Gentle Baby*

Cut a roll of paper towel in half (Bounty works well) and take the cardboard out. Soak half a roll in the solution and use as needed. Keep remaining wipes in a plastic bag or container.

### Diaper Pail Deodorizer

*2 tbsp uncooked white minute rice*

*4 drops Geranium*

*3 drops Bergamot, Cedarwood, and Lavender*

Place in a small organza sachet in or near diaper pail. Alternatively, you can drop 2–4 drops of oil on a felt pad and tape to inside of lid or under the bag.

### Foaming Bath Wash

*3 oz unscented liquid castille soap*

*2 tsp olive oil (or other moisturizing carrier oil)*

*10 drops essential oil (we love Gentle Baby, Lavender, Joy, Peace & Calming, or Chamomile)*

Water (ideally filtered or distilled, but I have used tap in a pinch). Combine the first 3 ingredients in a foaming hand soap container. Add water to within one inch of the top. Shake gently before each use.

**Sunscreen**

*1/4 cup Coconut Oil*

*1/4 cup of Beeswax*

*1/2 cup Apricot Kernel Oil (or Almond oil or Carrot Seed carrier oil)*

*2 tbsp of non-nano zinc (this is important)*

*2 tbsp shea butter (optional)*

*20 drops of essential oils of your choice (I used Lavender and Frankincense)*

Use a double broiler technique to melt the carrier oil, beeswax, and shea butter. Allow to cool. Add in non-nano zinc and essential oils. Whip to mix. Put in jar and refrigerate. Apply as you normally would a sunscreen.

**Teething**

Copaiba and Clove are the two essential oils that moms have used rubbed directly on the gums for a soothing effect. Copaiba is the milder option of the two and my favorite. It is gentle enough to use on the gums undiluted. I usually drop 1 drop into the palm of my hand and dip my clean pinky finger in just a little and then apply to gums. Afterward, I rub my hands together and disperse the remaining oil along baby's jawline where the teeth are errupting. For the really painful teething nights, I will add PanAway to the Copaiba (diluted 1:10 with carrier oil) and rub along the jawline. Clove oil is much stronger and needs to be diluted heavily (1:30). Apply on gums.

### Holistic Baby D.R.E.A.M.S Blend

(Yes, I created a special blend for my signature sleep course.)

*10 ml Roller Bottle*

*5 drops each of Peace & Calming, Stress Away, and Valor*

Fill the bottle with carrier oil. Apply to the bottom of your baby's feet and spine. You can also mix these and add 4 drops to a diffuser overnight.

### Sweet Dreams Cream

*1/2 cup coconut oil (melted). Allow to cool.*

*Add 7 drops each of Lavender, Cedarwood, Valor, and Peace & Calming*

Place in a small glass jar. Apply to feet and spine before nap and bedtimes.

### Monster Spray

*6 ounces water*

*20 drops Valor*

Mix together in a spray bottle and banish the boogeyman before bed.

If you have read this far and have been silently saying to yourself, "I need some of these oils in my life," or even if you are curious about learning more, I've got you. If you already have a Young Living account, you can grab any of the oils in this guide online with your member number and account. If you don't already have a membership with Young Living (trust me, it is not as scary as it sounds . . . think of it like a Costco membership), then let me help you get a member number right away. A membership allows you to purchase your oils and baby products for a discounted price (24% off) with your member number. Even though it is called a membership, you don't have to order monthly, although many people, myself included, choose to swap out all their consumables for toxic-free products with a customizable monthly wellness box. If you have a friend who has offered to help you with oil education, ask them for their member number as a referral. If you don't have one, I would love to be that friend for you.

Go to www.youngliving.com and sign up and use member referral number 1692595 or use this direct link: www.bit.ly/kailiYL. There are some pre-made kits for your convenience, or you can get started with whatever products you want.

# ENDNOTES

## SECTION ONE: THE INFANT BRAIN, ATTACHMENT, AND DEVELOPMENT

1.  Brink, Susan. *The Fourth Trimester: Understanding, Protecting, and Nurturing an Infant Through the First Three Months* (University of California Press; 1st edition, 2013), 17.

2.  Heller, Sharon, PhD. *The Vital Touch: How Intimate Contact with Your Baby Leads to Happier, Healthier Development* (Holt Paperbacks, 1997).

3.  Kirschenbaum, Greer, PhD. Bebo Mia's Infant & Family Sleep Specialist Certification program. Attended 2021.

4.  Goh, Carolyn, MD. "Chapter 3: Polyvagal Theory and Vagal Tone in Babies." From *An Integrative Approach to Treating Babies and Children: A Multidisciplinary Guide*. Edited by John Wilks. (Singing Dragon, 2017), 61.

5.  Buhler-Wassmann, Andrea C., and Leah C. Hibel. "Studying caregiver-infant co-regulation in dynamic, diverse cultural contexts: A call to action." *Infant Behavior and Development* 64 (2021). DOI: 10.1016/j. infbeh.2021.101586.

6.  Prochazkova, Eliska, and Mariska E. Kret. "Connecting minds and sharing emotions through mimicry: A neurocognitive model of emotional contagion." *Neuroscience & Biobehavioral Reviews* 80 (2017). DOI: 10.1016/j.neubiorev.2017.05.013.

7.  Hansen, Jessica C. "Attachment, Vagal Tone, and Co-regulation During Infancy." Theses and Dissertations (2014). https://scholarsarchive.byu.edu/etd/4320.

8.  Barthel, Kim. The Magic of Connection workshop. Attended January 2011. www.kimbarthel.ca.

9.  Faure, Megan, and Ann Richardson. *Baby Sense: Understanding Your Baby's Sensory World—The Key to a Contented Child* (Metz Press, 2002).

10. Faure, Megan, and Ann Richardson. *Baby Sense: Understanding Your Baby's Sensory World—The Key to a Contented Child* (Metz Press, 2002), 13.

11. Goodman, Brenda, MD. "Sensory Processing Disorder." WebMD. Accessed June 30, 2022. https://www.webmd.com/children/sensory-processing-disorder.

12. Barthel, Kim. The Magic of Connection workshop. Attended January 2011. www.kimbarthel.ca.

13. Barthel, Kim. Looking Beyond Behaviour in Early Intervention workshop. Attended November 2017.

14. Schore, Allan. "Effects of a secure attachment relationship on right brain development, affect regulation, and infant mental health." *Infant Mental Health Journal* 22 (2001), 7–67. https://www.allanschore.com/pdf/SchoreIMHJAttachment.pdf.

15. Champagne, Tina. "Attachment, trauma and occupational therapy practice." *OT Practice* Vol. 16, Issue 5. 2011.

16. Levy, Terry M., and Michael Orlans. *Attachment, Trauma, and Healing: Understanding and Treating Attachment Disorder in Children and Families* (Child Welfare League of America, 1998).

17. Tronick, Edward Z., and Andrew F. Gianino Jr. "The transmission of maternal disturbance to the infant." *New Directions for Child Development* 34 (1986). DOI: https://doi.org/10.1002/cd.23219863403.

18. Brumariu, Laura E. "Parent-Child Attachment and Emotion Regulation." *New Directions for Child and Adolescent Development* (2015). https://doi.org/10.1002/cad.20098.

19. Siegel, Daniel, MD, and Tina Payne Bryson, PhD. *The Power of Showing Up* (Ballantine Books, 2021), 34.

20. Attachment Parenting International Nurturings. "What Is Attachment Parenting." Attachment Parenting International. Accessed July 5, 2022. https://www.attachmentparenting.org/what-is-ap.

21. Kirschenbaum, Greer, PhD. Module 3: Parenting & Caregiver-Infant Relationships. Bebo Mia's Infant & Family Sleep Specialist Certification program. Attended 2021.

22. Leo, Pam. *Connection Parenting* (Wyatt-MacKenzie Publishing, 2005).

23. Neufeld, Gordon, PhD. *Hold On to Your Kids: Why Parents Need to Matter More Than Peers* (Knopf Canadian Publishing, Vintage Canada, 2013).

24. Ibid.

25. Cohen, Lawrence J., PhD. *Playful Parenting* (Ballantine Books; reprint edition 2002).

26. Siegel, Daniel, MD, and Tina Payne Bryson, PhD. *The Power of Showing Up* (Ballantine Books, 2021).

27. Neufeld, Gordon, PhD. *Hold On to Your Kids: Why Parents Need to Matter More Than Peers* (Knopf Canadian Publishing, Vintage Canada, 2013).

28. MacNamara, Deborah, PhD. *Rest, Play, Grow: Making Sense of Preschoolers (or Anyone Who Acts Like one)* (Aona Books, 2016).

29. MacNamara, Deborah, PhD. "The Surprising Secret Behind Kid's Resistance and Opposition." Deborah MacNamara (blog). Accessed July 3, 2022. https://macnamara.ca/portfolio/the-surprising-secret-behind-kids-resistance-and-opposition.

30. Neufeld, Gordon, PhD. Getting Bedtime Right presentation. Accessed July 3, 2022. Available for free on YouTube: https://www.youtube.com/watch?v=Y9ra898uoVM.

31. Neufeld, Gordon, PhD. Solutions to Sleep workshop series. Attended September 2021.

32. MacNamara, Deborah, PhD. "Taming Bedtime Monsters: When Sleepy Time is Scary." Deborah MacNamara (blog). Accessed July 3, 2022. https://macnamara.ca/portfolio/taming-bedtime-monsters-when-sleepy-time-is-scary.

33. MacNamara, Deborah, PhD. *Rest, Play, Grow: Making Sense of Preschoolers (or Anyone Who Acts Like one)* (Aona Books, 2016).

34. Majnemer, Annette, and Ronald G. Barr. "Influence of Supine Sleep Positioning on Early Motor Milestone Acquisition." *Developmental Medicine and Child Neurology* 47 (2007), 370–376. DOI: 10.1017/s0012162205000733.

35. Adolph, Karen E., and John M. Franchak. "The Development of Motor Behavior." *Wiley Interdisciplinary Reviews: Cognitive Science* 8 (2016). https://doi.org/10.1002/wcs.1430.

36. Ibid.

37. Majnemer, Annette, and Ronald G. Barr. "Influence of Supine Sleep Positioning on Early Motor Milestone Acquisition." *Developmental Medicine and Child Neurology* 47 (2007), 370–376. DOI: 10.1017/s0012162205000733.

38. Sears, William, MD, Martha Sears, RN, Robert Sears, MD, and James Sears, MD. *The Baby Book: Everything You Need to Know About Your Baby from Birth to Age Two.* (Little, Brown and Company; revised edition, 2013).

39. Ibid.

## SECTION TWO: FEEDING YOUR BABY

1. Stevens, Emily E. et al. "A History of Infant Feeding." *The Journal of Perinatal Education* 18 (2009): 32–9. DOI:10.1624/105812409X426314.

2. Minchin, Maureen. *Milk Matters: Infant Feeding & Immune Disorders.* (Milk Matters PTY Ltd., 2015).

3. International Affiliation of Tongue-tie Professionals. "About Tongue-tie." International Affiliation of Tongue-tie Professionals. Accessed July 3, 2022. https://tonguetieprofessionals.org/about-tongue-tie.

4.  Baxter, Richard, DMD, MS, et al. *Tongue-Tied: How a Tiny String Under the Tongue Impacts Nursing, Speech, Feeding, and More* (Alabama Tongue-Tie Center, 2018).

5.  Camaschella, Clara. "Iron-Deficiency Anemia." *The New England Journal of Medicine* 373 (2015), 485–6. DOI: 10.1056/NEJMc1507104.

6.  Food with Thought Nutrition. "Is a Deficiency in This Corrosive Acid Wreaking Havoc in Your Body?" Food with Thought Nutrition. Accessed July 3, 2022. https://foodwiththoughtnutrition.com/2021/07/28/insufficient-hcl-reflux.

7.  Hookway, Lyndsey. *Holistic Sleep Coaching. Gentle Alternatives to Sleep Training for Health and Childcare Professionals* (Praeclarus Press, 2019), 196.

8.  Ji, Xiaopeng, et al. "The relationship between micronutrient status and sleep patterns: A systematic review." *Public Health Nutrition* 20 (2017), 687–701. DOI:10.1017/S1368980016002603.

9.  Grandner, Michael A., et al. "Sleep symptoms associated with intake of specific dietary nutrients." *Journal of Sleep Research* 23 (2014): 22–34. DOI:10.1111/jsr.12084.

10. Healthline. "Zinc Deficiency." Healthline. Access July 3, 2022. https://www.healthline.com/health/zinc-deficiency#diagnosis.

11. Shafaghi A., Hasanzadeh J., Mansour-Ghanaei F., Joukar F., and Yaseri M. "The Effect of Zinc Supplementation on the Symptoms of Gastroesophageal Reflux Disease; A Randomized Clinical Trial." *Middle East Journal of Digestive Diseases* 8 (2016), 289–296. DOI:10.15171/mejdd.2016.38.

12. Healthdirect. "Foods high in zinc." Accessed July 3. https://www.healthdirect.gov.au/foods-high-in-zinc.

13. Hookway, Lyndsey. *Holistic Sleep Coaching. Gentle Alternatives to Sleep Training for Health and Childcare Professionals* (Praeclarus Press, 2019), 198.

14. Ibid., 195.

15. Hassall, Eric. "Over-prescription of acid-suppressing medications in infants: How it came about, why it's wrong, and what to do about it." *The Journal of Pediatrics* 160 (2012), 193–8. DOI:10.1016/j.jpeds.2011.08.067.

16. Faubion, W.A. Jr., and Zein N.N. "Gastroesophageal Reflux in Infants and Children." *Mayo Clinic Proceedings* 73 (1998), 166–73. DOI: 10.1016/S0025-6196(11)63650-1.

17. Nelson, S.P., E.H. Chen, G.M. Syniar, K.K. Christoffel. "Prevalence of symptoms of gastroesophageal reflux during infancy: A pediatric practice-based survey." Pediatric Practice Research Group. *Archives of Pediatrics and Adolescent Medicine* 151 (1997), 569–72. DOI: 10.1001/archpedi.154.2.150.

18. Martin, A.J., N. Pratt, J.D. Kennedy, P. Ryan, R.E. Ruffin, H. Miles, J. Marley. "Natural history and familial relationships of infant spilling to 9 years of age." *Pediatrics* 109 (2002), 1061–7. DOI: 10.1542/peds.109.6.1061.

19. Sutphen, J.L. and V.L. Dillard. "Effect of feeding volume on early postcibal gastroesophageal reflux in infants." *Journal of Pediatric Gastroenterol and Nutrition* 7 (1988),185–8. DOI:10.1097/00005176-198803000-00005.

20. Zeiter D.K., and J.S. Hyams. "Gastroesophageal reflux: Pathogenesis, diagnosis, and treatment." *Allergy and Asthma Proceedings* 20 (1999), 45–9. DOI: 10.2500/108854199778681503.

21. Faubion, W.A. Jr., and Zein N.N. "Gastroesophageal Reflux in Infants and Children." *Mayo Clinic Proceedings* 73 (1998), 166–73. DOI: 10.1016/S0025-6196(11)63650-1.

22. Homer, Aine. The Baby Reflux Certification course. Informal survey completed by Aine Homer, the Baby Reflux Lady. Course completed 2020.

23. Erlich, Katherine, MD, and Kelly Genzlinger, MSc, CNC, CMTA. *Super Nutrition for Babies, Revised Edition: The Best Way to Nourish Your Baby from Birth to 24 Months* (Fair Winds Press, 2018), 83.

24. Giglioni, Carrie, DC. Fearless Foodies course. Completed 2021.

25. Healthy Children. "Feeding and Nutrition Tips: Your 1-Year Old." American Academy of Pediatrics. Accessed July 3, 2022. https://www.healthychildren.org/English/ages-stages/toddler/nutrition/Pages/Feeding-and-Nutrition-Your-One-Year-Old.aspx.

26. Coleman, Erin, RD, LD. "Fatty Foods for Infants." Hearst Newspapers. Accessed July 3, 2022. https://healthyeating.sfgate.com/fatty-foods-infants-7165.html.

27. Erlich, Katherine, MD, and Kelly Genzlinger, MSc, CNC, CMTA. *Super Nutrition for Babies, Revised Edition: The Best Way to Nourish Your Baby from Birth to 24 Months* (Fair Winds Press, 2018), 87.

28. Ibid., 85

29. Giglioni, Carri, DC. Fearless Foodies course. Completed 2021.

30. Brown, A., and Victoria Harries. "Infant Sleep and Night Feeding Patterns During Later Infancy: Association with Breastfeeding Frequency, Daytime Complementary Food Intake, and Infant Weight." *Breastfeeding Medicine* 10 (2015): 246–252. https://www.liebertpub. com/doi/10.1089/bfm.2014.0153.

31. Nowak, Raymond, et al. "Neonatal Suckling, Oxytocin, and Early Infant Attachment to the Mother." *Frontiers in Endocrinology* 11 (2021). DOI: 10.3389/fendo.2020.612651.

## SECTION THREE: SLEEP

1. Saxbe, Darby, and Jennifer Hahn-Holbrook. "Human breast milk may help babies tell time via circadian signals from mom." USCDornsife: College of Letters, Arts and Sciences. Accessed July 6, 2022. https://dornsife.usc.edu/news/stories/3060/ breast-milk-helps-babies-tell-circadian-rhythm-from-mom/.

2. Tillman, Briana. "Breast Milk's Circadian Rhythms." La Leche League International. Accessed July 6, 2022. https://www.llli.org/ breast-milks-circadian-rhythms-2/.

3. Nowak, Raymond, et al. "Neonatal Suckling, Oxytocin, and Early Infant Attachment to the Mother." *Frontiers in Endocrinology* 11 (2021). DOI: 10.3389/fendo.2020.612651.

4. Stern, J. M., and S. Reichlin. "Prolactin circadian rhythm persists throughout lactation in women." *Neuroendocrinology* 51 (1990), 31–7. DOI:10.1159/000125312.

5. McKenna, James J., PhD, and Lee T. Gettler, MA. "Co-Sleeping, Breastfeeding and Sudden Infant Death Syndrome." *Encyclopedia on Early Childhood Development* (2010). https://cosleeping.nd.edu/ assets/33678/mckenna_gettlerangxp.pdf.

6. McKenna, James J., PhD, and Thomas McDade. "Why babies should never sleep alone: A review of the co-sleeping controversy in relation to SIDS, bedsharing and breast feeding." *Paediatric Respiratory Reviews* 6 (2005), 134–52. DOI:10.1016/j.prrv.2005.03.006.

7. McKenna, James J., PhD. *Safe Infant Sleep: Expert Answers to Your Cosleeping Questions* (Platypus Media, 2020).

8. Middlemiss, Wendy, PhD, and Kathleen Kendall-Tackett, PhD, IBCLC, FAPA. *The Science of Mother-Infant Sleep: Current Findings on Bedsharing, Breastfeeding, Sleep Training, and Normal Infant Sleep* (Praeclarus Press, 2014), 80–85.

9. McKenna, James J., PhD. *Safe Infant Sleep: Expert Answers to Your Cosleeping Questions* (Platypus Media, 2020).

10. Middlemiss, Wendy, PhD, and Kathleen Kendall-Tackett, PhD, IBCLC, FAPA. *The Science of Mother-Infant Sleep: Current Findings on Bedsharing, Breastfeeding, Sleep Training, and Normal Infant Sleep* (Praeclarus Press, 2014), 23–41.

11. Wiessinger, Diane, and Diana West, Linda J. Smith, and Teresa Pitman. *Sweet Sleep: Nighttime and Naptime Strategies for the Breastfeeding Family* (Ballantine Books, 2014).

12. Pennestri, Marie-Hélène, PhD, Christine Laganière, BSc, Andrée-Anne Bouvette-Turcot, PhD, Irina Pokhvisneva, MSc, Meir Steiner, PhD, Michael J. Meaney, PhD, and Hélène Gaudreau, PhD. "Uninterrupted Infant Sleep, Development, and Maternal Mood." *Pediatrics* 142 (2018). https://doi.org/10.1542/peds.2017-4330.

13. Weinraub, Marsha, Randall H. Bender, Sarah L. Friedman, Elizabeth J. Susman, Bonnie Knoke, Robert Bradley, Renate Houts, Jason Williams. "Patterns of developmental change in infants' nighttime sleep awakenings from 6 through 36 months of age." *Developmental Psychology* 48 (2012):1511–28. DOI: 10.1037/a0027680.

14. Hysing, Mari, PhD, Allison G. Harvey, PhD, Leila Torgersen, PhD, Eivind Ystrom, PhD, Ted Reichborn-Kjennerud, PhD, Borge Sivertsen, PhD. "Trajectories and Predictors of Nocturnal Awakenings and Sleep Duration in Infants." *Journal of Developmental and Behavioral Pediatrics* 35 (2014), 309–16. DOI: 10.1097/DBP.0000000000000064.

15. Neufeld, Gordon, PhD. *Hold On to Your Kids: Why Parents Need to Matter More Than Peers* (Knopf Canadian Publishing, Vintage Canada, 2013).

16. MacNamara, Deborah, PhD. *Rest, Play, Grow: Making Sense of Preschoolers (or Anyone Who Acts Like one)* (Aona Books, 2016).

17. MacNamara, Deborah, PhD. "When Saying Goodnight is Hard." Deborah MacNamara (blog). Accessed July 3, 2022. https://macnamara. ca/portfolio/info-graphic-when-saying-goodnight-is-hard-20-ways-to-bridge-the-nighttime-distance.

18. Walker, Matthew, PhD. *Why We Sleep: Unlocking the Power of Sleep and Dreams.* (Simon & Shuster, 2017).

19. *Time* magazine, *The Science of Sleep.* Time Inc. Special Edition (2020).

20. Barthel, Kim. Sleep Matters course. Attended August 2021.

21. Kirschenbaum, Greer, PhD. Bebo Mia's Infant & Family Sleep Specialist Certification program. Attended 2021.

22. Barthel, Kim. Sleep Matters course. Attended August 2021.

23. McKenna, James J., PhD. *Safe Infant Sleep: Expert Answers to Your Cosleeping Questions* (Platypus Media, 2020).

24. Bathory, Eleanor, and Suzy Tomopoulos. "Sleep Regulation, Physiology and Development, Sleep Duration and Patterns, and Sleep Hygiene in Infants, Toddlers, and Preschool-Age Children." *Current Problems in Pediatric and Adolescent Health Care* 47 (2017): 29–42. DOI:10.1016/j. cppeds.2016.12.001.

25. Acuña-Castroviejo, Dario, Germaine Escames, Carmen Venegas, María E. Díaz-Casado, Elena Lima-Cabello, Luis C. López, Sergio Rosales-Corral, Dun-Xian Tan, and Russel J. Reiter. "Extrapineal Melatonin: Sources, Regulation, and Potential Functions." *Cellular and Molecular Life Sciences* 71 (2014): 2997–3025. DOI: 10.1007/s00018-014-1579-2.

26. White, R.D. "Circadian Variation of Breast Milk Components and Implications for Care." *Breastfeeding Medicine* 12 (2017), 398–400. DOI: 10.1089/bfm.2017.0070.

27. Cohen Engler, A., A. Hadash, N. Shehadeh, and G. Pillar. "Breastfeeding may improve nocturnal sleep and reduce infantile colic: Potential role of breast milk melatonin." *European Journal of Pediatrics* 171 (2012), 729–32. DOI: 10.1007/s00431-011-1659-3.

28. Corbalán-Tutau, Dolores, et al. "Daily profile in two circadian markers 'melatonin and cortisol' and associations with metabolic syndrome components." *Physiology & Behavior* 123 (2014), 231–5. DOI: 10.1016/j. physbeh.2012.06.005.

29. Lavery, M.J., C. Stull, M.O. Kinney, and G. Yosipovitch. "Nocturnal Pruritus: The Battle for a Peaceful Night's Sleep." *International Journal of Molecular Sciences* 17 (2016), 425. DOI:10.3390/ijms17030425.

30. Mark, P.J., R.C. Crew, M.D. Wharfe, and B.J. Waddell. "Rhythmic Three-Part Harmony: The Complex Interaction of Maternal, Placental and Fetal Circadian Systems." *Journal of Biological Rhythms* 32 (2017), 534–549. DOI: 10.1177/0748730417728671.

31. Kurdziel, L., K. Duclos, and R.M.C. Spencer. "Sleep spindles in midday naps enhance learning in preschool children." *Proceedings of the National Academy of Sciences of the United States of America* 110 (2013),17267–17272. DOI:10.1073/pnas.1306418110.

32. Mazurek, Micah O., et al. "Course and Predictors of Sleep and Co-occurring Problems in Children with Autism Spectrum Disorder." *Journal of Autism and Developmental Disorders* 49 (2019), 2101–2115. DOI:10.1007/s10803-019-03894-5.

33. Appleyard, Katie, et al. "Sleep and Sensory Processing in Infants and Toddlers: A Cross-Sectional and Longitudinal Study." *The American Journal of Occupational Therapy: Official Publication of the American Occupational Therapy Association* 74 (2020). DOI: 10.5014/ajot.2020.038182.

34. Vasak, Mark, et al. "Sensory Processing and Sleep in Typically Developing Infants and Toddlers." *The American Journal of Occupational Therapy: Official Publication of the American Occupational Therapy Association* 69 (2015). DOI:10.5014/ajot.2015.015891.

35. Engel-Yeger, Batya, and Tamar Shochat. "The relationship between sensory processing patterns and sleep quality in healthy adults." *Canadian Journal of Occupational Therapy. Revue canadienne d'ergotherapie* 79 (2012), 134–41. DOI:10.2182/cjot.2012.79.3.2.

36. Jackson, Melinda, and Siobhan Banks. "Humans Used to Sleep in Two Shifts, and Maybe We Should Do It Again." Science Alert. Accessed July 4, 2022. https://www.sciencealert.com/humans-used-to-sleep-in-two-shifts-maybe-we-should-again.

37. Shoen, Sarah. "Biphasic Sleep: What It Is and How It Works." Sleep Foundation. Accessed July 4, 2022. https://www.sleepfoundation.org/how-sleep-works/biphasic-sleep.

38. McKay, Pinky, IBCLC. "Could Your Toddler's Diet Be Keeping You Awake at Night?" BellyBelly. Accessed July 4, 2022. http://www.bellybelly.com.au/baby/child-diet-awake#.UdMm4L8zw20.

39. Gupta, Ruchi S., MD, MPH; Elizabeth E. Springston, BA; Manoj R. Warrier, MD; Bridget Smith, PhD; Rajesh Kumar, MD; Jacqueline Pongracic, MD; and Jane L. Holl, MD, MPH. "The Prevalence, Severity, and Distribution of Childhood Food Allergy in the United States." *Pediatrics* 128 (2011), e9–e17. DOI: 10.1542/peds.2011-0204.

40. Ibid.

## SECTION FOUR: MAMA TOOLS

1. LaPointe, Melissa. Strong Beginnings: Occupational Therapy, Integrative Health & the Prenatal Client. Attended 2016.

2. Davis, Wendy N., PhD, PMH-C. Maternal Mental Health Webinars 2020: Resources for Professionals and Families. Attended 2020. Held through Postpartum Support International. www.postpartum.net.

# REFERENCES

The following sources have not been directly referenced in this book, but they have informed my writing and my work with mamas, so I've included them here.

Bowlby, J. *Attachment* (Basic books, 2008).

Cassidy, J. "Emotion regulation: Influences of attachment relationships." *Monographs of the Society for Research in Child Development* 59 (1994): 228–49. https://pubmed.ncbi.nlm.nih.gov/7984163.

Centers for Disease Control and Prevention. "CDC's Developmental Milestones." Accessed July 4, 2022. https://www.cdc.gov/ncbddd/actearly/milestones/index.html.

Cranston, Lynda. "Baby milestones: One to six months." Baby Center Canada. Accessed July 4, 2022. https://www.babycenter.ca/a6476/milestone-chart.

Dempsey, Moira (course creator) and Heidi McLarty (course instructor). Rhythmic Movement Training and Reflex Integration course (Levels 1 and 2). Attended 2017.

Developmental Milestones: *When It's Time to Be Concerned*. Patient handout. Advance for Occupational Therapy Practitioners. Retrieved June 30, 2017.

Dosman, Cara F. et al. "Evidence-based milestone ages as a framework for developmental surveillance." *Paediatrics & Child Health* 17 (2012), 561–8. DOI:10.1093/pch/17.10.561.

Freudigman, K. A., and E. B. Thoman. "Infants' earliest sleep/wake organization differs as a function of delivery mode." *Developmental Psychobiology* 32 (1998): 293–303.

Frick, Sheila. Building Blocks for Sensory Integration course. Attended 2013.

Folio, Rhonda M., and Rebecca R. Fewell. *Peabody Developmental Motor Scales Second Edition (PDMS-2).* Assessment tool. www.pearsonassessments.com.

Harper, Julia. Reflex Integration to Support Education course. Attended 2012.

Hazelbaker, Alison K. *Tongue-Tie: Morphogenesis, Impact, Assessment and Treatment* (Aidan and Eva Press, 2010).

Hermsen-van Wanrooy, Marianne. *Baby Moves: A Step By Step Guide To Enhancing Your Baby's Development Through His or Her Own Natural Movement* (BabyMoves Publications, 2002).

Kotlow, Lawrence A. *SOS 4 TOTS: Tethered Oral Tissues, Tongue-Ties, & Lip-Ties* (The Troy Book Makers, 2016).

Morea A., and J. Jessel. "Comparing the effects of varied and constant preferred items on improving tummy time for typically developing infants." *Journal of Applied Behavioral Analysis* 53 (2020). https://www.ncbi.nlm.nih.gov/pubmed/32026464.

Ockwell-Smith, Sarah. *Why Your Baby's Sleep Matters* (Pinter & Martin Ltd, 2016).

Parks, Stephanie, MA. *The Hawaii Early Learning Profile (HELP) Checklist: Birth to three Years.* Assessment tool. https://www.vort.com/product.php?productid=13.

Rapley, Gill, and Tracey Murkett. *Baby-Led Weaning: The Essential Guide to Introducing Solid Foods and Helping Your Baby to Grow Up a Happy and Confident Eater* (The Experiment, 2010).

Richter, Eileen. Using Gravity to Facilitate Sensory-Motor Development in Infants & Young Children course. Attended 2021.

Sadler S. "Sleep: What is normal at six months?" *Professional Care of Mother and Child.* 4 (1994), 166–7. https://pubmed.ncbi.nlm.nih.gov/8680184.

Skove, Ellynne. GoGo Babies: Developmental Movement & Baby Yoga Teacher Training. Attended 2015.

Solter, Aletha J., PhD. *The Aware Baby.* (Aware Parenting Institute; revised edition, 2001).

Toomey, K., PhD, Erin Ross, PhD, and Bethany Kortsha, OTR. Picky Eaters versus Problem Feeders: The Sequential Oral Sensory (SOS) Approach to Feeding course. Attended 2014.

# CHARTS AND CHECKLISTS INDEX

YGTMedia Co. is a blended boutique publishing house for mission-driven humans. We help seasoned and emerging authors "birth their brain babies" through a supportive and collaborative approach. Specializing in narrative nonfiction and adult and children's empowerment books, we believe that words can change the world, and we intend to do so one book at a time.

🌐 www.ygtmedia.co/publishing
📷 @ygtmedia.co
f @ygtmedia.co